Llewellyn's Practical Guide to Personal Power Series

The Sacred Power
in Your Name

Ted Andrews

1990
Llewellyn Publications
St. Paul, Minnesota 55164-0383, U.S.A.

First Edition
Second Printing, 1990

Cover Design: Terry Buske

Library of Congress-in-Publication Data:

Andrews, Ted. 1952-
    The sacred power in your name / Ted Andrews.
        p.   cm. — (Llewellyn's new age series)
    Includes bibliographical references.
    ISBN 0-87542-012-5
        1. Magic. 2. Names, Personal—Miscellanea. 3. Names, Personal—Religious aspects—Miscellanea. 4. Spiritual life—Miscellanea. I. Title. II. Series.
    BF1623.N3A53 1990
    133.3'3—dc20   89-77238
                                                                                      CIP

Llewellyn Publications
A Division of Llewellyn Worldwide, Ltd.
P.O. Box 64383, St. Paul, MN 55164-0383

Unlock the Sacred Power in *Your* Name!

Our names are much more than a label by which people can identify and stereotype us. Our individual names contain much power and subconscious significance. They are our most intimate energy signatures, and if used properly, they can lead us to spiritual knowledge, heightened consciousness, and higher initiation.

Our names trigger energy patterns that we have come to unfold, expand, develop, and overcome within this lifetime. Each soul comes into the world to learn certain lessons and to achieve certain goals to propel its evolvement. Our name and all of its elements serve as a catalyst for specific energies to play upon us throughout this incarnation.

Using techniques outlined in this book, you will be able to

- analyze the sounds and rhythms of your name.
- transmute your name into a magickal incantation.
- awaken creative energies inherent within your name.
- create an inner talisman.
- discover your purpose in life.
- use your name for personal empowerment and healing.
- and more!

Also included is a Dictionary of Names containing 196 names and their meanings, each with an affirmation and meditation.

Everyone is seeking some method to help them upon the spiritual path. Learning the power and energy inherent within our names is the ideal place to start. The name is a direct link to the soul. By learning how to use the name and its elements to more fully and more consciously communicate with the soul, we can begin to understand the rhythms and patterns of events within our life circumstances. We can then begin to control and direct our creative energies.

About the Author

Ted Andrews is a full-time author, student and teacher in the metaphysical and spiritual fields. He conducts seminars, symposiums, workshops and lectures throughout the country on many facets of ancient mysticism. Ted works with past-life analysis, auric interpretation, numerology, the tarot and the Qabala as methods of developing and enhancing inner potential. He is a clairvoyant and a certified spiritualist medium.

Ted is also active in the healing field. He is certified in basic hypnosis and acupressure and is involved in the study and use of herbs as an alternative path. He combines his musical training with more than twenty years of concentrated metaphysical study in the application of "Directed Esoteric Sound" in the healing process. He uses this with other holistic methods of healing, such as "etheric touch," aura and chakra balancing, and crystal stone and gem techniques, in creating individual healing therapies and higher states of consciousness.

He is a contributing author to various metaphysical magazines with articles published on such subjects as "Occult Christianity," "Working With Our Angelic Brethren," and "Metaphysical Mirrors in Our Lives."

To Write to the Author

We cannot guarantee that every letter written to the author can be answered, but all will be forwarded. Both the author and the publisher appreciate hearing from readers, learning of your enjoyment and benefit from this book. Llewellyn also publishes a bi-monthly news magazine with news and reviews of practical esoteric studies and articles helpful to the student, and some readers' questions and comments to the author may be answered through this magazine's columns if permission to do so is included in the original letter. The author sometimes participates in seminars and workshops, and dates and places are announced in *The Llewellyn New Times*. To write to the author, or to ask a question, write to:

Ted Andrews
c/o THE LLEWELLYN NEW TIMES
P.O. Box 64383-012, St. Paul, MN 55164-0383, U.S.A.

Please enclose a self-addressed, stamped envelope for reply, or $1.00 to cover costs.

About the Llewellyn Practical Guides to Personal Power

To some people, the idea that "magick" is *practical* comes as a surprise. It shouldn't!

The entire basis for magick is to exercise influence over one's personal world in order to satisfy our needs and goals. And, while this magick is also concerned with psychological transformation and spiritual growth, even the spiritual life must be built on firm material foundations.

Here are practical and usable techniques that will help you to a better life, will help you attain things you want, will help you in your personal growth and development. *Moreover, these books can change your life, dynamically, positively!*

The material world and the psychic are intertwined, and it is this that establishes the magickal link: that mind/soul/spirit can as easily influence the material as vice versa.

Psychic powers and magickal practices can, and should, be used in one's daily life. Each of us has many wonderful, but yet underdeveloped talents and powers—surely we have an evolutionary obligation to make full use of our human potentials! Mind and body work together, and magick is simply the extension of this interaction into dimensions beyond the limits normally conceived. *Why be limited?*

All things you will ever want or be must have their start in your mind. In these books you are given practical guidance to develop your inner powers and apply them to your everyday needs. These abilities will eventually belong to everybody through natural evolution, but you can learn and develop them now!

This series of books will help you achieve such things as success, happiness, miracles, powers of ESP, healing, out-of-body travel, clairvoyance, divination, extended powers of mind and body, communication with non-physical beings, and knowledge by non-material means!

We've always known of things like this . . . seemingly supernormal achievements, often by quite ordinary people. We are told that we normally use only ten percent of our human potential. We are taught that faith can move mountains, that love heals all hurt, that miracles do occur. We believe these things to be true, but most people lack practical knowledge of them.

The books in this series form a full library of magickal knowledge and practice.

Other Books by Ted Andrews

> *Simplified Magick: A Beginner's Guide to the New Age Qabala*
>
> *Imagick: The Magick of Images, Paths and Dance*

Forthcoming

> *Dream Alchemy*
>
> *Self-Initiation Through the Tarot*
>
> *Name Enchantment*

*Dedicated to Mom and Dad
for the magick of the
seven T's!*

Contents

Part Two: Sacred Seeds

"In the Name of . . . "   **103**

The importance of giving greater consideration to our names. Unveiling
the effects names have upon our lives. The reemergence of the ancient
naming ceremonies. How to use your name as the ideal tool to begin
your individual quest for the spiritual. The name analysis process. Sample analysis sheet.

Metaphysical Dictionary of Names   **111**

A listing of some of the more common names in use today. Each name
has its meaning given, a suggested affirmation for an incantation of
power, and other important esoteric elements associated with it.

Tables

Illustrations

INTRODUCTION

The Magick of Words

OUR VOICE IS our most creative instrument. With our words we can make others feel as if they are standing within God's shadow, or we can make them shrink as if they were some hideous being from Hell. It is no wonder that primitive societies considered language so mystical and magickal.

All the ancient mystery schools taught their students about the power of the word. They taught that when a thought is expressed in words, it forms the matrix of what will manifest within our physical lives. This is the reason they all stressed reticence in speech at all times.

Our myths and fables are filled with individuals seeking those special magickal words that will solve their life problems and bring them wealth and prosperity. Even today, people are fascinated with the possibility of discovering a magickal word or phrase. Stage magicians use "magickal words" in their acts of prestidigitation, and "abracadabra" and "hocus pocus" are familiar to every child and adult alike. What few people realize is that there abides within every man, woman, and child a deep-seated, ancient memory of the reality of the power of the word. Unfortunately, what has been lost is the understanding and the techniques for activating those levels of our consciousness that allow us to discover and use magickal words and sounds. We have permitted our rational minds to block access to those ancient techniques.

Every ancient society had its own hierarchy of gods and goddesses. All of these beings were specific manifestations of the *one divine force* that operates throughout the universe. By calling upon the various names of these gods and goddesses, societies could draw upon specific energies associated with that divine force. This allowed people to obtain energies from the divine Source that were more direct instead of general.

In the Hebrew Qabala, there were ten specific names for how the one God manifested and worked through the physical and spiritual universe. Hebrews used these names rather than the one name for God—what they called the Tetragrammaton. This one name was not used in their prayers because it was believed it could activate powerful energies that humans would not be able to handle. Tradition also said that if ever spoken correctly, it had the power to destroy the universe and create a new one entirely. Thus the Hebrews substituted specific names for it, such as Adonai and Jehovah. And of course, one of the commandments is "Thou shalt not take the name of the Lord thy God in vain," meaning in essence, don't use it without realizing the full significance of its power to work in your life.

Great respect and reverence was always given by initiates and mystics to the names of gods and goddesses outside their own belief systems. They recognized—as we must learn to do again—that all gods are part of the same God. These divine names have sounds and thoughtforms that trigger a release of energy into our lives. This energy may play a role in our lives in ways that are very subtle but also very real. A modern comic once hinted at this concept in explaining the population explosion. He commented that everything would be fine as long as we learned to keep quiet when having sexual relations. He explained that while in the throes of ecstasy, we utter such phrases as "oh, God! oh, baby!" Exclaiming "oh, God!" is like ringing His doorbell, getting His attention; by following this with the words, "oh, baby," God must assume that is what you are praying for, and being ever-giving and all-loving, He sets the process in motion. Although treated humorously, this example touches upon a very ancient principle.

In ancient and modern forms of both high and low magick, the essential power of sound and words is a common element. Many of the ancient languages had a very sonorous effect when spoken, and had sounds of tremendous transmutative potential. (This will be explored in chapter 2, The Mystical Vowels.) The words and sounds of these languages in many cases were designed for communication with the consciousness of the Angelic Kingdoms, and to keep the soul in communication with the Divine while in the physical body. It is why many people who begin to work with various forms of magick focus on the ancient languages, whether Latin, Hebrew, Greek, or Enochian. (Unfortunately, not everything is known about the ancient languages and their mystical associations, and unless caution and discrimination is practiced, the individual may invoke energies that cannot be controlled.) It is also why the Catholic Church lost much of its power when it changed from the Latin to the English. It lost the ancient thoughtforms and sonorous effects of the language, which even if not understood, still created alterations in consciousness during the service.

This does not mean that our modern languages have no power. They do. Unfortunately, the ability to give power to the figures and sounds of language has nearly been lost. This was one of the preeminent abilities of the magickal arts.

The process was simple. It began by attaching definite meanings to the sounds and their combinations so that every time they were used by the human voice, they would evoke energy. The script of those sounds—our written language—had attached to it specific meanings. Thus when combined with the sounds, an amplified and specific manifestation of energy would be projected into the individual's life circumstances. By "toning" the words in a specific, prescribed manner, the energy would be grounded into the physical. It is why one can often read about such processes as "audible sonics": the toning, letter by letter, of magickal words, thus giving the individual time to formulate the proper thought and meaning for each sound. It enabled one to attach spiritual significance to the words while performing the toning.

This art has not been lost. It may have been put aside, obscured, hidden from view, but it still exists. The art of empowering words is one that is able to be used by all people. Learning to use "Directed Esoteric Toning" is not something that only a few persons can learn. It can be learned by anyone.

Whether we realize it or not, when we were born we were each given our own Magickal Word. This word gives us the power to balance our bodies, both physically and spiritually, and enables us to awaken our highest soul potential. We can use it for energy, for abundance, or for prosperity. It is a word that has unlimited possibilities within this incarnation for anyone willing to put forth the effort to learn to use it. This Magickal Word is your name.

All words are magickal or nonmagickal, according to how much spiritual significance we attach to them. Our names have tremendous spiritual significance! If used and worked with in the proper manner, they can open up tremendous spiritual knowledge. Everyone is looking for some method or combination of methods to help them upon the spiritual path. Some have no idea where to even begin their metaphysical studies. Learning the physical and spiritual power and energy inherent within our names is the ideal place to start. All of the ancient mystery schools had one predominant precept—*know thyself!* Within our name are the reflections of our energies, potentials, capabilities, and our karma.

We do not have to depend upon the spiritual facts of others. We can learn to activate our own energies and open ourselves intentionally to higher states of consciousness in order to receive our spiritual instructions. Others can tell you how to receive the higher knowledge, but you have to receive it yourself. This book will provide the opportunity to begin to access the ancient knowledge of sound and names, as applied to you and your own unique life circumstances.

The responsibility is ultimately yours. You will be given the tools. You will be shown the doorway through which to enter. You will have the powers—innate and sacred—revealed to you in this incarnation. It will still be up to you to take these techniques and information and push forward to link your outer life with those inner realities of your spiritual essence. You must learn to see with your eyes and make greater sense of what you find about you through the magick of your name.

Tradition states that as we learn to align our energies and perceptions with the divine energies inherent in and reflected through our name, it will open up communication with one of those angelic beings who has chosen to work with us and with the creative expression of those divine energies within this incarnation. This being, of course, is commonly known as the Guardian Angel. The Guardian Angels are referred to in the mystical Qabala as the Malachim. They work at the heart of the physical universe and are known as the healers and miracle workers. When we learn to get in touch with the energies of our essence—as reflected through our names—we link with these beings, facilitating the play of miracles and wonder within our lives.

We enter the mysteries through the sphere of the mind, but only so we can worship at the temple within the heart. And it is our *name*—our own unique Magickal Word—that opens the heart of the universe to reveal the glory that is God and that God operating within us. We can discover just how unique we each are, and how to align ourselves with the unique plan of the Divine within our life!

Uncovering the mystery of the word and its effects within our lives is a high form of esoteric initiation. Learning to use our name, in our present language, opens one to what is called the Cosmic Language, the language of the Divine wherein rests all knowledge, all understanding, and all wisdom. For one who learns to use the symbolic language of his or her name to connect with the Cosmic Language, nothing is kept secret. The mysteries are revealed, the universal rhythms and patterns are understood, and the individual creative life force is expressed in all things and to all people with love and glory. It is the epitome of the spiritual path, which in the Western world is known as the Quest for the Holy Grail. It reveals our true spiritual essence, and it reveals how to express that essence within this lifetime.

It is often said that when the student is ready, the teacher will appear. Work with our name rings the doorbell of our inner teacher and activates that energy into our lives. To hear the angels sing, you must first hear the song within your own heart. It is this song that is echoed within your name. It is this song that can be released through the very same!

PART ONE

What's in a Name?

*Names belong to things by nature . . . and an artisan of words is
he who keeps in view the name which belongs by nature to each
particular thing!*

—Plato

CHAPTER ONE

The Divine Essence in Your Name

THE ANCIENTS RECOGNIZED that to know the name of something was to have knowledge and power over it, but it implied knowing all aspects of that name. Our individual names contain much power, and if we come to "know" them properly, we can discover much about our own soul's growth, its purposes, and how to release our spiritual energies more effectively into our physical lives. The meaning, the sounds, the rhythms, the nature of the letters and their combinations, all disclose secrets about the individual's essence—past and present, physical and spiritual. We are an integration of past energies and experiences, and the potential creativity within our personalities is reflected within the name we have taken upon us for this incarnation.

Our names reflect the energy signature—the energy patterns we have come to unfold, expand, and overcome within this lifetime. Numerology and nameology are based upon the idea that each soul comes into the world to learn certain lessons and achieve certain goals to round out its overall development and propel its evolvement. The problem arises when the soul takes upon itself the physical vehicle.

In the process of reincarnation, our true essence must slow its intensity and vibration down to the point at which it can integrate with the physical vehicle it has chosen. To do this it builds bands of energy about it—what is often termed subtle bodies. These bands of energy slow the vibration down so that our physical vehicles do not "burn up" in the process of integration, and they filter out the intense energy vibrations so that we can function and learn what we most need to learn while in the physical.

3

This filtering, along with the density of the physical body, causes us to lose much contact with our higher essence and consciousness. Our soul though, in its infinite wisdom, realized that the shock and density of physical form would create this problem, so it makes sure there are some built-in "reminders." It chooses a time and place of incarnation in which the universal energies can work in our lives to provide the learning circumstances, and it chooses a name whose vibration will serve as a catalyst for certain energies to play upon us throughout the incarnation. The soul knows that the letters and sounds and numerological correspondences of its particular name ties one to specific archetypal energies that it can respond to, consciously or unconsciously. In this manner, we set events and energies into play within our lives through our name.

The letters, the meaning, the sounds, and the configurations of the name you have taken upon yourself communicate with your soul essence in a very real and subtle manner. These subtle energy communications do not rule us, even though they can strongly affect how we respond to life circumstances. We always have free will. We do need to understand what kind of communications they are so that we can more consciously direct them. By learning how to use our name as a communicator with the soul, we can manifest the energies of the soul more powerfully. We can begin to understand the rhythms and patterns of events playing themselves out within our lives. We can initiate the process of unleashing our soul potential to create greater fulfillment, prosperity, love, joy and creativity. We can take in hand the divine process of accelerated initiation and heightened consciousness.

Our name gives a true indication of our purpose in this incarnation. It indicates the goals, the tools, and the handicaps, and it gives us information as to why we came into being on this planet at this time, what lessons we have chosen to teach ourselves, what gifts and abilities we have come to unfold, as well as some of the obstacles we will have to learn to overcome. When we understand this, and then learn to direct the communications with the soul from a conscious level, all life opens up to us. We discover the divine magick that lies within the essence and heart of each of us.

The question often arises, why are those with the same name so different? There are many deviations that influence a person's energy expression. Different birth dates and birth places create unique ways for the individual to manifest the energies of his or her name. We take upon ourselves nicknames and name changes that alter the manner in which the soul releases its innate divine energy. (These energy changes will be covered in greater detail in chapter 3.)

Learning to work with your name and with the power that can be released from the soul into your life by that name is the purpose of this work. Learning the esoteric significance and use of one's name as a tool for enlightenment and achievement was part of the ancient spiritual sciences taught within the Atlantean Wisdom Temples. For the New Age disciple, it must again form a part of the educational process.

The Masters of Israel were well versed in the law of vibration and how subtle energies are released into the physical life from the soul. The 22 letters of the Hebrew alphabet symbolize the 22 steps the soul must take in order to gain mastership and break free from the karma of incarnation. These letters—their forms, their sounds and their meanings—trigger vibrations within an individual's life, and the word, both spoken and written, is a physical manifestation of subtle spiritual energy. It translates the more ethereal, spiritual energies into tangible reality. Unless one becomes aware of this, it may be assumed that we are simply a victim of fate or of some form of divine omniscience that we can never be a part of.

Man has the innate power to create. The spoken word or name, when employed with potent thought, becomes a creative power that can be manipulated within one's life in any manner he or she desires. Learning to use that power is what gives dominion over matter.

Assigning a name to a child at birth is no longer given the proper consideration and care. It was once a ritual in itself, and the name would be selected to reflect the highest potential of the incoming soul. This is still reflected somewhat within the Catholic Church, where the newborn is given the name of a saint whose energies will be a guiding force within that child's life. On a subtler level, this choice implies the knowledge of the power of a name to call forth specific energies into one's life.

In the Western world children are given names in the custom of the ancient Roman and Celtic traditions.

The Romans were given (1) a *praenomen*, or first name, (2) a *cognomen*, a family or last name, (3) a *nomen*, or middle name indicating his *gens* (clan), and sometimes if a man was distinguished, (4) an *agnomen*, which was a surname often bestowed as a title of honor, or as a nickname.

> In Britain any noble Celt would also have three personal names, as we now see in Welsh: his *enwau personau: cyfenw* (surname), *enw bedydd* (a baptismal name), *llwyth* (a tribal name), or *tylwyth* (a family name, ancestral name), or *brychan* (his plaid or tartan name). Without a clan name, both Briton and Roman would have been scorned as a nobody (*sine gente*).*

It was not until the Romans and their elaborate civilization that there was felt a need for a hereditary title, a name to be passed from one generation to the next. Although initially popular, it was a practice that ultimately faded in Europe until about the 1500s, when middle names were again applied to individuals.

Originally, names were assigned for various practical and spiritual reasons. A name served as a way of distinguishing a person from others. It was given to symbolize a characteristic or a quality that the parent hoped the child would possess. Sometimes names were taken from the tribal or religious gods or from some animal or object associated with the time of birth. Other times a name was handed down through the family. In such cases some societies forbade the use of an individual's name while that individual was alive. This was a common practice among the early Hebrews. Judah the Pious decreed that a man's soul could not rest if his name were given to someone else in his lifetime.

To the ancient mystics, the assigning of a name was a process that was to be reverenced. Names were viewed as the spiritual essence behind the physical form and consciousness. Name counseling was prevalent for many centuries, especially in the Orient, where unique names were created for each newborn child. We are currently at a point in the evolution of humankind when it is again necessary to revive the ancient techniques of naming.

In many societies the naming of a child was conducted by the mother, as she had the greatest attunement to that incarnating soul. Even though the priest or priestess of a society played a major role, the mother ultimately had the final word. This is reflected within the Christian Bible in the story of the birth and circumcision of John the Baptist: "And it came to pass on the eighth day, that they came to circumcise the child, and they were going to call him by his Father's name Zachary. And his mother answered and said, 'Not so, but he shall be called John.' " (Luke 1: 59–60).

---

* Norma Lorre Goodrich. *Merlin* (New York: Franklin Watts Publishing, 1987), p. 8.

The ancients recognized that the time of pregnancy was a very mystical time. It can be a time when the parents, both mother and father, can attune themselves to the soul for which they will be the channels. They can discern the energies and purposes of that soul and thus the name that will assist in the manifestation of that soul's highest potentials.

Names label us and they represent us; they take on stereotypes and become thoughtforms. People will associate names with physical, mental, and personality characteristics. How often do we hear such phrases as, "You don't look like a Joe" or "You don't act at all like a Jennifer." We tend to become what others expect us to become. Humankind tends to conform to society's expectations, whether they are right or wrong. It has to do with what can be called forced resonance.

Resonance is the ability of energy—in any expression— to reach out and trigger a response in something that is of the same vibration or frequency. If one were to strike a tuning fork for middle C and a piano were in the same room, the vibrations of the tuning fork would reach out and trigger a response in the piano. By reaching in and touching the piano wire for middle C, we would discover that it was also vibrating, even though we could not hear it. *Forced resonance* is the ability to alter the vibration, or force a different vibration into harmony with a stronger one. A stronger vibration can force a weaker one into alignment and harmony with it.

Our name has resonance with a particular universal energy operating within our lives, an archetypal energy to which we have access. Society's thoughtforms and stereotypes about names can block your ability to access that energy and can force your innate energy potential into resonance with the societal thoughtform. This is more likely to happen if we no longer can identify the archetypal energy and the innate essence within our names. It is very easy to fall victim to forced resonance if we do not know how to express the energy and essence inherent within our names.

Most names in our present society have stereotypes associated with them. When we first meet people, we make assumptions about them based upon their names. This in turn affects how we communicate or connect with them. "For any child a name which interferes substantially with the normal interaction is a handicap. The expectations of one's society shape behavior" (Muriel Beadle).

Whether we are conscious of it or not, we all come into physical life knowing there will be some things that must be dealt with in one form or another. It doesn't mean that we can create a Caesar simply by assigning a name, but it does mean that we can choose a name whose meaning, sounds, and rhythms make the tasks of that new soul easier. That begins by recognizing there are stereotypes, but it also implies that we must learn to overcome them within the evolutionary process. We each must come to express our energies in a highly individual and creative manner. In order to do that, we must break the limitations that we have imposed upon ourselves and have allowed others to impose upon us as well.

It all begins with learning to identify and use the energies and essence within your name to which you have the greatest access. It means learning about those creative aspects and applying them so that you no longer fit the "stereotypes" but express an energy that is as unique as you are. It all comes down to making a choice within your life. Do you want to continue to be passive, allowing the energies and preconceptions of others to impose themselves upon you? Or do you want to be active, taking full responsibility to alter, awaken, and manifest the most creative aspects of yourself? The first way is easier, but it only delays what must evolve anyway, and it places you in a position of being blown by whatever whim and fancy the "fates" may bring. The second way returns control of what you do in your life over to you entirely, giving you the opportunity to awaken that divine aspect of yourself that ties your physical life to the Source of All Life within the universe.

"Know thyself!" This was the precept of the ancients and it still holds true today. The path to enlightenment does not lead into some blinding light that dissolves our troubles. It is a path that awakens the light of the divine within the physical. Within our name, within our essence, lies that light.

Our name opens up the path of spiritual knowledge. Others can tell us how to receive the higher knowledge, but only we can do the actual receiving of it. We must push forward to learn the inner realities. We must learn to see with our own eyes. We each must find our own doorways to the Source of All Life, and that doorway is no further than our name! *Man know thyself, then thou shalt know the universe and God.*

NAME MAGICK

In the seventeenth century, "name wizards" practiced the art of *onomancy*. Onomancy was a form of divination—determining a person's character and predicting his or her future by analyzing their personal name. Even before the seventeenth century, people recognized that names were more than just a label. They saw that names contained the spirit of the name bearer. Because of this, contaminated names—names that had been disgraced or were associated with anything negative—were avoided. Taking the name of another member of the family was also taboo, especially while the individual was alive. Some societies saw this as a siphoning off of the life of the first person. (An aspect of this will be discussed later in regard to "Juniors" and how they share the karma of their fathers.)

In ancient times, names were chosen for the distinction they carried. Many Chinese societies invented names for the incoming soul and child, giving each name a mixture of sounds and symbols with secret significance. Even today, many African names are created and given because of the significance of their sounds and meanings. This might involve blending the parents' names or choosing a name that reflects a quality that will suit the child.

Leslie Alan Dunkling defines "name magic" as the attribution of supernatural power to a name, or a belief in the extraordinary significance of a name. Belief in the magick of names still exists today but on a much more superficial level. How often do parents decide against a name because of what has been associated with it in the past? Which name conjures a better image of a lovely, dainty child—Jennifer or Bertha?

In ancient societies and schools of wisdom, people taught that to discover the name of a person or a supernatural being was to gain power over it. Our tales and legends are filled with individuals who needed to discover a true name of someone to be saved. "Rumpelstiltskin" is but one familiar example. Tradition says that to have power over any of the elfin or elemental kingdom one must first learn the name. Thus there arose the use of hidden or secret names. Many of the ancient gods and goddesses had secret names, which they revealed to people at times. That name could then be used to call upon the energy of that being, allowing a person to use it and fuse more intimately with it.

The great Archangels working for humanity all have secret names, and as one steps fully out into greater spiritual evolvement, these names are often given to an individual to assist him or her upon the path. When one receives the secret name of an Archangel, he or she knows that entrance upon the probationary path of discipleship has occurred. Ancient incantations and forms of high magick depended upon the exact knowledge of a name, particularly the "god-names." The name, if understood and used correctly, summons the character and essences that it represents.

The Opening of the Mouth was a ceremony of the ancient Egyptians that used a formula to reanimate the body of a person who had died in order to restore to it its Ka (soul). This spiritual process was known as "dying to be born again." Although it was a symbolic ceremony, it involved the proper use of *naming* to invoke the energies of the individual but also to align them with more divine energies, to open up the initiation process. These initiation names were kept secret.

Keeping secret names is a custom that has not passed with time. Many couples have sweet, secret "love" names for each other. These names are only uttered in the presence of the one they love. And if the name ever is made public, it is seldom used in private again—it loses its power. The power was the essence of its meaning for the individuals. It is why the ancient teachers cautioned "strength in silence" in all things, particularly in regard to names.

Part of the evolvement process must include a determination of our "real" name, which is sometimes referred to esoterically as the *soul* name. It is the name of our most creative and individual essence—not the name that we use during this incarnation, but the name that resides behind all of our names throughout all incarnations. "In the beginning was the Word . . . " In the beginning we had a signature that tied us directly to the Divine. We take upon our selves other names to connect with that divine aspect, to link to that "Word" from which we came forth.

The names we use or choose reveal only what we wish to reveal. They define the expressions of our energies for this incarnation. We are not bound to them, but unless we become more aware of their very real effects, we can never unfold the potentials we are capable of. Our names are special creations; inherent within them is the creative principle that operates throughout nature and the universe. It is what grounds our essence into a unique life of learning and expansion. We can awaken this creative aspect through our names and thus learn to control ourselves, our lives, and our evolution.

SACRED MEANINGS

Every name has its origin, and every name has a literal meaning. These meanings may have been obscured over the years, but then so have our ties to the divine essence that is part of each of us. Names traced far enough back will ultimately reveal their source within the seven sounds from which all sounds came forth—the OM, in Eastern parlance. It would be foolish to pretend that the meanings for our names are entirely accurate and in line with this incarnation's spiritual purposes, but the original meanings provide a starting point for self-exploration. They may now be more symbolic than literal, but as we will see, even this provides a means for unleashing the magickal essence within us.

Carlyle stated, "It is in and through symbols that man consciously or unconsciously lives, works, and has his being." Our names are symbols for us. They reflect us, they identify us, but they are *not* us. A name suggests a quality and thereby links us to the archetypal energy that lies behind that quality. It links us to an aspect of the archetypal energy that we once were and are again becoming. Just as spoken words express thoughts that are ethereal, grounding them in the physical reality for various purposes, so does our name begin the process of grounding our more ethereal energies into physical expressions of life. How much of our spiritual essence is ground into our physical life situations depends upon our knowledge of awakening and using our names. Just as we can increase our vocabulary to enhance our ability to communicate and learn, we can also increase our knowledge of how to use the "vocabulary" of our names (i.e., the meaning, the letters, the rhythms, and the sounds) to increase the manifestation of our spiritual essence within our physical lives.

It all begins with an awareness of the meaning of our birth name, as it appears upon the birth certificate. The name on your certificate represents the legal, physical grounding of your energies in the physical life. Many people find that the name they have been going by is often different—in spelling, essence, etc.—from the way it appears on the certificate. This alone often explains why many individuals have negative attitudes toward their names.

Often, too, there is confusion about what name to give a child. Questioning the parents can reveal much. It would benefit the individual to analyze any name that either parent had felt strongly about but did not give, for whatever reason. This name can reveal energies and essences you have come to evolve into by first overcoming and learning to manifest the energies of the given name. Part of the path of evolvement requires learning that *nothing* is insignificant, especially when it comes to something as intimate as one's name.

> Alice: Must a Name Mean something?
> Humpty Dumpty: Of course it must. My name means the shape I am. With a name like yours, you might be any shape, almost.
> (Lewis Carroll, *Through the Looking Glass*)

That which we in Western society call our Christian name—our *first* name—is the most powerful tool we have. It is the identifying, creative essence of the soul. This name, in conjunction with your birth environment and family karma (as reflected within the last name), sets the tone for how you will manifest your most creative and spiritual aspects.

The family name or surname indicates energies inherited from your ancestors, the karma associated with your family, and the qualities most available to a person through the family heritage—all of which help shape the expression of the individual's creative essence. It is a tool or form of energy given to you by others in the family. It is an optional gift, and it can be enhanced or ignored.

The middle name originally was a designation of the clan. Today, it is an elaboration of the first name. Its primary function in society is to facilitate identification, but it can also be used as a means of support for the creative energies of the first name. It can be used in all the same ways as the first name and has magick of healing and enlightenment.

Together these names indicate the motives, knowledge and potentials that you have come to awaken and use during this incarnation. They provide tools to assist one who knows how to use them in his or her chosen walk in life.

We have many names in the course of a single incarnation. Each one reflects energies and aspects of us at that time. We have family nicknames, nicknames from friends, adopted names, and others. We take the name of spouses and we align ourselves with their family names, thus sharing in the family karma.

There are also religious changes in names, such as during initiatory rites. Most modern initiatory rites involving names are formalized ceremonies that occur at set ages (i.e., baptism, confirmation, etc.), and they do not confer any particular power to the individual. Even baptism as it is often practiced occurs when the child is too young to be aware of the consciousness and energies being invoked. In more ancient times baptism occurred as an initiatory rite whereby the individual consciously takes upon himself or herself a new identity and consciousness. Certain awarenesses and capabilities were developed as a prelude to this rite. The names taken upon the individual at this time signaled the end of the old individual and the beginning of the new, in alignment with the energies reflected by the name itself.

Name giving was both an art and a science. Names were chosen with great care and reverence. People were conscious of the ways the sounds and their meanings could affect a new soul. "The Babudja people of Zimbabwe believe that a habitually crying child possesses an inadequate name. Crying is thought to be a sign from spirits that the name must be changed." *(Professor's Book of First Names)*

Does this mean that we can create a Caesar by the appropriate name? Probably not, but to deny that the name has no effect upon the individual is to admit foolishness. There are always names that are made light of because of what society has come to associate with it. This thoughtform of energy is something that the soul must overcome. It is amazing how many cruel names are given to children.

At one of the first schools in which I taught was a young black girl with the last name of Bodie (pronounced body). Her first name was Vanilla. The girl took a terrible teasing, and on some level there must have been some confusion for this beautiful black girl to be known as Vanilla Bodie. How much it ultimately affected her life is something that deserves serious consideration by her parents.

Most children know that if you want to hurt another child, all you have to do is find a way to make fun of his or her name. Children respond to this because at the early ages there is unconscious recognition of the link between our names and our essence. As we grow older, we develop a callousness out of self-defense. We build walls that separate us from the energies associated with our names. We lose that intimate bond with the energies of our name. It becomes for us just a title of identification, nothing more.

Because our names reflect us, there must be greater care in assigning them. We need to be aware of what our names mean so that we can awaken the power of our essence through it as we were originally meant to do.

Nicknames and shortened names limit our energies. One who goes by Tom rather than Thomas may be able to accomplish tremendous things, but how much more could be accomplished if the power of the *full* name were awakened and expressed by the individual. As we will see in the next two chapters, the extra syllable(s) has the capability of opening reservoirs of energy and potential.

In many cases the individual may find it easier to relate to the nickname. In cases such as these the nickname may be a bridge to the energies of the true first name. It can also indicate that the legal first name was a misnomer. It may not have truly reflected the energies you wished to work with. At the same time, everything in the physical life provides opportunity for growth and unfoldment, and it is possible that the lack of resonance with the name shows you have come to learn to work with new energies entirely and not coast with what has always been familiar and comfortable. Working with your real name in the ways outlined in this book will lead you to this information, and will help you recognize that the name you were given will further your education and evolvement during this incarnation.

In nicknames that use initials, a lot of power and energy is lost. As will be discussed in the next chapter, it is the vowels that carry the power within a name.

In the case of children who are given the same name as their parents, there is much to be concerned about. Many societies had taboos against naming children after someone who was still living, because it was believed that it drew the life force from the elder individual of that name. When a parent names a child after him or her, the child then becomes bound to the karma of the parent much more intimately than may ever have been necessary. Parents need to carefully consider their reasons for such actions. In many cases it is to fulfill some egotistical desire of the parent to relive his or her life through the child, which makes it difficult for the child to develop individual creativity and expression.

In such cases as adoption, the new name and family provides an opportunity for the soul to grow in an entirely new manner, free of the karma of the birth parents. This does not mean that the child is not karmically connected to the parents, but rather that he or she has learned to initiate new circumstances, to make leaps of change and awareness. This is symbolized by the leap into a new family. On an unconscious level it teaches the soul that it is not bound by anything in the physical, either past or present.

In many cases of adoption, especially with older children, it is only the last name that is changed. As previously discussed, the last name is the name of family karma and learning. At this point the child switches from the karma of the birth parents to the family energies of the adoptive parents with all its learning opportunities.

For children that are adopted shortly after birth and thus are not truly "named," it may simply be that they needed this time and place in order to enter incarnation for the sake of their own soul growth and development. They may have needed both the physical predisposition of the birth parents and energies of the new adoptive name to assist with their own unique lessons. The energies of the birth parents and the environment of the adoptive parents are often inherently critical for the intricate lessons that the child has come to meet. Often in cases such as these, both sets of parents agreed at some point to this unusual circumstance so that the child could learn and grow in a manner that would be best for its own soul development.

Many women ask about changing their names at marriage. My usual recommendation is to not drop the last name. Either keep the name the same, so that you do not lose your own individual identity in the marriage, or at least keep it hyphenated so that you retain individual essence while simply adding more to it, i.e., Mary Smith-Thompson.

If one were to interview 100 married couples and ask the question, Who had the most difficulty adjusting to that first year of marriage? the majority would unquestionably be the woman. It is the woman who changes her name, thus dropping part of her own individual energy and taking on an entirely new energy expression within her life. Until it is formally accomplished on a physical level—the new energies grounded and acted upon—the effects will not be truly felt. The man, on the other hand, does not change his name and thus does not change his energy. Life goes on pretty much as before, with little trauma.

In cases of divorce it is very important to drop the energies and the name of the partner. Any time there has been sexual intimacy, especially of an extended nature as in marriage, energy is exchanged and entwined between the two partners on an atomic level. The last name of the spouse keeps you tied to that energy, delaying the unentanglement of energy between the two. Divorce is never easy, no matter how the court proceeding may go. When there has been such an intimacy, it can take as much as seven years or more for the energies to untangle from each other at the atomic level.

Children of divorce should keep their names. Their names tie them to both parents, as they should. When they are independent adults they can then change their names as they see fit. For the wife though, it is important to understand that the last name can keep you linked to that individual's energy. Some women prefer this, which is fine also. They may have a wonderful relationship with their in-laws, and may have been married so long that the spouse's name is now more a reflection of their own energy. It must be remembered, though, that divorce is a separation of two to become one. It is the becoming of a single and individual energy essence again. That realization can be hindered by keeping a name that reflects an energy of duality.

We are at a point in which ancient techniques of name counseling and naming must reemerge. This was a procedure that was prevalent in the Orient for centuries. The children's rhyme, "sticks and stones will break my bones, but names will never hurt me" only refers to the physical. Names can hurt us in very subtle and very real ways, especially if we refuse to see their meaning and their effects on our lives.

Before we denigrate our names, before we choose to change them, we need first to explore their significance, both outer and inner. It is to assist in this that the last part of this book is dedicated. Hopefully, it will awaken a greater reverence for the name you have taken and the sacred meaning and power within it.

NAME CHANGING

It is much easier to unfold the magick within our names than to take on a new one. Changing names is not like changing tires that are worn out or don't seem to fit. They are intimate links to our highest essence. Realizing this aspect adds tremendous meaning to the words, "Hallowed be thy name."

Yet we cannot ignore the fact that people do make judgments based upon one's name. Some names sound older, more mature, particularly the full name as opposed to a contraction of it—for example, Timothy vs. Tim. Your name can reflect nationality, religion, etc., giving others clues about your personality and behaviors. Individuals also make racial judgments about people according to their names and the sounds within their names.

We can choose either to allow other people's judgments to limit us or to learn from them and grow. We can allow our names to label us or we can learn as much as we can about them, breaking the old labels and creating new perceptions in those you meet and deal with daily.

It begins with assessing your own attitudes toward your name. How do you feel about it? How do you react when others call you by name? Are you proud? Do you enjoy it? Do you hurry to tell them your nickname, so as to avoid dwelling on your true name? Do you even know what your name means? What effects do the sounds within the name have upon you and others, both physically and spiritually? Have you even explored the basic esotericism associated with your name and its significance in your life? If you have not explored the energies associated with your name, then you should not consider changing it to any other form.

Changing your name should be a last resort, because names are living and changing anyway. As you grow and unfold, so do the perceptions of others concerning your label. You break the old pattern and open new ones. A person who associates immaturity with any-one named Mary will change his or her perspectives as any Mary they are close to begins to unfold her potentials. Working with our names unfolds our potentials and enables us to empower our life so that previous assumptions and judgments can no longer be applied, be they others or your own.

Use your own full name first. Enforce its use. If you do not wish to be called by a nickname, correct others immediately upon their reference to you in that manner. Do not allow others to corrupt your name. With this simple act you begin to empower your life. If you must change your name, avoid fad names and be aware that dislike for a name may indicate low self-esteem or lack of realization of the innate divinity inherent within each of us.

SIGNIFICANT SUFFIXES IN NAMES

1. *a*—feminizes the name. It is the Latin feminine form of gender. (examples: Paula, Linda)
2. *ia*—feminizes the name. It is a Latin feminine form of gender. (examples: Patricia—the feminine of Patrick)
3. *e*—feminine French form. (example: Dominique)
4. *ette*—the feminine, diminuitive French form. (examples: Loretta, Lynette)
5. *ene/een*—Irish feminine form of gender. (example: Colleen)
6. *ine/ona*—the Greek feminine gender. (example: Pauline)
7. *ita*—Spanish feminine (diminuitive) gender. (Juanita = "little Juan")

These are a few examples of suffixes that alter names and their energies. As a general rule most names that end in vowel suffixes activate the feminine energies within the individual. We are all a combination of male and female energies, whether we define it as electromagnetic, assertive-receptive, or yin-yang, etc. Ultimately, we want to find a balanced use of both these energies within our lives. Most female names and many nicknames end with vowels, which keep the feminine energy more active in and around the individual.

In the case of nicknames (i.e., Joe, Kathi, Eddie, etc.) this vowel ending softens a person's energy, and activates his or her feminine, nurturing, intuitive and creative characteristics. This may enable one to relate more easily to others, and help ease the transition to handling the energy of the full name.

Two suffixes in particular, along with their sounds, need extra attention at this point in regard to activation of feminine energies within the individual. These are the *i* and the *y* endings of names.

Just as many suffixes activate feminine energies, shortened forms of the name can activate more of the masculine. A good example is use of the nickname Tom instead of Tommy, or even Tommi. Tom is more masculine and Tommy is more childlike, immature. Many male children will take upon themselves nicknames ending in *y*—Tommy, Timmy, Bobby, Johnny, etc. As they grow older, usually during the later teen years, they may use either the shortened name without the *y* suffix or their full first names. The *y* suffix softens the energy and awakens some of the feminine qualities without becoming unbalanced.

In our society there is much concern about masculinity and femininity. Males are still brought up to be somewhat macho. The *y* suffix is a temporary compromise because it allows the individual to be a little childlike and feminine while still retaining the masculine balance.

Rarely, if ever, will you see a masculine nickname spelled with the suffix *i* instead of the *y*, as is frequent with females. Robert is called Bobby, not Bobbi. Thomas is Tommy and not Tommi. As will be explored in greater detail in the next chapter, the *i* suffix activates the feminine energy.

The *i* suffix and vowel is a symbol of the feminine fires within the heart of us all. It strongly awakens the heart chakra and energy center and our nurturing, childlike and creative aspects. While it may be all right for males in our society to express a little love, as in "Timmy," it is too much to expect one to activate all his feminine energy through the name "Timmi." A male child using the *i* suffix in his name at the present time in our society will open himself to teasing and ridicule. This reflects much about the misunderstanding and unbalanced perceptions most individuals hold toward sexuality within our society. There is little true understanding of the masculine and feminine energies that are an inherent part of us all on more than just a physical, sexual level.

Hopefully, at some point individuals will come to realize the significance and power this one vowel can make when properly utilized within one's name. It has the capability of igniting the creative fires of love and idealism and lifting our energies and perceptions beyond the physical. It has the capability of linking the mind and the heart for greater creative expression within one's life.

AFFIRMING OUR ESSENCE THROUGH OUR NAMES

Sound is one of the most dynamic and powerful forces in the universe. Sounds, words and their meanings carry the ability to create or to destroy. It is a force that all of the ancient mystery schools taught in some degree to their students. Sound is creative and destructive, masculine and feminine, positive and negative.

When we use words, names and sounds as positive affirmations in conjunction with creative visualization, we amplify the activation of such energy within our lives. We can use our names as a powerful form of affirmation for health, creativity, higher consciousness and general empowerment.

All sounds and words have the capability of affecting us. Unpleasant sounds and words—careless and uncultured speech, for example—produce an atmosphere in which these energies constantly act upon the individual. Each word makes an energy form in the ethers. Some words are very objectionable, while others are intimately beautiful. Those words associated with our essence, our names, have the capability of transmuting conditions in our lives.

The first step is altering the way in which we communicate to ourselves. Generally, it is done in one of four ways:

1. Denial ("I can't ..." or "I won't ...")
2. Opposition ("I need to ..." or "I want to ..." In both of these cases there is an unspoken and strongly implied "but"—"I need to quit smoking *but* ..." or "I want to lose weight *but* ...")

While the first two ways of communicating with ourselves are negative, the second two are positive:

3. Reconstruction ("I no longer . . .")
4. Affirmation ("I am . . .")

We use affirmation with visualization to take advantage of all energies available to us. We work between the visible and the invisible, the mental and the physical, the spiritual and the material, and we learn methods that affect both. We use affirmations to draw forth energies from the less tangible realms that will manifest within the physical. We learn to awaken our more subtle energies so that we can more fully live within the physical world.

The most powerful affirmation you can utilize is one that involves your own name and its meaning. Everyone else uses our name, and we should too. We should feel comfortable saying our own names. We should feel powerful when affirming our essence through it.

Affirmations can be made in a variety of ways: (1) by meditating, (2) by speaking, (3) by writing, (4) in groups, or (5) by singing and chanting.

Using our names in the correct affirmation serves many functions:

1. It energizes us on all levels. (Five minutes of name affirmation with the appropriate visualization will replenish our energy after a difficult day.)
2. It is balancing to the entire metabolic system.
3. It stimulates greater healing in general.
4. It strengthens the auric field.
5. It keeps us linked to our spiritual bodies and energies, which atrophy from lack of use, as is the case with most people. Disuse can accelerate the aging process and the degeneration of the physical body.
6. It opens one up to higher consciousness and intuition.
7. It stimulates greater expressions of creativity.
8. When used in meditation, it will activate higher understanding of life circumstances.
9. It begins the building process for the Body of Light and Magickal Essence.
10. It can open one to communication with higher dimensional beings, particularly the Holy Guardian Angel.
11. It can awaken awareness of life purpose.

When using any affirmation, it is always best to use the "I am" phrase in the beginning. The "I am" phrase is a link to the highest spiritual energy operating within your physical life during this incarnation. In the ancient esoteric science known as the Qabala, specific names were given to God and how the Divine manifests within our lives. Instead of using one generic title for God, specific names/titles were used in prayer and scripture so that only the aspect of divine energy most needed would be activated.

In the Hebraic Tree of Life, ten names for God were utilized, covering the ten predominant areas of physical life. At the highest point on the Tree of Life was an aspect of God known to the Hebrews as EHEIEH. This is the name given to Moses at the time of the burning bush. "I AM THAT I AM!" It is the highest aspect of God to which we have access while in the physical. It is for this reason that the "I am" phrase is so powerful in affirmations. It serves as a call signal to that highest aspect of spiritual energy operating within our lives, which sets the energy of the affirmation into manifestation. Is it no wonder then that such statements as, "I am so tired of my job" and "I am always catching two colds every winter" become self-fulfilling prophecies. It activates that highest aspect of our consciousness to start work on our energies, which makes it possible for us to "catch those two colds every winter."

Using one's name with an "I am" phrase is strengthening, energizing, protective and releasing to our greatest power and creativity. It reestablishes the link between the you in your physical life and the divine part of you that is a part of all energies and light within the Universe.

Guidelines for Affirming Your Essence
1. Discern what your name means. Use part two of this book, and if your name is not listed and described, consult your library.
2. Always phrase in the present tense. There is no past, and the future is always future. We live in an ever-present moment, thus the significance of the "I am."
3. The shorter and simpler the affirmation, the better.
4. With many affirmations it is difficult to discern whether it is truly right for you. With name affirmations, this is no problem.
5. Remember that you are creating and manifesting something

new, reawakening the true you. You are not trying to override or change what already exists.

6. Affirmations are not meant to contradict or change feelings and emotions.
7. Create a feeling of belief.
8. Visualize yourself as the essence and being reflected in the meaning of your name.
9. Include references to spiritual sources for even greater power.
10. Sit quietly where you can be undisturbed.
11. Form your name and its meaning in an affirmation (e.g., Nancy means "gracious child," thus "I am Nancy. I am the gracious child of God!").
12. Sound the affirmation silently in your head as you inhale. As you exhale, sound it outward, audibly. Inward, silently. Outward, audibly. In. Out. Spiritual to physical. In this manner of Directed Esoteric Prayer we link the higher, inner self with the outer, physical reality. We bring our energies out into the physical.
13. See, feel, imagine yourself in all the glory, as in our example, as a "gracious child of God," replete with all the energies, potentials and capabilities you would imagine a gracious child of God would possess.
14. You may feel uncomfortable with this at first, especially referring to yourself by name. This passes. We are simply becoming reacquainted with our highest essence once more.

How long you take to affirm this each day is up to you. Ultimately we want to at least think the affirmation every day, so as to stay linked with our highest essence and be able to manifest it at any time within our day-to-day life circumstances. They actually become secret words of power, a formula for calling into being your greatest essence and energy.

With this formula we are manifesting divine light where there was none. You are expressing your divine essence. It ignites the aura as if awakening the great solar fires of the universe. You are bringing to life a new creation—the True You! It is like bringing light to an unlit and dark planet or an uncreated soul that was simply awaiting the touch of the Creator to bring the flames of life into manifestation.

This lighting of your inner fires through this name affirmation is an excellent prelude to meditation or occult work. It affirms the central presence of the Divine Spirit operating in and through you. The power that manifests rests within your own imagination and intention.

Other Techniques

One of the more ancient techniques for uncovering the power essence hidden within one's name is through the use of anagrams. An anagram involves the rearranging of the letters in a name (usually the full name—first, middle and last) to form words and phrases. These words and phrases provide clues to lessons, abilities, etc.

The making of anagrams from one's name was begun in the third century by a Greek poet named Lycophron. True anagrams come from all the letters, each being used only once. Sometimes the words that emerge are not preferred, but even these can unveil some character and personality changes necessary to the path of unfoldment and spiritual development.

Another system is one that was employed by the ancient Celts. For them it wasn't so much the whole name and its meaning as it was the significance of each individual letter. This system is similar to ancient Hebraic methods and Egyptian teachings. Part of the wisdom teaching involved the proper toning of "God-names" to manifest the play of that archetypal energy within physical life. The toning was performed ritualistically.

Each letter was sounded, one by one, along with the proper visualization for each letter. By toning individual letters in a name, one was able to formulate a creative image that facilitated the manifestation of the archetypal energy being invoked. The reading of the name was the sum of the individual letters within it. The dominant letters, most often the vowels, were given special attention.

(This book does not deal with the meanings of all the letters that comprise our alphabet. Its primary function is to enable you to link with the meaning of your name and utilize those letters and sounds that reflect your greatest energies, in this case the actual vowel sounds.)

Any technique that is to open and expand our awarenesses requires certain things:

    a. We must first determine our real name.

    b. We must note key words, meanings, even etymology of the name.

    c. Use such things as anagrams to unfold intricacies.

d. Analyze it according to letters, particularly the symbolic significance of the most important letters—the vowels.
e. Analyze your name according to the sounds of the letters and their effects, particularly again with the vowels.
f. Give attention to the rhythms of your name and the rhythms of the universe they are tied to.
g. Use as many other techniques for analysis as possible: meditation, numerology, musical correspondences, and even astrology to correlate, inform and confirm within your own mind the true potential of your highest essence.

Bonum nomen est bonum omen!
—Roman proverb
("A good name is a good omen!")

CHAPTER TWO

The Mystical Vowels

This is the very essence, the secret of modern Initiation: to get beyond words to a living experience of the spiritual. Precisely when we no longer think in language, we begin to feel it; we begin to have it streaming in us and out from us as an element of feeling.

—Rudolph Steiner
The Festivals and Their Meanings

IF WE WISH to understand the power of words and more particularly the power of our names, we must first pay attention to their sounds. Stuart Robinson and Frederic G. Cassidy in *The Development of Modern English* define vowels as "musical tones made by a regular vibration of the vocal cords and modified by varying the shape and size of the resonance chamber." Every society throughout the world has taught the power of sound and music, both as a healing force and as a force for alchemical change. What we are relearning is that all sounds within our names—especially the vowel sounds—are musical and can be used as widely and effectively as any form of music. (See chapter 4 for guidelines for transposing one's name into a musical melody.)

The vowel sounds in most ancient alphabets were sacred. The Hebrew alphabet—the forerunner of the English language by way of Greece—is comprised of consonants, because it was believed that the vowels were too sacred. Vowels have the activating or life-giving power. This concept is one that we need to rediscover for ourselves, and the following techniques will enable you to do so.

Opening the Doorways to Nature
The vowels are links to archetypal elements and energies within the universe. Many societies taught how to hum the various vowel sounds in order to link with the super-physical kingdoms. The primary vowel sounds within your name (especially your first name)

give you an indication of which elemental kingdom you have come to work with, and they can assist you in expressing your own creative essence during this incarnation.

There are other forms of life evolving and working together with humankind, and these beings embody creative intelligence. Whether we call them devas, angels or beings of the nature kingdom, part of their function is to assist with the maintenance of the Earth and the evolution of humankind. By learning to work creatively and constructively with the energies of the Earth, we are given impetus to bridge to the heavens. The vowels in our name tell us which beings of the nature kingdom we have the greatest facility with and what we must learn to work with to an even greater degree.

In the Hebrew esotericism known as the Qabala, it is one from the angelic or nature kingdom who will become our teacher-initiator when we more consciously step forward upon the path to spirituality. This teacher in one sense becomes our true Guardian Angel. It is one from a group of beings known as the Malachim—the healers and "bringers of light." By knowing which part of nature, with its associated elementals, that our name-sounds link us to, we can begin the process of calling forth the one who will ultimately step forward to teach and initiate.

Vowel	Element	Direction	Elemental Beings
E	Air	East	Sylphs
I	Fire	South	Salamanders
U	Earth	North	Gnomes
O	Water	West	Undines
A	Ether	All four	All four of the above

The above associations and correspondences are not rigid. They are guidelines that provide a jumping-off point for self-exploration.

The elements associated with the primary vowel in your first name are especially important when considered from an astrological point of view. As mentioned in the first chapter, when we incarnate we choose a time and place of birth and a name whose energies will play upon us to help us learn what we most need. We are not bound by them and can override them, but we choose that kind of energy "imposition" because it is easy to forget our purpose once encased within the physical flesh.

Each astrological sign is of one of the four elements as well. Our birth sign reflects those energies we hope to unfold within this lifetime—what we wish to evolve into. The element of that sign reflects what element of ourselves we wish to unfold and develop. Part of our life achievement and quest is in accessing that element within our world and learning to handle its energies.

The element associated with our name indicates what we brought with us to assist us in accessing the astrological element. For example, if we are a Water sign astrologically and have a vowel that is an Air element, then we might be trying to learn to link the Mind (Air) to the emotions (Water). It could indicate that one has come to use his or her mental energies to control the emotions.

If the two elements are the same, it can indicate that you may have come to double the work with that particular element, or even to learn an entirely new aspect of it. If the elements are opposite, it does not mean that they cancel themselves out. *All* elements can work well together. Fire and Water do not have to cancel. If worked with properly, Fire and Water create steam, which generates tremendous power and energy. Using tables 1 and 2 will provide some insight into the elements, their qualities and the vowels and signs of the zodiac that are associated with them.

Knowing the elements associated with your name and your astrological sign can help you utilize the energies of the Earth to aid your growth and to affect change within your life. In our search for a better life, we have grown less sensitive to the nuances of nature. We no longer see with a child's or seer's eyes. We must realize that the devic or angelic kingdom (which comprises the kingdom of nature) occurs side by side in the evolution of humankind. Their consciousness is open and more concerned with life itself and with its highest and truest expression, rather than with its form. Humankind centers upon the emotional and mental faculties; the beings of nature center upon the higher intuitive faculties.

We need to keep in mind one thing. In a universe of infinite energies and life forms, anything that expands our awareness can only benefit us. By opening ourselves to the possibility first and then the realization of such life, we open to ourselves worlds of wonders waiting to be explored. We are already open to such mysteries. The creation of our names opened the doors automatically. Learning to use our names enables us to walk through those doors.

The elementals are the building blocks of nature. The angels or devas are the builders. Most of the elementals act unconsciously, but

Table 1: Vowel and Astrological Elements

Element	Vowel	Signs of Zodiac	Qualities of Elements
FIRE	I	Aries Leo Sagittarius	Courageous, self-assertive, visionary, helpful, creative, strong, active life force; imposing, fanatical, self-indulgent, authoritarian. —Work with Salamanders
EARTH	U	Taurus Virgo Capricorn	Providing necessities, grounded, good sense of timing, stable, self-aware, understands emotions, miserly, controlling, coarse, no empathy. —Work with Gnomes
AIR	E	Gemini Libra Aquarius	Mental, inventive, intelligent, quick, alert, cooperative, humane, cold, aloof, imitative, nervous, superficial. —Work with Sylphs
WATER	O	Cancer Scorpio Pisces	Understanding, emotional, psychic, sensitive, artistic, romantic, reserved, impressionable, self-indulgent, exaggerates feelings, sensual. —Work with Undines
ETHER	A	Ether is substance from which all was created.	Ether is the spiritual aspect that overrides and influences all elements. It permeates all creation.

Differences of opinion exist as to the vowel associations of the Earth and Ether elements. These are only guidelines, but what is most important is how you associate and what correspondences *you* build. The author has used the *U* for the Earth element, as it also is a vowel whose sound correlates to the functions of the base chakra. The *A* is assigned to the Ether because of its connection to the heart chakra, which mediates all energies of the body, just as Ether mediates the energies of all the elements.

Table 2: Elemental Combinations

Combined Elements	The Qualities and Relationships
FIRE WITH FIRE	Tremendous impulse and stimulation; can burn self out; must find practical outlet; provides much energy toward life goal; must balance self-expression.
AIR WITH AIR	Excessively mental; not enough direction; whirlpool of ideas needing practical release; talkative and expressive.
WATER WITH WATER	Can give added depth; increased sensitivity; feelings easily hurt; intolerance; can lead to instability; requires a realistic focus.
EARTH WITH EARTH	Needs stimulus to manifest latent fruit; can cause inertia; materialistic; must work on self-expression and personal relationships; stabilizing; latent talents.
FIRE WITH EARTH	Learning boundaries of the activity of Fire; practicalize high ideals, inspiring greater mobility; can ground the Fire or stimulate expression.
FIRE WITH AIR	Very compatible; too much Air and Fire is out of control; Fire can change properties of Air for good or bad; strengthens and raises ideals.
FIRE WITH WATER	Fire turns Water to steam; Water puts out fires; when balanced they bring useful ideas/ tremendous activity; alchemical processes are to be learned.
EARTH WITH AIR	Air stimulates Earth qualities; fruit needs oxygen; Earth stabilizes volatile Air aspects.
EARTH WITH WATER	Very compatible, as the two are necessary for anything to grow; Earth stabilizes the restless Water element and Water prevents dryness and unfeeling nature.
AIR WITH WATER	Air keeps Water fresh; Water element can feel unfulfilled by Air not understanding the emotions; intellect modifies oversensitivity; Water broadens sympathies of Air.

The Ether element accentuates the aspects of whatever element it is associated with. It will enhance, or has the capability of enhancing, both the positive and the negative aspects.

the angels are more conscious creators. The celestial kingdom is as hierarchical as humankind.

There is often confusion regarding the difference between the elementals and the nature spirits—the ones referred to as elves, fairies, etc. They are all of the same hierarchy (the angelic), but they serve different functions at different levels. Most people link them all together under the same category, either as nature spirits or as elementals, but there is a difference. Those of the nature spirit position are more likely to display "personality," and the elementals have more of a "characteristic." For example, in any family there may be a particular characteristic or trait that all have—a tendency to baldness, thinness, dark hair, etc., but each person in that family, even though he or she may have a similar characteristic, will display a unique personality.

Because they are the basic building blocks of nature, the elementals are the closest to being true energy and consciousness. Men and women are energy systems, and if we come in contact with energy outside of us, it affects our own energy. Work around them and with them stimulates strong responses. It has been said that the way to heaven is through the feet. Implied within that statement is a realization that it is by working with the energies of the Earth and nature that we are given propulsion to the heavens. Learning to work with those elemental beings that we have the greatest rapport with will assist this process. It is for this reason that we need to be aware of the element of our name and the beings associated with that element.

GNOMES (Earth element; Vowel *U*)

This is a generic title, and it does not truly refer to our usual conception of the gnome. Elementals are all four-dimensional, in that they have nothing to obstruct their movements. They move through matter as easily as we move through air. The bodies of gnomes are comprised of the chemical ethers, and are "earthy" in nature. They cannot fly, and they can be burned in fire. They also grow old in a manner similar to humans. Various types of entities fall into this category, each with its own degree of consciousness. They maintain and work for the physical body—its composition, its assimilation of minerals, etc. Without them we could not function in the physical world. One is usually "assigned" to help us maintain our physical vehicles. As with many elementals, it is through their association with humankind that they can become ensouled and evolve. They are affected by what we do. If we abuse the body, we abuse the elemental that is assigned to us. The gnomes are needed to build the plants and flowers and trees. It is their task to tint them, to make the minerals and crystals and to maintain the Earth so that we have a place to grow and evolve. Those whose primary vowel is of this element will have a stronger resonance with this group than others.

UNDINES (Water element; Vowel *O*)

This is a classification of the basic life form of the Water element. They are composed of the basic "life ethers." Wherever there is a natural source of water, they can be found. Water is the springwell of life. The undines are also associated with the maintenance of the astral body. One is assigned to each person to help with the function of bodily fluids—blood, lymphatic fluids, etc. They are also subject to mortality but are much more enduring than the gnomes. How long they live depends upon their relationship with humankind and humankind's relationship with them. Abuse of our body abuses them, and once assigned, they must simply endure, which is why they are dependent on humans for growth as well. Diseases of the blood contaminate them, and many of the modern diseases such as AIDS, which affects the bodily fluids, tie those undines to the karma and effects of the disease, no matter how unwilling they may be. Because they have no control, in some respects it can be compared to selling a child into prostitution. Those who have the *O* as the primary vowel have a greater ability to establish rapport with those of this kingdom. All water upon the planet—rain, river, ocean—has tremendous undine activity associated with it.

SYLPHS (Air element; Vowel *E*)

On the hierarchical scale the sylphs are more closely linked to the angels than to any of the other elementals. They work side by side with them, and thus they too are made up of the "light ethers." They are part of the creative element of Air, and it is their work that results in the tiniest of breezes to the mightiest tornadoes. Not all are restricted to living in the air, and most are of high intelligence. Some have much to do with humans, often helping alleviate pain and suffering. They also serve as temporary guardian angels until we open ourselves and draw to us the one who is *the* Guardian Angel. One of their special tasks is to help children who have just passed over. Certain of the sylphs are also assigned to the individual human. They help to maintain the mental body, and thus our thoughts (good or bad) are what most affects them. They work for the assimilation of oxygen from the air we breathe and with all functions of air, in and around us. Exposure to pollution and to smoking, etc. affects their appearance and their effectiveness in our physical lives. Those whose primary vowel is an *E* have greater ease in developing rapport and resonance with them. They also work to cleanse and uplift our thoughts and intelligence.

SALAMANDERS (Fire element; Vowel *I*)

These are the Fire elementals. They are found everywhere. No fire is lit without their help, but they are mostly active underground and internally within the body and mind. They are responsible for explosions and volcanic eruptions. They also function within the physical body, particularly in circulation and in maintaining the correct body temperature. Outside of the body, they work less intimately with humankind. Fire is a powerful vibration and esoterically has been described as having the sound of a harmonic invocation. Salamanders have a strong love for music and are foremost an agency of nature. They have the ability to evoke *powerful* emotional currents in humans. They also can stimulate fires of spiritual idealism. The inner fires can be expressed for either good or bad, as in all things. Their energies are very stirring, and it takes tremendous ability to control and direct them for the most creative results. Those whose primary vowel is an *I* have the ability to establish resonance with them more easily.

Almost all the elementals and nature spirits require some contact with humankind, and there are, in fact, many who require this contact and human assistance to help with their own evolutionary process. For this reason it is important that we try to establish a more harmonious relationship with them, and develop a greater perception of their interaction within our lives. Working with the sounds within your name as described within this book will initiate the process.

Those who have a vowel that aligns them with the Ether element have a greater responsibility. The Ether element gives wider access to all of the elemental kingdoms. This implies that there is not only an increased ability to work with all of the kingdoms but also an increased ability to be affected by all of them (meaning a greater need to be watchful of balance).

Element	Vowel	Archangel of Element	King of the Element
Earth	U	Auriel	Ghob
Water	O	Gabriel	Niksa
Air	E	Raphael	Paralda
Fire	I	Michael	Djin
Ether	A	Christ	None

The process of linking with your element is easy. You should always begin when you're relaxed and can remain undisturbed. As you relax, breathing slowly and rhythmically, silently sound the letter of the element. Alternate the vowel with your first name and with the name of the archangel and king: vowel, your name, the archangel, the king and then end with the vowel again. You now have five "elements" (vowel, name, archangel, king, and vowel). Five is the number of the microcosm—the energies of the universe manifesting in humankind.

This fivefold formula serves as a call signal, a flare to let those elementals and beings working with you know that you are now open to greater ministrations from them and with them as well. After calling them, allow yourself to focus upon ways you can more constructively utilize those energies throughout the rest of the day.

THE SYMBOL OF THE VOWELS
AS AN INNER TALISMAN

The path of our return to the primal point of creation is marked in the language of the symbols. These symbols both hide the path and reveal it. No one is helped by an outward symbol. The outward symbol is a sign that must be transferred to an inner symbol, then we build that symbol within our own hearts and consciousnesses. It is also a building process. When we build it within us and then become everything the symbol is, we also become what it stands for on spiritual levels. We become one with the archetype that works through it.

Speech is the real language. It is the real power for us while in the physical. The written form of speech is secondary in that it leads us to the inner power of the Word. The written word reflects humanity's evolvement. From an anthropological viewpoint, speech raises us above the beasts, but writing (the means of recording and passing on human knowledge without the necessity of direct contact) is the mark of a high level of human society.

There are primarily two systems of writing: (1) pre-alphabet (pictographs, hieroglyphics, etc.), and (2) alphabetic (syllable scripts, single-sound scripts, etc.). Drawing becomes writing when the picture ceases to stand for an idea and instead comes to represent a combination of sounds. In working with the symbols of our names, especially the vowels, we must rediscover the idea that lies behind the script itself.

The form the primary vowels take within our names can show us much concerning our potentials, life lessons, and goals on physical and spiritual levels. We need to begin exploring the symbolic form of the vowels and the concepts, ideas and energies associated with such forms so that we can draw them into us, reawakening them so as to re-express them as a divine force within our lives. In this way they become personal inner talismans.

SYMBOL OF THE *A*

The first vowel is one that is associated with the element of Ether. Esoteric tradition teaches us that from the ethers came all the other four elements, comprising the five elements of nature and of man—the microcosm in which all energies of the universal macrocosm have the potential of manifesting.

Its form is triangular, pyramidal. It has an apex out of which issues the energies of the other elements to manifest upon the Earth and in turn rise up again to the ethers. On another level it is like a ladder, its cross bar to steady and support us as we climb to the heights of our divinity. It reflects levels to which we can attain in our development.

The letter *A* is comprised of three lines. Three is the creative number within the universe. It comprises the male, the female and the Holy Child of their union. It is a symbol of the trinity and of law. Something may occur once or twice in nature coincidentally, but a third time that it occurs, it begins to reflect a law of occurrence. It reflects the heavens, the Earth (the two polarities of life on Earth) and the realm that bridges the two. Learning to walk that middle line between the worlds is difficult. It is a razor's edge, but it reflects the lesson of balance in some area of an individual's life who has this letter as the dominant vowel within his or her name.

The line between the two poles (positive and negative/male and female, etc.) is a line of balance. It reflects the need to learn to work between all poles of life, to balance polarities at all times. It reflects the infinite variations of male-female energy expressions. It is the process of learning to shapeshift with one's energy in order to maintain balance in the growth process, particularly in day-to-day circumstances.

The line that cuts through the center of the *A*, which cuts through all that manifests from the ethers, is the Thread of Life. The Thread of Life binds all things together. It links all peoples and it joins both sexes. It is what builds to androgony. It serves as a reminder that in the process of raising ourselves to the pinnacle, there will be a threshold to cross.

This is the threshold from the outer to the inner sacred worlds and energies. It marks the point where no one may enter without proper preparation or invitation. It reflects that at some point within the incarnational cycle, the individual will have to come to terms with the meeting of the natural and the supernatural.

It also indicates that one has come to learn to shift consciousness on some level, to learn to open to new levels of awareness, symbolized by the two levels of the letter itself: the creative level above the horizontal line and the level of the Earth below it. Learning to pass and work from one to the other ties one to Jacob's Ladder and the two-way traffic of Earth and Heaven.

While a vertical line reflects desire, activity and dynamic energies, the horizontal line is stabilizing. It is the shortest distance between two points. If *A* is your primary vowel, then it tells you that you have come to shorten the evolutionary process in some manner during this incarnation. As to which area of life this will play itself out in, it will vary from individual to individual. Personal reflection will reveal much. Examining which aspect of your life seems to recur more often and contain more problems may provide some answers.

Because the horizontal pole reflects the linking of the downward emanations from the heavens, it also indicates that the individual has come to rebuild the ladder to development, to form a new pattern of growth within his or her life. This can reflect itself in change that forces growth in the life circumstances. In order to do this, one must face all aspects of himself or herself. This includes those aspects that you have painted over, closed off, pushed to the back of the closet, saying, "No, that's not me!" It is part of what is often called Meeting the Dwellers on the Threshold. We must face these shadow selves, love ourself in spite of them and transmute them so that we can cross to the upper threshold of heavenly energy.

The color associated with the letter *A* is white. White has all frequencies and all colors of the spectrum within it. The ethers have all elements within it. It reflects the energies of the Sun, as the Sun is our primary source of life in this solar system. *A* is the symbol of divine unity, the linking of the heavens and the Earth. It is the unity of the male and female, learning to express the creative principle fully and powerfully. It can make one very versatile (shapeshifting quality) but can also be scattering. Again, it reflects the lesson of balance in some area of the individual's life. It gives one the potential to work from all planes of life and with all elements. It amplifies the energies, potentials and abilities of whatever vowel it is next to.

There is a heightened sensitivity in those with this dominant vowel, and thus there is a greater need to work for balance and to withdraw. If physically weak, this individual will tire much more easily and quickly, although he or she will seldom admit it.

Its energies manifest a striving for truth and the expression of many talents. Like the glyph itself, the individual will be open to everything upon Earth. Thus there will be a tendency to scatter energies and to become immersed in activities while neglecting the spiritual. Working to awaken the Creative Intellect, the apex, will keep an individual from losing himself or herself in the activities of the physical. Until work is done on the Creative Intellect, the activities and relationships of the physical will not be entirely satisfying or fulfilling. Unity in the physical will occur most beneficially when there is unity within the individual. Thus it is not uncommon to have difficulty in relationships with others.

Positive Traits of *A*	**Negative Traits of *A***
1. ambition	1. cynicism
2. intellectuality	2. sarcasm
3. versatility	3. scattered
4. inventiveness	4. lack of concentration
5. concentration	5. immersion in sensuality
6. aspiration	6. overly critical
7. truthfulness	7. disharmony
8. idealism	8. hypersensitivity
9. sensitivity	9. possessive
10. broad-mindedness	10. lack of will
11. creativity	11. easily hurt
12. organization	12. always planning, never manifesting

A opens the doors to higher wisdom and illumination. It manifests opportunities within one's life to develop purity of ideas. It activates the enlightened mind, and it creates opportunity to balance and parallel reasoning and intuition. It can give one musical gifts and eloquence. Its energies can be activated to manifest healing, especially related to chest, heart and breath. On a spiritual level, it gives one the ability and potential for higher clairvoyance, levitation (which is working with all elements), and it can at a high level give one command over storms, which involves all elements of the Earth.

THE SYMBOL OF THE *I*

I is the second of the five primary vowels. It corresponds to the element of Fire—the spiritual fire that operates upon the Earth and within all life. We must distinguish between fire and flame. Fire is the force that lies behind the physical manifestation of all flames, be they the flames of candles or the flames of inspiration.

As humanity as a whole evolves, so do the energies and significances of the vowels. At one point in the evolution of humankind, little was known about the fifth element of Ether, or Akasha. It was believed that Fire was the highest of the four elements. Because of this, the *I* vowel was assigned to the heart, as the heart is the seat of all that manifests within the physical. There is much to support its attachment to this chakra center. The physical heart works with circulation and keeping the temperature of the body at an appropriate level. It is love and its passionate fires that are traditionally associated with the heart.

What we must understand is that the glyphs for the vowels must be distinguished from the sounds of the vowels. The glyphs provide insight into energies operating within our life; the sounds provide a means of activating the energies so that we can bring out what we have recognized. The vowel sounds provide a way of manifesting the spiritual that resides behind the physical. Because of this, the vowels can be assigned in different manners. What is most important is not to lock oneself into it. We want to become flexible enough to use our energies on all levels and express them anywhere. We use associations to give us a starting point.

The *I* is not a vowel that is actually associated with one of the seven major chakra centers, although as stated it can be aligned with the heart. As we evolve and the symbols we use evolve, the associations and correspondences and intricacies of using them will also evolve. The *I* may have been appropriately assigned to the heart chakra at one time, but for the New Age aspirant the *I* is a glyph that works much more effectively in a very important "minor" chakra.

At the base of the stem of the brain—the medulla oblongata—is a minor chakra center. This center is one that brings clarity to the mind and emotions. Fire brings warmth, but it also brings light, clarity by which to see. This is a center that was very important in the Egyptian Mysteries. When this center is fully awakened and functional, it creates what the ancient Egyptians called "intelligence of the heart." It stimulates the mind over the emotions, linking the head to the heart so as to give greater individual creative expression through the throat chakra.

The *I* fuels the fires so that we can begin to burn away the dross of emotions and mental attitudes that hinder expression of our higher energies and potentials. As the glyph itself, it is a direct line of dynamic energy linking the Earth and Heaven. The Earth is the bottom line; heaven is the top. In this sense, then, the *I* represents the true Tree of Life. Those whose primary vowel is the *I* itself have come to build a life that resembles the Tree. You must have your roots in the Earth and your limbs stretching toward Heaven.

The tree and thus the *I* are a symbol of regeneration and resurrection. In legends and myths the tree is usually guarded by a monster or dragon that must be overcome before the treasure can be gained. The *I* reflects this lesson for the individual's life. There is difficulty in overcoming one's lower nature, but it must be done if one is to achieve enlightenment. It is a symbol for one who has the capability of communicating and working on both levels, for themselves or for others.

Learning to balance the physical and spiritual will always be a task encountered by those with this vowel. Finding the proper means to do so is what becomes the Quest for these people. In this quest, the individual will find himself or herself encountering situations and people that will test their ability to harmonize opposites. It begins with realizing that everything in the physical is connected to some spiritual principle that must be learned. It is why the bottom line is identical to the top. Working with the concepts of the microcosm and the macrocosm and the Hermetic Principle of Correspondence ("As above, so below; as below, so above") will facilitate this.

Every Tree has the capability of bearing great fruit and shedding its knowledge upon those around it. Because of this it is always considered a sacred symbol. Learning to be as fruitful as the tree is part of the lesson of those with this vowel. For many, life situations involve the search of many paths to find one in which fruitfulness can be manifested.

The small letter *i* is also significant. Again we have the line rising up to re-achieve that point in Heaven. We try and raise our energies incarnation after incarnation in order to reattain the Primal Point of Creation—Heaven or Nirvana. On another level it reflects the image of a candle and its flame, which is a guide to the force of fire within the Universe. Fire has always been regarded as something holy. Everywhere in the world smoke from a fire has been believed to melt into the air in a magical manner, as if being taken to the heavens.

Even the origin of fire was considered magical and mysterious. The world abounds in tales and myths of the firestealers. Prometheus and his stealing of fire to save humankind is but one. For his act he was punished, chained to a rock forever at the mercy of birds of prey who tore at his flesh, only to have it healed and torn again. Many of those with the *I* vowel find themselves following their inner fires strongly, and as a result encountering strong consequences.

The Baptism of Fire is what many of those with this vowel have chosen to undergo in this lifetime. The Baptism of Fire is the discovery of our relationships with others and what these relationships teach us about ourselves. They may create changes and turmoils, but these are what we call the fires of experience. Each one of us is like a rough diamond when we start our journeys in life. The effects of others and our interactions with them serve as a polishing agent that cuts new facets into our stones. It is then that we sparkle with light and *fire*! This is the reflection of those with this vowel. They have come to burn away the old and to give birth to the new. They have come to learn to rise from the ashes like the phoenix.

As these individuals learn how spiritual and physical fire operates within their lives, within their consciousnesses, they find that their "limitations" diminish. Perceptions extend, and they begin to focus upon the infinite possibilities for new growth created by the fire of life's circumstances. It is then that the fires within become a channel of light for others to see by.

The *I* is the vowel for Divine Love. Its color is red and red-violet. It lends one strength (physical, mental and spiritual) that can be used for strong healing. It enables one to link the heart and the mind for the greatest manifestation of healing energies. Those with the *I* have natural healing ability on some level. It gives them a unique mentality that seems to stand out for most others.

Those with this vowel have come to develop new perspectives on self-sufficiency. This involves lessons on *becoming* rather than possessing. *I* gives one great ability for attracting love and great reservoirs for the outpouring of love for the enlightenment of humankind. This can be overdone, so one must be careful. Just as the two cross bars on the *I* are equal and balanced, we must balance what we pour out with what we draw in.

Some people with this as the predominant vowel will learn to temper the emotions and selfishness, and to properly express love— physically, as in sex, and spiritually. It can give endurance or it may manifest as tests of endurance. It holds the lesson of learning to transcend disharmony.

Creative energy is very dynamic in these individuals, be it expressed through healing or through artistic endeavors. Either way, unless there is positive expression in some form, it will take the opposite manifestation. Often its energies will manifest repetitiously until every aspect of the lesson is learned. It is a symbol that invokes perfection and the opportunities to manifest it. Perfection only comes after we have been tried and have transmuted that which can hinder.

Positive Traits of the *I*
1. Healing ability
2. Self-sufficiency
3. Selflessness
4. Greater love
5. Stimulating
6. Faithful and loyal
7. Active and energetic
8. Demonstrative
9. Intuitive certainty
10. Outspoken

Negative Traits of the *I*
1. Stifled creativity
2. Overly emotional
3. Selfishness
4. Possessiveness and jealousy
5. Obliviousness to others
6. Stubbornness
7. Impulsive and erratic
8. Apathetic
9. Distrustful
10. Indifferent

On a spiritual level, those with the vowel *I* are very memory conscious, and they work well with the laws of cause and effect. There is an innate ability to bring it to life and have it work for them. When it does not, it usually teaches the individual something about hindering himself or herself. These individuals are capable of linking the astral with the spiritual, the astral being the activating principle for most life upon the planet. Learning to work with breath benefits all. They have an innate ability to comprehend the metaphysical laws of life affecting them.

THE SYMBOL OF THE *E*

The *E* represents the second of the more commonly known elements, although it is the third of the five. It is the element of Air. It reflects the importance of intellectual activities and mental energies in the growth of those who have this as the primary vowel within their name.

Initiation by Air is understanding the workings and powers of the mind. Air is what separates Earth and Heaven, and thus it is the link between our own spirituality and our physical consciousness. It is coming to an understanding of what a new life (and in the case of many upon the planet now) and what the New Age is really about.

This understanding does not occur through mere accumulation of facts. Although an integral part, knowledge does not elicit understanding. The Air initiation is the opening of new wisdom, wisdom based upon higher intuition. Because of this, many individuals with this letter as the predominant vowel are highly sensitive. This psychic sensitivity needs to be understood and transmuted into a spiritual intuitiveness before true wisdom unfolds. If not understood, this sensitivity will act itself out in an individual's life through lack of will, over-emotionalism, and in other ways listed under Negative Traits of the *E*.

We live through breathing, and we breathe in air. Whatever air is blowing around us is what we will take in, unless we learn to control our surroundings. Learning to control what is allowed within one's life is a prominent lesson for those with an *E* as the primary vowel. In the glyph of the *E* itself there are three cross bars, which emanate from the one activating pole. It reflects the winds blowing out eastward, like signal flags.

The eastward direction of the three "flags" of the *E* is significant. It is to the east we must focus, for the Sun rises in the east, and the Sun is our primary source of life. It fills the air about us with energy to strengthen and nurture us.

The fact that there are three flags is also important. Three is the magical number. It is the number of the manifestation. From the one Source of all life (the vertical bar) comes three manifestations— mental, emotional and physical. Together, all four comprise our being. Without the spiritual, the others could not be. This is a spiritual lesson for all of those of this vowel to keep in mind throughout their incarnation.

The lengths of the three cross bars are significant as well. The first or upper emanation from the Source is the mental. It is the same length as the bottommost bar, the physical. This tells us that on the path to higher initiation, it is the mental that is as important to our overall evolvement as the physical life experiences. The bottom pole is a mirrored reflection of the upper. Thus whatever manifests within the physical is a result of the mind. The mind sets the matrix, the blueprint of what is to manifest within our physical lives.

Much research has been done concerning how our thoughts affect our actions. How often do we tell ourselves or others that we "catch two colds every winter"? The mind sets the physical energy in motion so that we are more susceptible to catch the two colds.

We have a tendency to believe we are ruled by the emotions. And yes, they do affect us strongly, but it is the mind that sets the energy in motion, which is then given impulse by our emotions, making it easier for our thoughts to manifest on some level in our physical life. Learning to control the mind and develop positive thought processes and then empowering them with the correct emotion will create a straight, strong physical life as depicted in the vowel. The bottom bar (physical) will only be as straight as the upper. They parallel each other.

The keynote of those with this vowel is strength and self-mastery. It is why three has always been a sacred number. Strength is the union of power and love. It takes strength to overcome the struggles and sorrows for greater creative expression within one's life. When this is accomplished, we begin to understand the beauty and wisdom lying beneath true strength. The three pillars of the Masonic temple are the pillars of wisdom, strength and beauty.

Those with this vowel have the lesson of discovering strength through overcoming. It is the lesson of harmony. Harmony occurs in the physical when the mind is strong enough to keep the emotions in control, thus the significance of the smaller middle bar in the glyph. It is the astral or emotional side of humanity kept in control. It reflects the lesson of the mind controlling the desire rhythms in the body so that those desires can be transmuted to spiritual power and aspiration.

The mind in motion—air in motion—is a force. It is the wind. The wind can be used for either good or evil, for our benefit or for our detriment. By learning to use this faculty correctly, we can link with the real self while in the physical. Thus the significance of the bars touching the vertical pole. The pole is our true self, which has access to both the energies of the Earth and those of Heaven and everything in between.

It is important to note also that there is movement outward from the vertical pole in three directions. This is a reminder to those with this primary vowel not to become focused on self alone. We must awaken our energies and let them flow forth to touch others. Three is the first number capable of reconciling opposites (the one and the two) and creating more numbers as a result.

Because the E is associated with the element of Air, it is also associated with those chakras of the head—the throat (creative expression), which reconciles the brow (feminine energy) and the crown (masculine energy). Upon the ethers, it is the color of blue, and it is associated with the planet Mercury.

E reflects lessons in gaining perception through chastity. It has the energies of the poet, the mystic, the lover of truth and intellect. It can give one the ability for inventiveness and philosophy. When developed, on the higher planes it gives wondrous strength. It can also express itself through hypocrisy, treachery and deceit.

The vowel E denotes action, either physical or mental. It can reflect an almost hyperactivity. This ability to manifest activity lessens when it appears at the end of a name silently (Grace). Its energy gives one the ability to illumine others if desired. It also can denote nervous energy. Those that do not work to develop the creative aspects inherent within its energies will go through a loss of friends, worldly goods and encounter business problems.

Positive Traits of the *E*	Negative Traits of the *E*
1. Strong intellect	1. Hypocrisy
2. Intuitive	2. Treachery
3. Logical	3. Deceitful
4. Philosophical	4. Aversion to studying
5. Attracts friends	5. Restlessness
6. Mechanically minded	6. Argumentative
7. Inventive	7. Narrow-minded
8. Outgoing	8. Self-righteous
9. Determined	9. Lack of self-control
10. Persistent	10. Nervous afflictions
11. Strong	11. Impurity
12. Electrical	12. Easily irritated
13. Strength of will	13. Stubbornness
14. Genius	14. Dogmatic
15. Mystical	15. Cruel

The *E* gives one opportunities to develop universal consciousness. It opens one to divine ideas, ideas that link our normal consciousness with the universal. It evokes the highest form of intuition, although if undeveloped it will manifest as an uncontrolled psychism. It can enable one to move into those realms where physical time and space are nonexistent.

Part of the lesson for those upon this path is learning to control the astral consciousness, the lower desires. *E* sounds a vibration that opens true clairaudience, the hearing of beings, communication with the angelic hierarchy. It can also awaken the ability to understand the language of all animals. Development will open perception of the past, present or future. One will learn to make ideas physical and visible, and will be able to apply the knowledge in practice. It can open the opportunity to develop true materialization and dematerialization—the manifesting of things from the air to the Earth. It is the manifesting of a universal consciousness within the physical life, inherent with all its abilities.

THE SYMBOL OF THE *O*

The vowel *O* is linked to the element of Water. Inherent within all its lessons is control of the emotional aspect. Initiation into the Water element, as with all elements, may take many lifetimes before all its spiritual truths are revealed. The *O* is a circle. Our lives are journeys, each adding to the circle of knowledge, experience and ability.

The initiatory lessons of those aligned with this element deal with the emotional side of humanity, the power of intense feeling and those desires to express that feeling within the outer world. *O* has inherent within it joy and sorrow and finding balance in all polarities. It involves lessons throughout life in balancing any of the 12 pairs of opposites:

1. Keeping silent and talking
2. Receptivity and resistance to influence
3. Obeying and ruling
4. Humility and self-confidence
5. Lightning-like speed and circumspection
6. To accept everything and to be able to differentiate
7. Ability to fight and peace
8. Caution and courage
9. To possess nothing and to command everything
10. To have no ties and to have loyalty
11. Contempt for death and regard for life
12. Indifference and love

When we are undeveloped, the emotional nature is very overpowering and can drown us. We may constantly desire excitement, noise, activity and novelty. We may lack poise and may express our feelings in extremes of unbalance. Those with this lesson and this vowel have come to learn to bring balance to the emotions.

This does not mean bottling them up, but learning to expend them on important and beneficial objects and goals. Initially this may begin with just a moral purification, but it builds to finding ways of expressing the emotions in a creative or artistic fashion, as suits the individual. In essence, we must learn to be in the world but not of it, as the Buddha taught his students.

The *O* vowel is also a circle, and the symbolism of the circle has been a part of all life and all cosmologies. It is the archetypal symbol of wholeness. It has no end and no beginning, a reminder to the individual that you start this life's learning wherever you are at. O is the wheel of life that turns constantly and signals perpetual movement within our lives. If we try and hinder the wheel, it grinds, resulting in physical, emotional, mental and spiritual breakdowns.

The circle has an inner and an outer part. The inner is hard for many to express. It is the part that does not want to be revealed, that likes being snug and safe inside, untouched by the outer. For this reason many individuals with the O vowel have difficulty expressing their emotions, their true feelings. They keep everything bottled up inside, whether there is room for it or not. Learning to bring it out and let others in is part of the lesson. The O people must learn to work within the circle and outside of it as well.

The circle is a symbol for the Sun. The Sun revolves through the heavens, and represents wholeness that comes from balancing the opposites—the inner with the outer. The merging of the two is known in esoteric parlance as the Dance of Life. It balances the hemispheres of the brain, the polarities in the body and the systems of health and life.

Sacred circle dances are very ancient. The more ancient dances were repetitious, continually circling, which implies a lesson for those of this vowel. Unless the lesson is truly learned, you will be destined to repeat it again and again. When we merge the outer circumstance and reality with higher inner awareness, the lesson is at last learned and the situation resolved. If not, it reoccurs in a different manner.

The energy centers in the body are known as chakras. This is a Sanskrit word meaning "wheel." These "wheels" work intimately with the body in directing energy for our various functions, and they depend upon our emotional balance to a great degree. Mental and emotional balance will create a mis-flux of energy in the body, which can manifest as a breakdown, illness, or dis-ease in some manner.

Working with balanced emotions and thought visualization is of key importance to the welfare of individuals with this vowel. Physical imbalance will manifest more quickly and easily from mental and emotional imbalance than in others. Learning to mark off sacred time and space—finding time and places where you can occasionally withdraw, recoup, etc.—is of key importance.

This was part of the ancient magickal dance. Making a circle was an act of creating sacred ground for an individual or a group. The O vowel is a reminder to create a sacred space in the mind and in the emotions, a point where the spiritual can mix with the physical. The center of the circle is the point of focus. Depending upon what your mental and emotional focus is, a vortex of energy is created, which brings those thoughts and emotions into manifestation in the outer world. Again, it is the lesson of control of thoughts and emotions. It is a symbol of learning to awaken deeper, inner consciousness through physically enforced concentration.

O is the vowel for Saturn in astrology. Saturn is the great teacher, particularly of cause and effect. The implication for those with the *O* vowel is that they must learn to recognize that all effects they are experiencing within their lives are the result of some previous cause triggered by their own thoughts and emotions. These effects can manifest either beneficially or positively. This is the lesson of cause and effect, of the ideal versus the real.

Individuals with this vowel have powerful imaginations and visualization capabilities. As has previously been discussed, our thoughts create a matrix of energy that will ultimately play itself out in physical life circumstances if given enough strength. Those of this vowel group must be cautious to keep the mind on the positive, because they have an innate ability to manifest quickly and strongly what they think about. That gives these individuals a tremendously powerful creative tool that can be developed and applied to all aspects of their lives.

The *O* gives one the ability to absorb and concentrate life. It has a capacity for binding together, connecting, but it also makes one sensitive to criticism. Individuals with the *O* often need encouragement in creative self-expression, but once started, they are faithful and tenacious.

The color is black, which like the white has the whole color spectrum within it. Black is the womb from which all life comes forth, and there is a natural ability for those of this vowel to give life and life opportunities to others. It may not be in dramatic ways but through normal life activities and responsibilities. Because *O* has all colors within it, individuals who have this vowel can affect and be affected by everyone and everything.

Positive Traits of the O
1. Stability
2. Power
3. Sensitivity (psychic)
4. Organizing
5. Steadfast
6. Faithful
7. Imaginative
8. Love of music/art
9. Sympathetic
10. Strong-willed
11. Orderliness
12. Sense of justice
13. Sociable
14. Generous
15. Initiative

Negative Traits of the O
1. Melancholy
2. Lack of will
3. Dogmatic
4. Nagging/fault finding
5. Poverty is agonizing
6. Critical
7. Domineering
8. Acutely sensitive to criticism
9. Resents opposition
10. Arbitrary
11. Fear of failure
12. Aloof
13. Suppressed feelings
14. Lack of concentration
15. Failure to take advantage of opportunities

The O brings lessons about justice, particularly divine justice. A lesson many must deal with is recognizing that what works and harmonizes for them individually may not work for others. O gives an innate ability to attain high spiritual judgment and to comprehend legalities. Therefore those with this vowel must learn to not condemn unjustly. It gives one the power to evoke energy and response on many levels, for good or bad, and awakens through the course in life opportunity to achieve satisfaction, security and success. Learning to understand relationships between events—causes and effects that play out in life—is of key importance. Once achieved they can then teach this to others and make moves to become masters of metaphysics.

SYMBOL OF THE U

U is the element of Earth and the initiation of the same. The initiation of Earth can be the most difficult, because it involves freeing ourselves from all of its limitations in our path to the spiritual. Those with this vowel seem to lead lives of great variety.

Earth and matter are not evil. We have chosen to come and live upon the Earth to grow and learn and to develop our highest potential and power. To do this we must learn about all expressions of matter and the archetypal energies that exist behind it. In order to learn of it and utilize it, we must develop discrimination, aspiration, etc. without it becoming imbalanced.

The *U* is like a womb in which life is born. Through the Earth we can be born again. This realization begins with recognizing that matter is not inert. Everything is alive and is made up of energy expressed in one form or another. Everything is a manifestation of the Divine. Part of the evolvement process involves recognizing that the metaphysical resides behind the physical.

Those with this vowel must learn to recognize the power within, and he or she must direct it outward toward understanding life and death upon the physical plane. It is with this initiation that one learns to draw the light out of the well of truth that lies within each of us, symbolized by the glyph *U*. We can get lost in the well, or we can learn to dip from it to assist us on our paths.

The *U* is shaped like a cup, and cups in all occult traditions are associated with feminine energies. The Earth itself is a feminine planet (Mother Earth) that gives birth to the opportunities for us to grow. A cup holds and contains elixirs of all kinds. It can also be used to pour them out. Learning when to hold and when to pour forth in life is part of what those persons with this vowel must learn. It is called discrimination: when to act, when not to, how much, where, who to trust, etc.

The cup, and the *U*, shapes whatever is in it according to its own shape, and yet it can still pour forth the liquid and life. Those with this vowel must learn to recognize that they are not limited by the environment or the physical. The creative, birth-giving energies must be awakened, stirred and poured forth into one's life.

The cup is but one symbol for the Holy Grail, the quest of which leads us to find our spiritual essence and the best manner to express that essence within this incarnation. This vowel should tell the individual that the only thing limiting him or her is his/her own perceptions.

Mother Earth is the microcosm of the universe. In the Qabalistic Tree of Life, it is represented by Malkuth. When the universe formed, it did so in stages, until all life and energy emptied down from the Divine to manifest in the Earth. Thus the opening at the top of this vowel. It symbolizes the individual as the recipient of all divine energies.

Part of the lesson for those with this vowel is overcoming jealousy and envy and recognizing that no one has anything that you also cannot obtain, and that there is no one doing anything that you also cannot do yourself if you learn to pour forth your energies. Learning to pour forth those energies and potentials from the inside to the outside is difficult, but it is something that can be accomplished by anyone with this as the primary vowel who is willing to put forth the effort.

Cup, cauldron, womb, Grail and *U*. They are all the same. The *U* represents *you* on the Earth in your quest for the Grail Chalice. They are inseparable. You cannot separate what you do from who you are. Choosing an appropriate occupation and appropriate companions and activities in life is essential for those with this vowel. Others are more likely to make judgments about those with the *U* according to their work, activities and companions than they would about others.

It is easier for you to be influenced by the environment than many others, thus the containing form of the letter itself. Choosing the correct environment—and the choice is always yours—will assist in manifesting your highest potential. If in an environment of impurity and imbalance, you will assume a resonance and rapport with it. If in one of high spirituality and creativity, you will likewise assume an empathetic rapport with it. Recognizing this aspect and then using it to your benefit is part of the life lesson for all those with this vowel. It doesn't matter what the environment may have been in the past. There exists a natural resilience and an innate ability to revivify one's life if one chooses. It may not be easy, but these individuals often learn to do so on a multitude of levels.

Just as with the cup, the Grail and the cauldron, the *U* is also linked to the energies and symbology of the Horn of Plenty—the cornucopia. The original cornucopia was from the horn of the goat Amaltheia, who became the constellation for Capricorn. It is a symbol of infinite supply of whatever is contained within. The cornucopia serves as a reminder to those of this vowel that whatever you focus and bring into your life has the potential of being multiplied. It also reminds us that as we give more out, we get more. Giving never diminishes our energies or supplies. Learning to work with the universal Law of Abundance is a priority. The Law of Abundance simply tells us that there is an infinite supply for our infinite demands. There is no eleventh commandment that states, "Thou shalt do without." The essentials of life are always there for us.

The vowel *U* represents protection through resistance. Just as there are two walls on each side of the vowel, there is energy in those with this letter to resist outside dangers and threats while still being able to draw down energies from the heavens.

Those of this vowel need love, patience and gentleness to stay open to the new. If not, the walls will close in. There is strong intuition in these individuals. They are instinctive and conservative and can be excellent judges of character.

Like the vowel—opened at the top—these individuals are open to strong impressions through the dream state. Much attention should be given to dreamwork and understanding the relationship of dreams to their physical lives.

Earth colors are assigned to this vowel—greens and browns and their various combinations. In the Earth are all the treasures and minerals for great wealth, reflecting what can be achieved by those of this vowel. These individuals must keep in mind, though, that everything upon and within the Earth reflects energies beyond the Earth itself.

Because of their empathetic abilities, they are very clairsentient. There is an innate ability to sense the thoughts, feelings and motives of others. They need to learn to trust their feelings and not resist their opportunities.

Positive Traits of the *U*	Negative Traits of the *U*
1. Strongly intuitive	1. Harshness
2. Conservative	2. Feelings easily hurt
3. Proud	3. Selfish
4. Visionary	4. Overly protective
5. Lucid Dreaming	5. Resistant to change
6. Tenacious	6. Resentful
7. Poised	7. Haughty
8. Trustworthy	8. Bragging
9. Protective of others	9. Sensitive to criticism
10. Quiet and unobtrusive	10. Narrow in ideas
11. Gentle	11. Secretive
12. Patient	12. Deceitful and dishonest
13. Progressive	13. Misuse of power
14. Reliable	14. Clannish
15. Nurturing to children	15. Miserly

At the highest level, this vowel opens the faculty of comprehension of the creative act and the ensuing karma. It opens one to the highest forms of intuition and clairvoyance. It can stimulate inspiration and awaken the energies and strength to master the karma of the Earth experience. It is a vowel, if worked with, that opens the energies and opportunities for developing conscious astral projection. It manifests opportunities to understand all life's mysteries and how they operate and are reflected through normal, day-to-day life circumstances. Thus, control of the Earth experience begins to manifest.

It is from these five predominant vowel glyphs that our language derives its many vowel sounds. The sounds are important in that they help activate the archetypal energy that resides behind the glyph of the vowels (as will be seen). All symbols, images, sounds, colors, etc. have an archetypal energy that works through them. It is this archetypal energy and combination of energies that we are trying to activate through the work with our names.

There is another vowel that we have not discussed but it is very important to our study. It has no sound of its own per se, as the other vowels do, but its glyph reflects strongly the transition of consciousness occurring in all humanity at this time, particularly in the Western world.

THE SYMBOL OF THE Y

The Y is related to the Fire element, as is the letter I. Where I would be the fire, the Y is the flame. The I represents the force, the Y the form. Individuals with this as the primary vowel learn the lessons of Fire and its transmuting force in physical situations.

The Y represents the primal love and how it manifests in earthly expression. Because of this, individuals with Y as the primary vowel will undergo and experience both poles of love. They will see both balanced expressions (passion, lust, jealousy, etc.). This may manifest in them or in those around them.

Learning to balance both aspects and remain upright is part of what is relected through the glyph of the Y. The upper portion is a downward-pointing triangle, representing emanations from the spiritual into the physical that must be balanced and used through proper expressions of the heart.

Relationships will be very important, and often these individuals will not feel they are whole until they are in a relationship, whether it is good or bad. This is reflected in the two upper lines joining with the vertical pole. It is the balancing of the male and female that gives birth to their higher expressions of love. Whenever the male and female are joined, their union gives birth to the Holy Child within us. Until those with this vowel can find balance and contentment within themselves, they will not find it in others, thus the road of relationships can be rocky.

The ancient mysteries were broken into three categories: the Lesser, the Greater and the Supreme Mysteries. Learning to open to these is reflected in this glyph of three lines. The Lesser Mysteries were those lessons to help the individual unfold and develop his or her own personality. They bring tests for the development of character. These tests always involve other people and our relations to them. The greatest learning comes through groups. This relationship to others unfolds and helps us realize who we are. It forces us to strengthen the mind and control the emotions (the two upper lines) so that the vertical line (ourselves) does not get toppled from imbalance of either the mental or the emotional.

The Greater Mysteries were those that unfolded a person's individuality. It involved awakening one's creative energies and learning to balance psychic sight with spiritual insight. The focus of the Y turns from the outer to the inner realms. This is reflected in the narrowing of the lines, which merge with the vertical pole. The two become one. The physical cannot be separated from the spiritual.

The Supreme Mysteries involved understanding how everything works and learning to set energies and fires in motion for the benefit of all. It is looking beyond immediate effects and recognizing that everything is significant. It is realizing that the purpose of our unfoldment is to render ourselves more useful to humanity. For those of this letter, the occult axiom, "I seek to know that I may serve" is of tremendous importance. Knowing and serving must be expressed.

This aspect is reflected through one of the most ancient symbols of the spiritual path, the Quest for the Holy Grail. This quest is the search for our true essence and how best to express it in this lifetime. The Y glyph is shaped like the chalice of the Grail Mysteries. It is a reminder to those of this vowel that there is much more significance to their life circumstances than what may appear on the surface, and that if the Grail can be seen, it can also be attained. It is a reminder to us that all those who step out onto the path will achieve it. Unfortunately few have the wisdom to recognize this.

As mentioned, love has two poles—that of the spiritual and that of desire and the emotions. Keeping the two balanced is part of the life lesson for those with this as their primary vowel. When the emotions get out of control, one of the best things that those of this vowel can do is to see themselves as the golden Grail chalice. This image stimulates a release of spiritual energy into one's life to help balance the emotions.

Transmutation of energies is the keynote for those of this letter. Learning to transmute the lower into the higher begins with balance. It is a slow progress. It involves learning to mix Fire and Water without extinguishing either. If done properly, it creates steam, which is a powerful generator of energy.

The Y is only a vowel when sounded in a name. The fact that it is sounded and is the key vowel is of great importance. It indicates that you have come to make a split with the old patterns (again reflected in the form of the glyph itself), but most importantly it indicates that at some point within your incarnation you will make some major decisions concerning spiritual and religious matters. They will be of major import, enabling you to initiate new patterns of growth.

The color associated with this vowel is a light golden brown. This reflects the ripened wheat, the food of physical life ripened by the warmth of the sun fires. It also reflects the color of the Grail. We are beginning to see the gold of the Grail, and as we grow, we will open to expressing our spiritual essence even stronger, which will enable us to become a channel of fire and inspiration to others.

Y holds the lesson of freedom from bondage, of breaking the old outworn patterns—from this life and past. The Y person must be guided gently, as he or she is ruled by the fires of love. This individual has strong desires for mental, spiritual and material freedom within his or her life.

The stem of the Y is also significant because it represents not only the self that has balanced itself from working with the opposite poles of love but also the early life of the individual, where at some point separation from the old patterns occurs. It is the traditional "parting of the ways."

Astrologically, Mars is often associated with this letter. Mars is the planet that gives one energy, strength and courage. This is energy for the tearing down of the old and the building up of the new. Mars is passion for change and activity of change.

Positive Traits of the Y
1. Loving
2. Building of mental power
3. Insight and intuition
4. Potential for manifesting great power
5. Mechanical ingenuity
6. Healing
7. Patience
8. Wisdom
9. Aspiration
10. Self-sufficiency
11. Loving guidance
12. Positive

Negative Traits of the Y
1. Lustful
2. Overly emotional
3. Overly dependent
4. Easily hurt
5. Impatient
6. Lack of common sense
7. Inability to make decisions
8. Egotism
9. Negative
10. Restricted freedom
11. Imposed bondage (self or others)
12. Inability to manifest

On its highest level this vowel can ultimately be used to reveal the origin and rhythms of all life. It can awaken the most profound intuition and aspiration. It has a power for opening the macrocosm. It can stimulate the aptitude for prophecy with *no* possibility for mistake. It can be used to spiritualize the astral body so as to see the fate and patterns of all life forms. It has the potential for opening the gift of prophesying in the tradition of the greatest prophets taught in the secret schools. One tradition speaks of its ability to be used for invisibility. It can open to one the sight of the archetypes that exist behind all life in the material world.

AWAKENING THE LIFE OF THE LETTERS

1. Determine the primary vowel of your first name. This is the vowel that has sound in the accented syllable of your name, the stronger stress. If two vowels are together, it is the vowel that is sounded. In the descriptions of specific names given in Part Two, the primary vowel is listed.
2. Familiarize yourself with the correspondences and symbology of the vowel itself. Although methods of toning the vowels to bring them to life will be discussed, it is most important to concentrate on the aspects of the vowel and feel them coming to life within you.
3. Allow yourself to relax, undisturbed.
4. Visualize the vowel around you and in you filling you with its energy, awakening within you the abilities and poten-

tials associated with it. Visualizing yourself filled with the color associated with it will facilitate the process. Imagine yourself as the letter, the glyph with all its inherent energies. Use the diagrams on page 57 to assist.

5. With each breath in, pull the letter and its energy color into you to fill you. With each breath out, imagine the energy pouring forth from you to be given expression in your day-to-day life. In, out. Spiritual, physical. We are manifesting and bringing to life the energies you came in to unfold and express.

6. Repeat until you begin to feel the energy changes. This will be felt first in different parts of the body—according to which element is associated with the vowel:

Fire (head and heart)	Air (chest and head)
Water (abdomen and groin)	Earth (feet and legs)
Ether (throughout the body)	

The letters of each element can be practiced by focusing and concentrating on them in their corresponding areas of the body. If you work with the Fire element (*I* or *Y*), visualize that part of the body as an infinitely open space, like the heavens. As you breathe in and out, imagine it coming to life and being filled with the energy and color of the letter. Seeing the color come to life in that part of the body like a new sun is extremely effective.

Ten minutes a day spent on this exercise will bring the energies awake in a relatively short time. For some it may take a month, for others it may take six, but be assured that it will create the effects. It will bring to life your innate energies and abilities.

In the imaging process we want to see the physical, astral, mental and spiritual bodies and energies of ourselves being affected. By doing so we begin the process of activating the Light body—linking the spiritual with the physical. Practice at this will enable you to ultimately evoke those inner energies. It will enable you to picture and perceive the corresponding virtues and energies consciously at work in your day-to-day life.

Changes will be felt first upon the physical level, but they will carry over to other levels as well. Take time at the end of the exercise to contemplate ways in which you can apply this new energy to correct situations in your life and to bring creativity out for you and others.

A = Ethers
Keynote = Illumination
Colors = White or Light Blue

I = Fire
Keynote = Divine Love
Colors = Red Violet or Opal

E = Air
Keynote = Strength/Self-mastery
Colors = Blue or Dark Violet

O = Water
Keynote = Justice/Balance
Colors = Black or Dark Ultra-
marine

U = Earth
Keynote = Birth Giving
Colors = Earth tones and
Ivory Black

Y = Fire
Keynote = Transmutation
Colors = Lt. Golden Brown and
Pink

Special Hints

1. You will be learning to pronounce and tone the letters in order to quicken the process. It is important to see a letter take shape around you as you tone it. You want to see the energy fill your body, your room and then your universe.

2. You want to be able to visualize a letter into activity and then also dissolve it. In this manner you are learning to activate and deactivate the energy according to your needs. We don't need faucets to be turned on and left on. All we need do is learn to turn it off and on at will.

3. In absorbing the letter and its energy into the body, do so by seeing it form in the area of the body associated with the element and then radiate outward as a force.

4. In learning to fill the room and the universe with the letter and its energy, one must first activate it within the body. Then as you breathe out, feel and see the energy radiate out from your body to begin the process of filling the room or universe. With each inhalation, the letter becomes increasingly intense and vibrant so that there is more to breathe out. We are learning to work from the microcosm to the macrocosm and back again.

5. Assuming the postures as depicted on page 57 while performing the exercise will enhance the effects. Physical movement creates electrical responses in the body and brain, which facilitates access to the energy. It enables you to build a thoughtform around the symbol, empowering it just as you would a talisman. In this case, though, it becomes one that is always carried within you, simply waiting to be invoked.

CHAPTER THREE

The Sacred Sounds of the Vowels

*In the spheres a wonderful harmony of sound is being produced
eternally, and from that source have ALL things been created!*
                                                    —Florence Crane

NAMES AND THE glyphs and sounds that comprise them are
poorly understood. Misconceptions about names abound. It is pre-
sumptuous to think that our natures are self-evident and that we
know everything about our names simply because we use them.
Philosophers have always been interested in names and their psychological connections. Names are critical to understanding our
spiritual aspects and how they interplay in our physical lives.
Linguistics is the study of human language in general, but there is also
what can be termed metaphysical linguistics—how language (and
names in particular) affect humanity beyond the physical realm.

The study of language and its various sounds has a long and
ancient history. It is generally believed that our modern language has
its roots in forms of Sanskrit. Sanskrit, in and of itself, is dead, but
Indian yogis still use sounds and words from Sanskrit because of its
potential to release energy. The languages of many of the ancient
traditions and rituals are still considered sacred, and any changes in
the words, names or their pronunciations is felt as threatening the
power within them. The power of names and the spoken word was
commonly recognized among the ancient traditions. Knowing the
real name of a being (knowing all of its aspects and significances) is
still believed to give the possessor of this knowledge a certain power
over that being.

The ancients used symbology in names and languages to communicate many of their teachings. Glyphs and symbols were selected
and assigned to names, words and prayers to attract blessings, give
power, bring release from difficulty, give courage and strength and to
heal and comfort. The students of the past had the task of trans-

59

lating the sounds and glyphs into their own set of symbols. They had to learn to build the symbology into the words and names, thus empowering them to work in their lives. It was this ability that would ultimately be tested by the Masters to ensure that a student had achieved the proper depth of understanding, thus releasing the archetypal energies into play within his or her life.

The Masters of Wisdom were careful in imparting knowledge of sound and names to their disciples. Students had to learn to speak, when to speak, how to speak and when not to speak. If they wished to learn the higher knowledge of sounds and names, they had to first unlearn their previous way of using words and refrain from ordinary methods of talking. In the Pythagorean schools of Wisdom, the neophytes were not to speak for two years. This was to help teach them reticence in speech, and to develop an ability for mental silence so as to imbue their words with power. They were taught three uses of sounds and names and speech:

1. Intuitive: sounds that enable the soul to turn more to its universal and divine aspects. Part of this involved affirming the essence through the meaning of the name, as has been described.

2. Scientific: the effects of sounds upon the physical body of individuals, as well as the subtle energies of man. This included understanding which sounds were most accessible to the individual based upon the individual's name.

3. Astrological: the sounds, names and tones used to evoke energies of the planets, in order to diminish or increase their effects within the day-to-day life circumstances. This has been briefly touched upon in regards to the elements of the names and the elements of the astrological signs.

What then makes a name powerful? Is it its meaning? Is it its sounds? Is it its rhythms? Is it the way it is used? In essence, all aspects add to the power of a name. When a person can employ all aspects simultaneously, then the name becomes MAGICKAL!

THE POWER OF THE VOWEL SOUNDS

The human voice can produce two aspects of sound—vowels and consonants. It is the vowels that contain the real power, for consonants could not be discerned without the vowel sounds. The vowels are sacred. The sounds that the vowels take within our names provide ways of awakening the archetypal energies for greater health or enlightenment. The glyphs and their corresponding sounds can be used to transmute current energies and conditions, awaken greater perceptions and open realms, the likes of which we have only dreamt. They reveal which energies we have the greatest access to.

Languages and names constantly change, but they do not decay, because the sounds are inherent within them. It is often believed that only words within a language have meanings, and individual sounds do not. They too have effects, and can be used with the glyphs of the letters and the meaning of our names to assist us in manifesting beneficial conditions in life.

The vowel sounds hold the strongest influence upon us. Each vowel opens a particular part of the human body when visualized and sounded silently during the inbreath. This inner sounding (intoning) is the key to many metaphysical teachings concerning sound. The exact process in using it with your name will be explained later in this chapter.

The opening of our body's energies by means of vowel sounds in names is easily understood if we realize that breath penetrates into any region according to our thoughts and focus. *All energy follows thought!* The inbreath draws air and prana into the body, and the vowel sounds open regions of the body enabling the prana or energy to penetrate. With the aid of our thoughts and imagination (focusing upon the symbolism of the letters and their sounds), we can suffuse our whole body and consciousness. We bring to life every fiber and spark with the energy that lies within our names.

Many find it confusing that we have but five primary vowel glyphs (six, if you include Y), and yet we have a multitude of vowel sounds. For many, working with just the sounds will be easier because it is easier to experience effects from the sounds. They are more tangible and not nearly as abstract as the form of the letters themselves, but if we wish to understand the true power of names and words, we must learn to pay attention to all aspects. This is not accomplished all at once. Initially, it may be easier to work with the sounds within your first name. As we learn to feel the energy, we can then add to it the energies of the glyph as well.

While the glyphs may be abstract, the sounds can be felt. For this reason in many mystery schools, according to Rudolf Steiner, "learning to write was prohibited until the 14th or 15th year of age; so that the form, the mechanism which comes to expression in writing did not enter human organism. Man only approached the form of the letter when his spiritual vision was developed." The form of the letter could activate energies because it more closely resonated with archetypal energy.

The sounds within our names help prepare us to activate the full impact of the divine essence that lies behind our names. Learning to use the sounds, then link them to the glyphs and give them and their meanings expression, is giving expression to our own divinity. It is the Initiatory path.

The sound of the primary vowel in your name provides even more information about your potential and the path you have chosen to walk in this life. It also provides a means by which you can awaken the archetype that resides behind the name you have chosen.

To most people, the vowels each have two sounds—a long sound and a short sound. Actually there are many sounds for the vowels; some can have five or six variations. No two vowels and no two sounds are exactly alike, but the difference may be insignificant to one trying to become aware of their energies. The table of correspondences on page 63 uses the more generic phonetic spellings that can be understood and used by anyone. If you are looking for the actual breakdown of sounds per vowel, a chart is given in Appendix B with appropriate phonetic spellings and sample words for clarification.

Table 3: Vowel Correspondences

Vowel Glyph	Vowel Sounds*	Chakras**	Effects of Energy When Activated
A	ay (hay)	Heart	Chest, lungs, circulation, heart, blood (love, healing, balance, Akashic memory)
	ah (cat)	Throat	Throat, respiration, mouth, trachea, etc. (creative expression, clairaudience)
	aw (saw)	Solar Plexus	Stomach, digestion, left-brain, intestines (inspiration, clairsentience, psychism)
I	I (eye)	Medulla Oblongata	Balanced brain function, mental clarity (Mind over emotions, "Intelligence of Heart")
	ih (bit)	Throat	Throat, respiration, mouth, trachea, etc. (creative expression, clairaudience)
E	ee (see)	Brow	Head cavity, sinuses, brain, pituitary, glands (clairvoyance, Third Eye, spiritual vision)
		Crown	Skeletal system, pineal (Christ Consciousness)
	eh	Throat	Throat, respiration, mouth, trachea, etc. (creative expression, clairaudience)
O	oh (note)	Spleen	Muscular system, reproduction, navel area (creativity, reserve energy, higher emotions)
	aw (cot)	Solar Plexus	Stomach, digestion, left-brain, intestines (inspiration, power, psychic sensitivity)
U	oo (boot)	Base	Genitals, pelvis, lower body, circulation (vitality, life force, kundalini)
	uh (but)	Throat	Throat, respiration, mouth, trachea, etc. (creative expression, clairaudience)

* Vowel sounds given are generic references. See Appendix B for actual phonetic spellings.
** For a greater clarification of what chakras are and how they function, refer to Appendix C.

SOUND MEANINGS

1. Determine what the primary vowel is in your first name.
2. Review the significances of it as described in Chapter 2.
3. Using Table 3, determine what your primary vowel's sound is.
4. Using the descriptions below, add the information of the power in your name's primary sound to the information of

your name's primary vowel.

5. Keep a journal of Name Awareness and Empowerment. Jot down the key ideas, meanings, etc. for each aspect of your name. As you read through the descriptions, certain ideas and experiences will come to mind that verify some aspect of the elements found in your name. Write these down as well for later contemplation and meditation. You can also jot down how you can use the power of your name, once realized, to correct problems in the future and prevent them from reoccurring. Other ways you would like to use your power will also come to mind. No matter how far-fetched they may seem, jot them down as well. Remember, by working with our names, we are trying to awaken the magic that lives within us all, so nothing is too farfetched. We may not be able to do it at this point, but we are awakening to the possibility.

What follows is a description of the primary sounds associated with the vowels. This will include the physical and metaphysical effects of the sounds. If the sound is one that is associated with your primary vowel, it will provide clues to your lessons and your hidden potentials. Later several techniques will be explained that use these sounds with your vowel glyph and your name's meaning to bring to life your highest energy and thus empower your being.

As a general rule, most long vowels are considered masculine, while short vowels are feminine. We are all a combination of male and female energies. The male in us is the assertive, electrical, initiating energy. The feminine is the receptive, magnetic and intuitive aspect. If the primary vowel is masculine, it can indicate that you have come to assert your essence in a unique way. If it is feminine, it can mean that you have come to awaken it and absorb the essence into your life.

The masculine can be catalytic and the feminine life-giving. Finding ways to balance them within our lives is part of the growing process. Bringing together the male and female aspects of our lives is what results in the birth of the Holy Child that resides within each one of us. This is a creative principle that operates within the universe on all levels, not just on a physical, biological level. Thus the masculinity and femininity of the vowels does not reflect whether you are more masculine or more feminine in physical life. It provides clues that enable you to participate in the creative process that will give birth to yourself, by activating more of the male or female energies.

Sounds of the primary vowels provide clues to strengths the individual has come to develop and weaknesses that may need to be overcome. Understanding this can shed light on many of our previously "misunderstood" life circumstances.

SOUNDS OF *A*

The Long *A* (as in "ay")

The long *a* sound is one that activates the heart chakra, which is a center for higher love. It is the balancing center of all the chakras, and it corresponds to the element of Ether, as discussed previously. It helps link our intuitive consciousness with our normal physical consciousness. It bridges the lower with the higher.

On a physical level it is linked to the heart and the thymus gland. It directs the circulatory and immune systems. It corresponds to the assimilation of all nutrients and to all heart-related and all childhood diseases. If properly balanced and activated—a task often more easily achieved by those with this sound in their name—one can attain mastery of the immune system and thymus gland.

This is a center for awakening compassion, and those with this sound in their primary name will find it something to be developed or expressed. It can be used to awaken higher forms of healing.

There are weaknesses that we all must overcome in our paths to enlightenment, and strengths that we need to obtain. The primary vowel sounds provide clues to which strengths and weaknesses will be predominant during this incarnation.

The long *a* as a primary vowel sound can indicate that the individual may have to overcome insecurity, self-doubt, possessiveness and fear. He or she may find themselves needing self-confirmation and recognition in all things. It can reflect lessons in false pride as well.

It also indicates that the individual will have opportunities to develop a strong sense of security and great compassion. Occasion will arise to awaken devotion, high idealism and greater reverence. Nurturing will become an important aspect, and opportunity to awaken healing energies and abilities will also arise.

Balance in all aspects of life is tested often for those of this primary vowel. This is often reflected through the relationships, whether good or bad, so that learning to maintain balance in all things will manifest. The Ethers involve all of the elements, and thus balance will involve all aspects of the individual's life as well. In this manner we learn to breathe life into all elements of our life circumstances.

The Short *A* (as in Pat)

The short *a* sound is one of four sounds that are close enough to all activate the throat chakra. The others are the short *i, e,* and *u*. This is a center for creative expression and higher communication, and it is associated with the gift of telepathy and clairaudience.

On a physical level, this chakra is linked to the functions of the thyroid and parathyroid glands. It controls much of the respiratory system, particularly the functions of the bronchials, and it affects the whole vocal apparatus. When properly awakened and balanced, diseases of the throat and upper bronchials are relieved, and the immune system is strengthened. This center can be awakened to strengthen the entire endocrine system, especially by those whose primary vowel takes this sound.

Psychosomatic illnesses and problems are often a part of those who have this vowel sound, either in themselves or in those around them. Learning not to suppress the self is thus an important lesson for those of this sound.

This chakra center is sometimes referred to as the cornucopia center. Depending upon the person's focus, it has a capability of manifesting either an abundance of joy or sorrow, fulfillment or lack of.

This center is one that needs to be activated to link with the more spiritual "bodies" or bands of energy surrounding the physical. If it does not operate properly, there is no link to those more spiritual energies, which then begin to atrophy. Consequently, aging accelerates and the degenerative process progresses. Those of this vowel sound need to work with something of a creative nature or this atrophy is more likely to occur. This center, and thus this vowel, controls higher wisdom and creative expression in all forms.

Individuals with this vowel sound—or those of the short *i, e,* and *u*—need peaceful situations and times in everyday life. There will be a tendency in such individuals to cling to the old way of doing things. They may find themselves needing rules and supervision. There may be a need to deal with dominance, either in themselves or in others.

And there is often a conflict between a strong desire for contentment and the tense conditions and "excitement" of discontent.

Dogmatism and its imbalances is often a lesson for those of this sound. In fact, there can be a leaning toward ultraconservatism. There may seem to be an inability to manifest things in his or her life, and lessons in efficiency, envy and forgetfulness are common.

On the other hand, there is ample opportunity to develop and unfold powerful strengths. Initiative, inspiration and intuition are powerfully prevalent in these individuals. They can be farsighted and visionary, with a capability to open up and read the Akashic Books of Knowledge. These individuals also have an innate ability to tune into the hidden rhythms of the inner worlds. There lies many opportunities to unfold and realize their inner hidden abilities and also to unveil the same in others. The creative instinct is strong and can be applied to all situations and fields of endeavor for those willing to put forth the effort.

The *A* as in "aw" (Paul, Margaret)

This sound for *a* is similar to the short *o* sound, as will be discussed later. Both apply to the solar plexus chakra, and although they are different, the difference is minimal in the sounds. What is important is that the sound here is even more powerful than the short *o*. When the primary vowel is an *a* with this sound, the effects are intensified.

With this sound of the *a* vowel, the solar plexus power is linked to the heart and the throat for greater expression within one's life. This can manifest, of course, in either a beneficial or detrimental manner.

We have spoken of the vowels being masculine and feminine in regard to their sounds. This *a* is the sound of the male and female energies coming together with great creative force. Whether that force is dissipated or used to conceive much within the individual's life is entirely up to the individual. It is the energy of the male uniting with the female to give birth. The solar plexus was an area of the body that the ancient Essenes referred to as the "manger," the place where the Holy Child is given birth. Much significance lies in this for those of this sound and this *a* vowel behind it.

In the physical body the solar plexus is linked to the stomach, lower diaphragm, liver, gall bladder, pancreas, etc. It mediates left-brain activity and all mental activity in relation to the physical body. Emotions are integrated into the soul through this chakra, so it increases and activates early intuition with those whose names have this sound. The solar plexus is that center for psychic activity known as clairsentience, or feelings and hunches.

This center controls the digestive system, so it is important that individuals with this as the primary sound take extra care with proper digestion. White corpuscles and the assimilation of nutrients are also affected by it.

This sound often indicates lessons in balancing anger and resentment. Compulsiveness, a fear of loss, and feeling deprived of recognition are aspects that must be dealt with by those with this sound. There can also manifest an aloofness and a tendency toward dogmatism, criticalness and bullying. There is often a need to balance insecurities with greater self-confidence. Often individuals with this sound will find themselves in a position of defending narrow viewpoints, either their own or others'.

This sound gives individuals the opportunity to develop with greater facility certain strengths. Again, it must be remembered that often the strengths manifest by overcoming a weakness. Strength of will is but one that is prevalent among those of this sound. Strength and power to manifest are also inherent. Critical judgment—without being nit-picky—is a lesson that is common to many of this sound and vowel. Flexibility and novelty in perception often manifests as well. Mental clarity unfolds through the day-to-day life experiences, experience being a very powerful teacher to those who fall into this category. This sound and vowel give one the power for great success and fame if used in a creative manner.

SOUNDS OF *I*

There is a long *i* sound and a short *i* sound. There is also a sound for *i* when used with another vowel, most often the *e*. When the *i* is placed beside the *e* within a name, the *i* usually loses its energy of individuality and instead expresses itself through a heightening of the energies of *e*. In names such as Kath*ie* and Sus*ie*, the *i* is silent, and the *e* takes a long sound. Use the long *e* description as a basis in such cases, and remember that the *i* with the *e* will intensify the effects. Sometimes the *i* has the long sound without having the *e* present—such as in Bobbi or Candi. In these cases, use the sound of the long *e* as a basis for understanding how the fires of the *i* will manifest in your life, or use the information on the specific name in Part Two as a means of beginning to understand.

The Long *I* (as in Irene, Elisa)

The long *i* sound is not associated with any of the seven major chakra centers. It is associated very strongly with one that helps bridge the upper four chakras. It is a sound that activates lessons in life associated with a minor chakra point, located at the stem of the brain.

This sound, and thus those names with it, entail learning to maintain mental clarity. It will activate lessons in controlling the emotions through the mind. It can often reflect the continuation of lessons begun during Egyptian or Atlantean times in which the awakening of this chakra was known as Awakening the Intelligence of the Heart. The mind and the heart work together to give greater expression of creative energies within one's life. This involves learning to balance the emotions.

Inherent within this sound is the lesson of devotion and committedness, which urge us to maintain balance. It reflects lessons in learning to overcome discord—not through emotional love alone nor rational thinking alone, but by both processes. It has to do with learning that there is abundance in all forms in the universe, and it has a capability of being expressed within one's life, if allowed to develop. It involves learning to overcome melancholy and to develop contentment.

On its highest level it can awaken true spiritual understanding and discipline. It activates higher forms of intuition, and it manifests many opportunities throughout one's lifetime to overcome hidden fears. It helps one to understand the importance of restrictions and can open one to the understanding of the life and death processes, and not just on the physical level.

Individuals with this as their primary sound will find lessons on confidentiality, impatience, superstition and faith. It can mean that the individual must learn to walk on his or her own, in faith that all will work out. It gives one the opportunity to refine the bridges between the physical and the spiritual. It gives one the opportunity to either control all aspects of one's life or be controlled by it. It reflects learning to do what Rudolph Steiner referred to as "grabbing the serpent of Wisdom by the neck." It involves learning to control all energies on all levels and direct it where you wish them to go, rather than allowing them to twist and meander in their unfoldment and awakening.

On the physical level, it has to do with the functions of the medulla oblongata of the brain. It also has to do with coordinating the functions and activities of the hind-, mid- and forebrains. This is symbolic of coordinating the energies and activities of the body, mind and soul. These are the three flames of our spiritual fire, Fire being the element associated with the letter *i*.

The Short *I* (as in Bill, Phillip, Phyllis)

The short *i*—just like the short *a*, *e*, and *u*—is linked with the energies, tests, lessons and strengths associated with the throat chakra. (Review what has been written about the short *a*.) The short *i* will also activate the throat chakra, but it does not mean that its sound is identical to those other vowel sounds that will activate this same chakra.

The short *i* gives more fire to the creative expression within the throat chakra. *I* is a letter of the element of Fire. Fire is creative and destructive. It burns away the dross to reveal the gold beneath. The lessons thus associated with the throat chakra are often intensified for those of this vowel sound.

The fires of creative expression run hot, and if not channeled properly, they may be expressed in unfulfilled passions. Psychosomatic illnesses can be a problem, but curing them in the self or in others is often more dramatic. There is usually a powerful, although not understood, drive to find something that is fulfilling in one's life, and this may manifest in life circumstances that test one's ability to be stable and fulfill normal obligations while still searching for the ultimate.

One of the primary lessons for those of this sound is recognition that our growth and unfoldment does *not* occur in artificially contrived situations, but through the normal day-to-day activities and our infusion of fire into them. There seems to often be, at least until some beneficial form of creative expression is found, a conflict between the drive for fulfillment and for change and a vague sense of emptiness.

Those of this sound, as with all of the *i* sounds, have a tremendous healing ability. Using creative expression as a healing modality is important. Working with sounds, music, voice, counseling, teaching, or vocal expressions of any kind is very beneficial. Many of those with this sound have a capacity for activating the throat chakra through conversation and voice-toning to impact tremendous healing upon those with whom they come in contact. It is easy for others to talk to them and thus be opened to be healed by them.

THE SOUNDS OF *E*

The Long *E* (as in Gene or Eve)

The long *e* sound is one that gives the individual opportunity to activate two chakra centers—the brow (third eye) and the crown. Both are centers of the head, and even the short *e* sound is of the lower head and throat. Thus the chakras for the *e* will be one of the upper three. They all reflect lessons and abilities in awakening and using the higher mind. In the discussion of the glyph for the letter *e*, we assigned it the element of Air, which reflects mental energies or energies of the higher mind.

The brow chakra center is linked to the pituitary gland, the seat of the feminine energies in the body, the intuitive and imaginative side. The crown chakra is linked to the pineal gland, which the ancient Essenes termed the Sun center, the center for the masculine energies. Again we have the male and female. When they come together, they give birth to a creative expression in some form. The throat chakra is the seat of creative expression. Thus, we begin to understand the powerful significance and potential of the *e*. It, along with the "aw" sound of the *a*, provide those of this sound with opportunities to balance and unite the male and female energies in order to give new birth to their life and to their soul's development. All are associated with the head, which provides insight into the occult teachings of the mind, which is at the heart of what manifests within our physical life.

The brow chakra itself is the seat of our conscious awareness. It mediates the energies of our spiritual self into physical awareness. It is the center that assists us in learning to live free from negative energy expressions of fear and vulnerability. This center balances the hemispheres of the brain for greater utilization of potential. It is a center for high spirituality, creative visualization, imagination and vision. It is linked to powerful insight, clairvoyance and intuition.

In the physical body the brow chakra is connected to the pituitary gland and the functions of the entire endocrine system. It affects the synapses of the brain, the sinuses, eyes, ears and face.

Those that have the sound of the letter *e* in their name may find themselves envious of others' talents, impatient, forgetful, undisciplined and oversensitive to the impressions of others. It brings with it lessons in using power for personal ends and problems associated with avoiding trials and growth. Fear of the dark and the unknown can be strong in children with this vowel's sound. Learning not to martyr oneself nor to belittle others can be part of the lesson of unfolding this center.

Individuals may have to deal with feelings of being misunderstood. This is usually the result of a seeming inability to have enduring relationships. There may also be manifestations of intensely erotic imaginations, a desire to dominate and overwhelm others, and it can manifest opportunities to deal with negative self-images and the need to feel popular. There may manifest a need to deal with daydreaminess, self-illusion and self-denial. There may be experiences of lack of tenderness and sympathy as well, in themselves or in others. Either situation still requires one to come to terms with it.

This center gives those who activate it higher understanding, patience, intuition, and it can open the mysteries of birth and death. It stimulates initiative and farsightedness, with an ability to manifest what is envisioned. Intuition and aspiration are strong, but they can be undermined by inefficiency and fear of the future. It awakens abilities and the lessons of decisiveness, and opens one to initiate the process of inner alchemy. There is usually a drive to right wrongs and an innate ability to defend the weak. It is that protective mothering energy being given assertion. Those whose name has this sound can create a balanced manifestation of higher understanding and higher wisdom.

It also gives facility (if it is developed) in opening the crown chakra and manifesting its energies. The crown chakra links our divine essence in its truest form to our physical consciousness. It takes many lifetimes of concentrated evolvement to become conscious of the energy connection between the two and to utilize them to the fullest. We can still experience it in varying degrees though, and those whose primary name vowel has the long *e* sound have come to do so in some form.

When properly stimulated, this sound aligns us with all of the higher forces of the universe, and it can purify all of our energies, both subtle and physical. It is the center of our highest spirituality and it is often referred to as the Cosmic Christ Consciousness Center. It is our link to the Divine within the universe.

This sound also opens the door to manifesting some powerful strengths and potentials. The creative imagination can be applied effectively in all situations and endeavors. There is a tremendous ability and potential for transformation and for restoring order. A true sense of charm can unfold. Many of these individuals have a true sense of wonder about everything and everyone in life. There is a wonderful ability to ignite spiritual fires in others, as all of these individuals are instinctively mystical.

These lessons associated with both chakras will manifest in some degree in the lives of those whose primary vowel has the sound of the long e. This can be difficult because, unlike the other vowel sounds, this one affects two chakras instead of just one. This is usually an indication that the individual has done some strong preparatory work in previous lifetimes or has come into this one to insure that new ground be opened to them. It brings accelerated learning and thus it also can manifest amplified rewards.

The Short *E* (as in Betty, Fred)

The short e is a sound found within many names, and it has its own unique lessons and potentials. As with the short a sound, the short e also activates the throat chakra. This is a center of higher creativity. As discussed, the e sounds all pertain to the head area and the mind. The throat chakra, activated by the short e sound, can enable one to express the higher mind's inspirations and ideas. It enables one to bring the thoughts out of the ethereal realm of the mind into physical manifestation.

The throat chakra activated by names with this sound has many of the lessons that are found in the short a sounds. It does have its differences though. There are more concentrated lessons on communication and on being grounded. There is often so much inspiration that discrimination is very important. Often these individuals keep trying to unfold their intuition and psychic abilities, and don't realize that they often come into the world with such abilities already active. They often search for ways of "clicking the lights on"—as they have often heard others describe the experience—and they don't realize that theirs are already on.

Lessons in being grounded are also important and prevalent. Individuals with this sound within their name are often accused of "being in another world" or "flighty." Their perspective on life is often unique, and it has to do with the creative inspiration that they are so open to.

Those with this sound have an inherent gift of verbal or artistic communication, but they are often overly sensitive to criticism. At the same time, they often have to learn not to be overly critical of others. The names that have this sound as its primary vowel come into this life with the throat chakra active, giving expressions greater strength and power. This means that their words will be felt more strongly by others. Things said more lovingly will be felt much more intensely. Things said cuttingly will cut more deeply. Strength in silence is often a test for these individuals.

This is a sound that opens knowledge of the higher realms for those willing to work for it, but they will have to learn the ability to discriminate about that knowledge (what's real, what's illusion, etc.). The search for higher knowledge by those with names of this sound will bring with it unique tests and learning situations. For the highest knowledge to manifest, it will be necessary for them to be able to independently test their knowledge and intuition, while giving it the appropriate respect and devotion.

Learning to come to terms with doubts and fears is a preeminent lesson for those of this sound. Dealing with superstitions and negativity, self-imposed and otherwise, often occurs at various points within his or her life. Knowledge means breaking the old patterns and asserting one's own will to express that knowledge in a creative manner. For this to occur, these individuals often have to realize there is as much to unlearn as there is to learn.

There is a need to develop detachment from personality desires, and the lessons surrounding the desires are often the most difficult. Doing what one feels he or she must do is part of this lesson, even if it means being cut off from the mainstream of society. Learning to develop a confidence in the future is often a lesson as well. This confidence is developed through greater knowledge. Learning not to get lost in one's misery and overcoming doubts, apathy, fear of the future, and "know-it-all" attitudes are but some of the lessons inherent in this sound.

On the other hand, it enables one to open to the deepest levels of the subconscious so as to clean out the inner fears and "demons." It can give one access to knowledge of all deeds, both past and present. These can be revealed and brought to full consciousness for those willing to put forth the effort. It gives one an innate ability to utilize knowledge for the benefit or detriment of self and others. The choice is always there. It gives an inherent healing ability that can be developed, particularly in regards to emotional problems. It gives illumination and intuition.

This sound within the name links one to the will force and creativity. It can open the secrets of generation and regeneration. It can open one to the true power of sound as a dynamic force within the universe.

THE SOUNDS OF O

All of the O sounds deal with the bottom three chakras. These are powerful centers and they work with the basic life force in one degree or another. They are no less important or powerful than the upper ones. Upper and lower denote a hierarchical evolvement, but in this case they denote location within the physical body. The long sound is associated with the spleen chakra, and the short o sound is associated with the solar plexus chakra, which has been discussed in some degree in relation to the "aw" sound of the a. A third sound of the o will be covered in the section on the long u. When two o's or an o and a u come together in a name (as in Doone or Lou), the o will take on the long u sound. Referring to its description will assist. Specific names with the o vowel and the u sound will be covered in Part Two.

The Long O (as in Joseph, Rose)

Names with the long o sound will be working with the energies, lessons and potentials of the spleen chakra. This involves all the energies associated with the element of Water, as previously discussed. It involves the emotions, balancing polarities, accessing the astral plane, creativity, psychic sensitivity and sexuality.

This chakra is our sensation center, a center for our emotions and our reserve energy forces. It brings with it lessons in integrating emotions and expressing them on higher levels. It brings opportunities to heal emotions and physical problems aggravated by them. Those with this sound often have strong instinctual healing ability.

In the physical body this sound is linked to the adrenal glands, the sexual organs. It works intimately with the reproductive system and the muscular system as well. It also affects the functions of all the organs surrounding the spleen area of the body. It is a center that works for the body's detoxification. When properly opened and balanced, it eases sexual diseases and problems of fertility. It eases arthritic diseases that stem from protein deficiency and overall stiffening of the skeletal system. It alleviates all problems linked to stress from internalized anger.

Learning to balance it through proper creative expression is part of the lesson for those with this sound in their name, along with developing the ability to integrate the emotions. Most of the lessons involve balancing the polarities of the body, mind and soul. The twelve pairs of opposites discussed in relation to the glyph of the o is usually a part of it.

Selfishness, arrogance, conceit and superficiality is often a lesson, whether it is with the individual or in those around him or her. It still must be dealt with. Worrying about what others think is also something that can arise. There is usually a strong desire to belong to groups and a love of social contact. These individuals can be very ostentatious and mistrustful.

The sexual energies are usually very prominent. They may be very strong or may manifest as "undersexed." Balancing this polarity is part of this individual's lesson. Possessiveness, introversion or extroversion, overemotionalism, impatience, idleness and impulsiveness are all lessons that may have to be dealt with. Lust, impurity, and obsessive sexual energies may also need to be dealt with at some time by those with this sound in their name.

On the other hand, this chakra gives opportunity for manifesting very powerful gifts and potentials. A sense of independence and self-awareness can unfold. Extremely strong psychic and intuitive feelings are prominent. Individuals with this sound have an innate ability for working with and using the dream state for knowledge, enlightenment and resolution of problems. The ability to develop conscious astral projection is there as well.

There is often a strong tie to the nature kingdom as well. Learning to work with the elves, fairies and nature spirits is something those of this sound have a facility for, if willing to work upon it. There is often a tremendous amount of learning that occurs through relationships, and many individuals of this sound have difficulty balancing relationships until they find the balance within themselves.

There is usually very strong artistic energy available, and when they are positive and optimistic, it has repercussions on everyone and everything around them. The healing energies are very strong, and spontaneity and innate expressiveness can make life an adventure and joy for those who are around such individuals. They can sense others' feelings and can stimulate love and idealism if they choose.

The Short *O* sound (as in Bob, Donna)

The short *o* sound corresponds to the solar plexus chakra and the lessons and abilities associated with it. As was discussed with the "aw" sound of the *a*, the solar plexus is a powerful center. It is the "manger" in which the Holy Child within us can be born.

In the physical body it is linked to the digestive system, so those of this sound need to be extra careful concerning diet. It affects the functions of the pancreas, liver, gall bladder, etc. It also is related to the functions of the left hemisphere of the brain—the logical side. Those with this sound may find lessons that surround this brain function: either there is distrust of the intuitive side or there can be a tendency toward "flightiness," or lack of a sense of logic or common sense.

Developing common sense is usually a lesson for those of this sound. The solar plexus controls clairsentience, our psychic feelings, which is usually considered the "sixth sense." This is a misnomer though. There are actually seven senses—the five physical senses (taste, touch, smell, hearing and sight) and the sixth sense, common sense, which is learning to integrate what is learned through the other five senses to enhance one's life. This then leads to the unfoldment of the seventh—intuition.

Many of the lessons and abilities associated with the "aw" sound of the *a* as previously discussed also apply to the short *o*. Along with these are lessons in impatience, being overly critical, being separative and always planning but never manifesting. If activated properly, it unfolds wonderful abilities for the individual.

Those with this sound can unfold a facility for learning. A strong sense of truthfulness is important to these individuals. There is an innate ability to communicate, and a strong sense of practicality can manifest. There is the potential to take even the most abstract and strange ideas and make them practical on some level.

There is usually a strong sense of idealism in some area of this person's life. At the same time there will often manifest lessons surrounding what works for them as individuals but not for others. They usually have to realize that what worked for them may not work for others. Implied is a lesson in recognizing that we are all unique and must live our lives in unique manners.

There is an ability to prosper through visualization and proper focus of the mind. These individuals have excellent imaginations. Sometimes they run off the deep end with their imaginings, but it is a wonderful ability. If applied correctly it can set the Laws of Manifestation into play for them. They have an instinctual knowledge of the workings of the Law of Cause and Effect. With the power of their minds, they need to focus on the positive, because their thoughts intensify and manifest whatever is being focused upon.

There is an ability for great prosperity through knowledge. They also have an ability for enabling others to prosper as well. They often choose lives in which they can effect changes and institute opportunities for family members and friends in and through normal life circumstances. They often choose lives in which they can help others to give birth to their Holy Child. Thus they may not seem to always lead a glamorous life, but the power to affect others is there, even if it is unacknowledged. They do need to come to terms sometimes with the idea that although they can envision so much, they themselves do not always seem to get. When they don't "get," it is usually because they are denying themselves. Optimism is a keynote for these individuals.

They have come to be catalysts in the lives of others, providing opportunities for them to turn their lives around and take new directions. By enabling others to transform themselves, these individuals thus transform themselves on a soul level, which begins the spiritual process of igniting the Body of Light—the weaving of the Golden Wedding Garment that gives access to the spiritual planes.

SOUNDS OF *U*

The Long U (as in Hugh, Ruth)

The long *u* sound is linked to the base chakra and its energies and lessons. Those who have this sound in their primary name will deal with those lessons in some form or another. There is also the opportunity to unfold the energy potential associated with this chakra to enhance one's life.

The base chakra is located in the area of the coccyx at the base of the spine. It is linked to our basic life force, the testicles and ovaries, and it works for the assimilation and distribution of our basic life force. It is linked to the reproductive system and the circulatory systems as well. It affects the energies of the pelvis, the hips, and the lower extremities.

The base chakra mediates our life-promoting energy. It is a center tied to talents and abilities developed in past lives. It is the seat of the kundalini, the serpent of wisdom which when awakened brings enlightenment.

> Chakras were first associated with the goddess called Kundalini. She is described as a sleeping serpent coiled three and a half times around the first chakra at the base of the spine. Her name comes from the word *kundala*, which means coiled.
>
> In the Hindu traditions this Goddess, when awakened, climbs upward, chakra by chakra, until she reaches the crown chakra at the top of the head. As she pierces each chakra, she brings awakening to her subject. When her journey is complete, her subject is said to be completely enlightened. (Anodea Judith, *Wheels of Life*, p. 36)

The base chakra brings lessons in power and aggression. This may be in ourselves or in others. Unbalanced, it can make one aggressive, power conscious, sexually obsessive, impulsive, manipulative, and domineering. Lessons dealing with fear, worry, anxiety and general disorientation may arise to be dealt with by individuals of this sound.

Recklessness and an inability to recognize limitations may also reflect lessons of this sound. These individuals may seek and need the approval of others. They may be focused entirely in the present and be unaware of the past or the future. Over-practicality may diffuse the natural intuitiveness of this person.

On the other hand, if the sound is used properly, it can stimulate greater discrimination and discernment. It will elicit greater physical energy and vitality. It can awaken strong psychic energy and ability. A spontaneity can unfold that adds color to their lives.

Inherent within all individuals with this sound is a dramatic ability to heal. If it is developed they can stimulate their own life force and use it to balance out the physical life force of others. It can be used to restore homeostasis to the metabolism of others.

It is easy for those of this sound to be "at-one" with the Earth and its elements. Working with things of nature is essential to these individuals. In fact, the best thing they can do for their own health and well-being is to spend time outdoors around things that are green and growing. There is a natural link between them and the nature kingdom and its beings. This link can be, and often is, the result of past-life experiences. This can be unfolded to an even greater degree in this lifetime, opening communication and fellowship with the Devic and Angelic Kingdoms.

The Short *U* (as in Russell, Gus)

The short *u* sound (as in the short *a*, *e* and *i*) also ties one to the operations of the throat chakra. Although they all have certain lessons and abilities in common, there are some differences. The information for each of the others needs to be reviewed for this one as well.

The throat chakra, as has been discussed, is linked to creative expression and opening to higher knowledge. This sound also links one to those lessons and potentialities, but it is a little different. Often individuals with this as the primary sound have come to lay a new foundation by balancing the karma of the past. For many this is done in the early years, and thus the early lives of these individuals seem to be filled with strong lessons. After about the age of 30, these individuals seem to truly come into their own. They are often the so-called late bloomers. The early years are spent taking care of past-life business so that the way can be cleared for the new.

Past-life exploration for these individuals is often beneficial in that it can put the present into its proper perspective. There is a need to discriminate and not just blindly accept things. These individuals have come to learn to integrate the philosophical with the practical. They have come to integrate the past with the present to give birth to a new future.

There is an ability, for those willing to develop it, to read the Books of Life of the Akashic Records. This can help them integrate their normal life experiences with the evolvement of the soul. Learning to listen to that inner voice is important for these individuals so that they do not repeat old patterns that are unhealthy. For this reason, individuals with this as the primary vowel will often find themselves repeating situations and encounters until they pay heed to those inner promptings. First impressions are important, and they need to be trusted. This allows them to avoid situations that can create entanglements. Their intuition is strong, and it enables them to be excellent judges of character.

It must be remembered that all the chakra centers and the name sounds interact, and although discussed as singular sounds and centers, they are a unit. Many names also have more than one vowel sound within them. This is an indication that you have come to work not only predominantly with one, but with all the others reflected within the name as well.

Every atom of our being is a sound resonator. This means that the sounds within our names reach out and trigger responses within us.

Learning to work with these energies from all perspectives and use them fully within your life was taught in the ancient mystery schools. It comprised an area of learning and training for higher initiation.

TONING OUR NAMES

Every atom of our being is a harmonic resonator. Each has the capability of responding to sounds and tones, particularly those associated with our names. If an area of our body is out of balance, we can use musical tones or vowel sounds to restore its balance. All we need do is vibrate or tone the sound, visualizing it going out to that area of the body, restoring homeostasis. Working with toning, especially toning of the sounds within our name, returns to us the ability and responsibility for the care and maintenance of our health. Toning can assist the healing process and open us up to higher consciousness. Toning is cleansing, harmonizing and stimulating to new cell growth and unfoldment of higher potentials.

Voice releases power! It releases it in the direction of our thoughts. Everyone else uses our names, for good or bad, and because our names are attached to us, the energy associated with that expression of our names will also attach itself to us. We need to learn to utilize our own names—in affirmations and in the toning process—to activate the highest vibrations possible around us. Then others who use our names in negative ways will be unable to affect our energy. It will be too strong, vibrant and pure.

The sounds within the name are vibrated or toned in the manner best for the individual. There is no specific length to hold the tone, nor is there any specific volume. We allow the voice to vibrate the sounds in the manner best for it. One can even sing the vowel sounds. Using Table 4 on page 82 will assist in this process. Buying a simple three to four dollar pitch pipe at any music store will enable you to easily combine the vowel sound with the appropriate musical note.

By discovering the method or variation best for you, you release your own creative force—that force reflected in your name. This innate spiritual potential is taken out of the ethereal realms and grounded into the physical plane by the use of your voice.

The tones will burst through any negative energies that we have allowed to impose upon our energy fields. They will shatter those we have created for ourselves. When the tone is allowed to pass freely, it will cleanse the entire body and release tensions, blockages and re-

Table 4: Tone Correspondences

Chakra	Tone	Vowel Sound	Mantram	Color	Attribute	Healing Property
Root	Middle C (Do)	u (ooo)	Lam	Red	Vitality, Kundalini, life force	Circulation, low blood pressure, colds and shock
Spleen	D (Re)	o (oh)	Vam	Orange	Creativity, reserve energy, sexuality	Muscles, reproduction, detoxifying, emotional balance, sexuality
Solar Plexus	E (Mi)	aw/ah	Ram	Yellow	Inspiration, intellect, wisdom, psychism	Digestion, laxative/ constipative, headaches, adrenals
Heart	F (Fa)	a (ay)	Yam	Green	Love/healing, balance, Akashic memory	Heart trouble, lungs, ulcers, hypertension, blood/ circulation
Throat	G (Sol)	e (eh) (a/uh)	Ham	Blue	Clairaudience, cooling, relaxing	Throat, fevers, asthma, lungs, thyroid, antiseptic stimulation
Brow	A (La)	i / e (ih/ee)	Aum/ Om	Indigo	Third Eye, clairvoyance, spirituality	Purifier (blood), obsessions, coagulant, sinuses, headaches, stroke afflictions
Crown	B (Ti)	e (ee)	Om	Violet	Christ Consciousness, inspiration	Soothing to nerves, stress, confusion, neurosis, insomnia, skeletal problems
* Soul Star (Transpersonal/8th chakra)	High C (above middle C)	——	Om	Purple or Magenta	That part of Soul linked to matter, Link to our true spiritual essence	Building the Body of Light, key to burning away negative thoughtforms that hinder physical and spiritual health for discipleship

strictions within the flow of our energy, physical or otherwise.

TECHNIQUE #1—Directed Esoteric Toning

The purpose of Directed Esoteric Toning is to restore the vibrational pattern of the body (physical and subtle) to its perfect electromagnetic pattern so that the spiritual essence can more fully manifest within our physical lives.

All aspects of toning are related to breath. Breath refers to that quick intake or gasp that carries an image or thought to the subconscious. Breath is life. When we become aware of our breathing patterns, we can have better control of our life energies. As we consciously work with tones and breath, we become more balanced and our breathing becomes more fluid, healthy and harmonious.

1. Take the primary vowel within your name and review the significances of it. Visualize it larger than life, overlaying your physical body. Assuming the positions as described on page 57 will help. Visualize it in its appropriate color.

2. Close your eyes, and as you inhale, sound the vowel silently within your mind. Imagine it echoing within your head and across the realms of inner space. As you do, feel the color grow brighter and more intense around you.

3. As you exhale slowly, vibrate or tone the sound audibly. Sound it slowly, allowing it to find its own volume and length. Do not try to initially hold it to a specific pitch. As you work with it, it will find its own natural pitch.

4. Repeat the toning. Inhale, sounding it silently. Exhale, sounding it audibly. In, out. Silent, audible. In, out. Spiritual, physical. This process activates the spiritual aspects of the name and brings them out into the physical life. It links and bridges the two worlds. The effects are amplified by visualizing the colors intensifying as you audibly tone them.

5. Repeat for about ten minutes. The sound will begin to assume the same pitch with each toning. The inner, silent sound will connect and become inseparable from the outer, audible sound. This is an excellent preliminary to the next technique.

6. This is especially effective if focus upon the appropriate chakra is done as well. As you inhale, feel the chakra associated with

your name's primary sound accumulate and build up reservoirs of energy. As you exhale, see and feel this energy surround you, filling your entire being with its color and radiance. Imagine your entire aura filled with its brilliant intensity.

7. At the end, visualize the aura ignited and the chakra of your name's sound fused with energy. In the core of the chakra, visualize the glyph of the vowel radiating energy eternally outward to you and for you. As you work with this exercise, all you will need to eventually do is close your eyes and visualize the glyph shining within the chakra, and it will activate the release of its energy into your life. You have created the internal talisman of light and spirituality!

   Pause and meditate upon its energies and all that you are able to do, or will soon be able to do, as a result of calling forth your true inner essence in this way. You have begun the process of integrating your Higher Self with the physical self.

TECHNIQUE #2—Toning and Affirming

We have learned to create an affirmation of tremendous power based upon your name and its meaning. This in essence becomes a powerful prayer and spiritual incantation in its truest sense. We can combine the toning with the affirming to give greater strength to the affirmation and to intensify its effects.

Basically we are developing the tools of the magician, tools that are uniquely your own. These include your own magickal incantation and your own magickal inner talisman. These tools, in conjunction with your visualization and the symbology that you build into them, creates a magickal body, or field of energy around you that ultimately will help enable you to integrate with the archetypal energies of the universe. With practice this magickal body develops, transmuting your lower energies and unfolding your highest potentials. It makes other planes, dimensions and awareness accessible to you. It opens you to higher understanding, knowledge and wisdom and is only as limited as you allow it to be.

1. Prior to performing the affirmation, visualize the primary vowel and perform the toning of it as described in the preceding techniques.

2. Next, tone your entire first name, extending out the primary vowel sound in it. For example, if your name is Fred, you visual-

ize your primary vowel, *E*. See it in its color, radiating energy around you. Then perform the esoteric toning of the sound. In this case it is the short *e* sound (eh). Next insert the tone back within the whole name and tone the whole name: "Fr-ehhhhhh-d," "Fr-ehhhhhh-d," etc. In this way, the name becomes more energized. You also become more at ease with using your own name. Over a period of time, it will make you more cognizant of how others use your name. You will respond very strongly when others call you by name. This is a positive indication that you have started to realign yourself with your true essence. Hearing others use your name after this has been accomplished will give insights into how those individuals feel about you. You will get definite impressions when you hear your name come from others' lips.

3. Next go into your affirmation, using your name and its meaning. (e.g., "I am Fred. I am the peaceful child of God.") Do not forget the visualization with the affirmation. Remember we are re-creating our true magickal and spiritual essence.

4. Do this as long as you feel appropriate. There is no set number of times to repeat the toning of the vowels, the names or the affirmations. Then take time—at least three to five minutes—to absorb the energy, meditate and contemplate about the changes you are setting in motion. Write your responses in a journal. Think of ways you can express your true creative essence within the next 24 hours.

TECHNIQUE #3—Healing with Your Tones

This technique can be use to heal one's self and to increase self-awareness. As with all healing, relaxation is the key, and in the process of toning your primary vowel sound, relaxation will occur as a natural part of the process. You cannot use the sounds without them producing relaxation and relieving stress.

When this procedure is applied to yourself, it opens up an increased awareness of how energies play upon and within our physical and subtle vehicles.

1. Take a seated position and close your eyes.

2. Tone the primary vowel sound within your first name in your natural voice. Allow it to find its own natural pitch. Hold the tone as long as is comfortable.

3. Open yourself, paying attention to its effect upon you. Can you feel it in any particular part of the body as you repeat the tones? What is the effect? Is it comfortable? Uncomfortable? Agitating? Energizing? Determine what the feeling is as best you can. Do not be discouraged if you are unable to label what you are feeling. This is a learning process, and for many the doors to self-awareness have been closed for a long time. Because of this you may have no boundaries by which to determine and label the effects. This will pass shortly. Consciousness is wonderful in this manner. It never leaves us without some guidelines, some barometer by which to begin to understand and respond.

4. As you notice which part of the body is more strongly affected by the sound, think about the chakra that is linked to that part of the body. It may not be the chakra normally assigned. Remember that all the chakras work together and there is an interrelationship, even if we don't initially understand it.

5. Visualize the chakra growing brighter, stronger and more balanced. What kind of energy or force does it seem to stir? Does it stir extra energy? If so, what kind of energy? Is it calming or firing? Does it draw you into harmony? Does it heal? As you pay attention to how it is affecting you, you will begin to understand how sounds and tones can be used as a dynamic healing force.

6. Focus upon your emotional and mental energies as you tone. What emotions are being affected? It may be subtle, and there is often a tendency to not give due credit to our feelings. Trust your impressions! Is this response constant or does it seem to fade as you continue to work with the tone? Overall, how does it make you feel? Try to define it. Try to find that one word or phrase that most encompasses that feeling.

7. Experiment with the dynamics of the toning. Try different pitches and musical tones with your vowel sound. What effects do they have upon you? What happens if you soften the tone? What happens if you tone it louder? What happens if you sing it? Play with its rhythm. Hold it for longer lengths of time and then shorter lengths of time. How does it change? Pulse the tone. Mix the tones. What are the differences? Every change within the tone creates changes in how that tone affects us. The more we learn about it, the more tools we have in our magickal closet to impact upon our lives.

8. Work and combine the vowel sound with the musical notes. Use your vowel sound with each note of the musical scale. Does the vowel sound work better or have a stronger effect upon you with a particular note? Sing the sounds. Play with them; have fun with them. (Yes, we do have to put forth effort in the growth process, but we can enjoy that effort also.)

9. Use the tones in group healing: Place an individual in the center of the group and have the group tone or sing his or her primary vowel. It is an excellent way of harmonizing a group, and it amplifies the experiential aspect of the toning process. Each individual of the group can take turns sitting or lying in the center of the group prior to the group activity.

10. Doing this process prior to sleeping is very powerful and allows the subconscious to further activate your highest energies while sleeping. If done regularly, the dreams will provide great insight into how those sounds reflect lessons and potentials.

TECHNIQUE #4—Balancing the Male and Female

We have discussed the fact that we are all a combination of male and female energies. We have also discussed how the vowel sounds are usually assigned masculine or feminine energies. The chakras to which the vowels are assigned are neither male nor female—they can manifest either. They can be more electrical or more magnetic, more assertive in their energies or more receptive. We can learn to control these aspects. To assist in this we can use toning to keep the energies of our primary chakra balanced.

1. Relax and sit comfortably.

2. Determine your primary vowel and review its significances.

3. Determine the masculine and feminine sounds for that vowel. (These are the short and long sounds. Review the significances of both.)

4. Begin with either one, the male or the female. Begin the process of Directed Esoteric Toning. For example, the vowel *E:*
   a. Inhale, toning silently the long *e* sound (masculine).
   b. Exhale, audibly toning the long *e* sound.
   c. Repeat three times and then switch to the short *e* sounds (feminine).

    d. Do the short *e* sound three times as well.

    e. Repeat the whole cycle—both long and short sounds—two more times for a total of three. This is the creative number, the number which reflects the male and the female coming together to give birth to the third—the Holy Child within.

5. Go into your affirmation with all of its visualization.

6. Begin with either the feminine or the masculine, whichever suits you.

7. Since the feminine is the receptive and the masculine is the assertive, a powerful technique involves using the feminine or short sound on the silent inhalation and the masculine, long sound on the audible exhalation. To assist this process, you should visualize yourself filling with beautiful energy with each inhalation, and see that energy pouring forth and surrounding you and your world with each audible exhalation. We are learning to control all aspects of our energy and direct it to where we wish. We are learning to assimilate and accumulate our energy and express it and dispense it in conscious awareness.

CHAPTER FOUR

The Magickal Rhythm
and Music of Names

> God has left for us an eternal memorial of Himself, our music
> which is the living God in our bosoms. Hence we will preserve
> our music and ward off from it all sacrilegious hands, for if we
> harken to frivolous and insincere music, we extinguish the last
> light God has left burning within us to lead the way to find
> Him anew.
>
> —Richard Wagner

All life is imbued with rhythm and music. Rhythm is found in
everything, from the tiniest of atoms to the great stellar movements.
It is found in the protons and electrons of all matter, both animate
and inanimate. Rhythm, be it in a game, music, dance or name, is by
its very nature part of man's constitution.

The Western traditions in regard to language and its occult
significance can be traced to the ancient Greeks, who raised the question of whether there is something essential in the relationships between a word, a name, its sound and rhythms and that which it
represented. They questioned whether the sounds and rhythms carried the meanings or if the meanings were already inherent.

Speech—in the form of words, sentences and even names—has
rhythms. These rhythms reflect general states of being and can be
indicators of qualities and energies that can be unfolded. They can be
used to enhance the physical body's metabolic rate, its natural
rhythmic system. An excellent experiment to work with from time to
time is to listen to the speech of another without listening to the
words. Listen to the rate of speech, the volume, the pitches and the
timbre. It takes some practice to do this without allowing the words
to intrude, but by learning to listen to the musical expression and
rhythms of voice, we can initiate the process of recognizing the music
and rhythms within our own names.

We each have the capability of experimenting and detecting the music and rhythms of our names: Softly speak your full name. Do it slowly and audibly. Look upon your name as a musical phrase. (Later in this chapter you will learn how to translate your name into music.) How do your names flow together? Is there a smoothness between your first and your middle name? What about between your middle and last? What about the first and last? Try different combinations to determine which combination sounds more rhythmic to you. Note the rhythm, the tempo, the rise and fall. Note the number of syllables or beats to your name.

TECHNIQUE #1—Discovering Your Name Rhythms

1. On a piece of paper, print your full name out, as it appeared on your birth certificate. If you go by a name different from your name at birth, this indicates that you are developing a link to the energies and forces other than what you came to do. This is neither good nor bad. It is a demonstration of free will, but we must keep in mind that it does not cancel out your basic rhythmic signature from birth. It now becomes somewhat secondary and influences more subtly.

2. Divide it into syllables, just as you need to divide words in school and total them up. In determining the syllabic rhythm, we will use a numerological method. If the number of syllables is greater than nine within your name, it must be reduced. This is accomplished by adding the digits in the number total. For example, if there are 12 syllables in your full name, add the 1 + 2. This gives you a name rhythm of 3. The number of syllables is the key to your basic rhythmic energies.

3. Take a look at the rhythm of your first name, your most creative potential. What energies does it align you with in the universe? What are the positive and negative aspects of it, the ways in which it may manifest or express itself in your life? Remember that the rhythms of energy operating within us are neutral and impersonal. They may manifest in either a positive manner or a detrimental manner. They can also take alternative ways of manifesting. They help us recognize our potential for learning and power. Using a journal to record your impressions, as was suggested with the vowels and their sounds, is helpful. Add the information on your name's rhythms to it as well. You will by

now be forming a good indication as to the energies, potentials and lessons you have come to work through and manifest. You should be coming to some conclusions as to why some things have happened to you in your life and what they were supposed to teach you.

4. Softly chant or even sing your name. Allow it to find its own natural pattern. As you do this, you will notice that your name takes on rhythm. After a few minutes you will find yourself chanting your name in a repeated pattern. This is a pattern that will be picked up each time you do it. Usually, after about a week of working with it, warming up into that rhythm will not be necessary. It becomes automatic and natural to speak your name in that rhythm. This is a positive indication that you have accessed your basic life rhythms. This serves to restore the metabolism of the physical body to its basic primal pattern. It assists in aligning and reintegrating the physical with the spiritual.

5. Chant your name as a prelude to the visualization and meditation upon your integration of the energies of the universal rhythms found in Table 5 on p. 92. Learning to adjust your name and its rhythms to more closely attune and balance with the energies of the vowels and their sounds can help smooth one's life. Odd-numbered rhythms are masculine, even-numbered rhythms, feminine. If your primary vowel is masculine, experiment with the rhythm of the name so that it is more in line with the masculine energy of the vowel. If it is more feminine, adjust it to an even-numbered rhythm. Keep that name and its rhythm for at least six months to a year, or at least until you can determine how it is affecting you and your life situations. There will be an effect! How strong and quickly it manifests will vary from individual to individual. Performing the chanting every day for one month will activate the new rhythm much more quickly. (One month is given, as this is one cycle of the Moon's rhythm. The Moon is a symbol of our subconscious, which is what we are trying to activate to a greater degree so as to manifest its energies more intensely.)

   This can also be done with the letters in the first name. Instead of counting syllables, count the number of letters in the first name. This can give the potential rhythm that can be manifested. At one time, many esoteric societies invoked energies

Table 5: Rhythmic Correspondences

Rhythms	Energies, Effects, and Lessons
1	Aligns one to archetypal male energies; initiator; strength of will; discrimination; inventiveness; self-centeredness; laziness; fearfulness or fearlessness; lessons and energies of confidence; search for answers; independence and originality.
2	Aligns one to rhythms of astral plane, archetypal feminine energy and dream consciousness; cooperative; kindness; psychic sensitivity; hypersensitivity; can be scattering; need to focus on details; vacillation and lessons of divisiveness; passion.
3	Aligns one to rhythms of saints and blessed souls; energies of art/inspiration, creativity; lessons of wastefulness and repression; spirituality and the awakening of the inner child; expressiveness (good or bad); optimism.
4	Aligns one to the rhythms of the Devas and Divine Men; energies of harmony/balance; building with patience; restricting and insensitive; narrowmindedness; impracticality; solidarity; integration of energies, learnings from four corners of Earth.
5	Aligns one to rhythms of Mother Nature herself; awakening of the microcosm of soul; lessons of freedom and purity; versatility; scattered; resists change and imposes rules; healing; adventuresome; freeing from limitations; psychic powers.
6	Aligns one with the feminine/mothering energies of the universe; nurturing energies; healing; birth-giving energy rhythms on all levels; rhythms of the educator; cynical and worrisome lessons; responsibility and reliability.
7	Aligns one to energies of all people and all planes; rhythms of healing for all systems; lessons of self-awareness and truth; rhythms of strong intuition; lessons of self-criticism, melancholy and inferiority; wisdom and knowledge.
8	Aligns one to the energies of the gods and goddesses as they worked through nature in the past; unites physical rhythms of individual with spiritual ones; confidence; occult power; lessons of carelessness and authority; awakens true judgment of character.
9	Aligns one to all healing energies and experiences; rhythm of empathy and transitional forces in the universe; lessons of being hurt and overly sensitive; pessimism and indifference; intuitive love; rhythms of at-one-ment.

by pronouncing and toning names letter by letter. The alignment with the energies in the table of rhythmic correspondences seems to work more consistently with just the first name, rather than the full birth name. The first name is our most creative and individual energy. Experiment with both if you feel inclined. These are guidelines by which you can begin the process of aligning yourself with the archetypal energies within.

TECHNIQUE #2—Balancing the Rhythms

In the table on page 92, you can identify which energy rhythms you have the capability of manifesting, as well as which lessons may manifest within the life circumstances of one with those rhythms. If there are problems arising, chanting the name will help restore the balanced rhythm. Energy that is disrupting our lives reflects a discordance in the rhythms. When we chant our name in its natural rhythm, it sets the energy around us back into its normal balanced pattern, smoothing out its rhythms, which will have positive effects within our lives.

1. Take a few moments to chant your name, making sure you have allowed it to find its natural rhythm.

2. Pause and reflect upon what has disrupted your life in relation to that rhythm. For example, if you have a name rhythm of three, and you feel you have been too wasteful in your time and energy, reflect upon this.

3. Slowly return to chanting the rhythm of your name. Visualize the wastefulness coming to a stop and being replaced with a greater fertility. This can be done with any negative expression of energy associated with a particular rhythm. Exploring the significances of numerology will give even greater information on the positive and negative potentials associated with the number for your name's rhythm.

    We are in essence using the name, its sound and its rhythm to shatter the negative expressions of energy. We clean them up and restore our auric field to its primal energy pattern, enabling its energy rhythms to work for us rather than against us.

TECHNIQUE #3—Cleansing the Aura
1. Take a seated position, and remove all distractions (phone off the hook, etc.)

2. Review some of the major significances of your name.

3. With eyes closed, begin rhythmic breathing. Breathe in for a count of four, hold for a count of four and exhale for a count of four. (One can also use the name's rhythm to determine the count for the breathing. If your name has a rhythm of six, inhale for a count of six, hold for a count of six and then exhale slowly for a count of six.)

4. As you inhale, sound your primary vowel silently. Visualize it drawing the appropriate color energy down and around you. As you hold, feel it permeating your physical body and becoming a ball of colored light around you. As you exhale, sound the tone audibly, seeing and feeling the energy vibrating more strongly. Repeat at least three times to insure you have invoked a good amount of pure, strong energy.

5. Begin a slow rhythmic chant of your name. Visualize the energy fluctuating, vibrating, massaging your entire body and energy field. It is as if the chanting is a cleaning and polishing agent. We invoked the energy through the toning, but now we set it in motion to purify and cleanse us through the name's rhythms. See it dissipating and dissolving all negative emotions, mental attitudes and physical problems, leaving you filled with and surrounded by a polished pure essence.

6. Again begin breathing and toning as you did before the chanting. This invokes more energy to replace the negative energy that has been dissolved. You are filling your aura with the pure energy of light and health.

You may do this two to three times. It is recommended that you do this at least once a week, repeating it for however many times that your name rhythm indicates. If you have a name rhythm of eight, repeat this exercise eight times once a week.

We are putting our energy through a wash cycle. We go through as many wash cycles as is necessary to keep our energy clean. We accumulate a lot of energy debris throughout a week's period. This procedure prevents it from attaching itself too strongly and thus being able to get a hold and trigger greater resonance, manifesting physical and spiritual problems. This procedure can be used to clean out much debris and garbage we may have accumulated throughout this life. With practice, this will allow opportunity to clean out the attics filled with limiting fears, doubts, emotions, etc. It is comparable to one of those winter scenes that when tipped over sets all the snowflakes into activity. We are loosening up and setting it all free so that we can skim it off and restore our natural energy patterns and expressions.

THE MUSIC IN OUR NAME

One of the most powerful ways of working with our name and activating its energy is through music. We can apply musical notes to the letters of the alphabet, and our names can be converted into a musical phrase. This assignment is somewhat arbitrary, as there are various ways of doing it. We will work with one of the easiest to give you a starting point. Again, we must keep in mind that we are learning to explore our essence from new perspectives, and the more significance we can attach to it, the more power and magick it will awaken within our lives.

Any musical instrument can be used for playing the names, as long as it has a chromatic scale (i.e., as long as it can play the sharps and flats). Inexpensive synthesizers and keyboards are available at most discount stores and are easy to learn, so no true musical training is necessary for this. Or if one likes, one can always purchase a pitch pipe, which can do the same thing.

Modern society views music in basically two ways: (1) as an art form, and (2) as a commercial product. Music needs to be considered in a third way, especially when applied to one's name. It is a *power* or *universal force*. It is a force that was treated with great respect in ancient times. The ancients recognized that music demonstrated the natural laws of physics and metaphysics. They recognized that the "physical emission of a sound was an outer and audible agency of an inner, Transcendental Power." They knew that all music was a relation of one tone to another, and that all life was the relation of one individual to another.

The power of music works because of a secret content that lies in the expression of the sound. This secret content was the pattern of sounds emitted through various techniques. For example, inspiration and intuition occur through a repetition of regular musical structures, tones and patterns. It was the order and rhythm of the tones, combining them into specific successions of melody, that was the source of magick. Learning to combine specific tones to link energies of the body together for healing purposes, for higher intuition, for dream enlightenment, for communing with spirits or for the invoking of divine presence was all a part of the ancient mystery schools, and it must again become part of the modern mystery teachings.

It was recognized by the ancients that certain modes of music were very powerful. As a general rule, the minor modes were the carriers of greater force and power. Some modes and their variations were considered so powerful that they were banned by the Church. They were derived from ancient practices that utilized music to invoke unseen beings and power.

The difficulty today in reawakening much of the ancient knowledge of music and the powerful applications of it to one's name lies in relating the old models to modern awareness and consciousness. Our own energy and expression is much different from those of a thousand years ago. This is why we must build our own significances into our name, its symbols and its sounds. We, as humans, have evolved much, and so what worked for the ancients may not fit us today.

CONVERTING YOUR NAME TO MUSIC

1. Print your full birth name.

2. Using the following conversion table, write down the musical notes associated with each letter in your name. It is based upon an octave of notes, beginning with middle C (designated as C^1).

C^1	C#	D	D#	E	F	F#	G	G#	A	A#	B	C
A	B	C	D	E	F	G	H	I	J	K	L	M
N	O	P	Q	R	S	T	U	V	W	X	Y	Z

3. Begin by playing each name separately. Each name—first, middle and last—is a musical phrase. Remember, though, that the first name reflects our most creative essence and potential.

4. Experiment with the sounds. Play all the notes of your first name simultaneously as well as separately. Take the notes of your first name and mix them up, playing them in various orders and sequences. Note which sound good to you and which don't. As you play with the music of your name, you are calling your higher essence to attention.

5. Give the tones associated with the vowels greater stress. Hold them longer than the tones associated with the consonants. Don't worry if the sound seems discordant. Eastern music sounds discordant to many Westerners, but it simply has its own rhythm and tonal value. The more you work with it and become familiar with it, the more interesting, pleasing and powerful it will begin to sound.

Learning to combine the tones in a more harmonious manner is part of the alchemical process. We are trying to combine our energies in more harmonious ways with all life and all life situations.

Just playing the tones in your name for five to ten minutes will balance your energies. This is especially effective at the end of a long day. The most effective way of restoring balance is through sound and music. It is part of a spiritual lesson and exercise we all must deal with at some time. In music it is known as the principle of "neighboring keys." Like neighbors in the physical, the notes within our name touch up against one another. Some of these tones sound good when played together; others do not. The more that we use them, the more familiar they become. We get to know our neighbors, and the walls of discord break down, for they are all part of the same neighborhood. Working with our neighbors builds harmony and health.

SINGING THE NAME

Singing is one of humankind's most creative acts. It links us with our underlying substance and being, and it is a means by which we can enter into a relationship with our most occult powers and abilities. Names in and of themselves have power, but when those names are placed within a melody, the power becomes universal.

Singing involves full use of the voice—our most creative musical instrument—and our whole self. We are an instrument of music and sound. Singing helps us to breathe more fully. It improves the posture, enhances our speaking voice and helps bring emotional awareness and fulfillment. It assists us in toning for greater health, and it serves as a grounding mechanism.

Music and singing awaken the creativity reflected within our name. It releases our stresses and limitations. There are many ways of using singing and your own name in a creative manner to enhance your health. We produce sound the way God produced the world, but we have lost the joy of this creative process. Singing with our name is a fun way of restoring that childlike ability to create at will.

Yes, we do have to put effort into our development, but there is no metaphysical clause or spiritual rule that prohibits enjoying the process. By learning to play with our names through song, we can affect everything about us.

> The song word is powerful; it names a thing, it stands at the sacred center, drawing all towards it . . . The word disappears, the poetry is gone, but the imagined form persists within the mind and works upon the soul! (Halifax, J. *Shamanic Voices*)

TECHNIQUE #1—Opening to the Name Song

1 Pick a simple melody that you enjoyed singing as a child.

2. Sing the song, varying the volume in different parts of it. Insert your name into the lyrics of the song while you are doing this. Don't worry if it does not make sense. It doesn't matter; we are just learning to sing out our name.

3. As you sing the song, make dramatic pauses.

4. Instead of lyrics, sing only your name to the melody of the song. No other words should be in it.

5. Now pretend you are singing your name in that melody to a lover or special friend.

6. Sing your name in that melody as if a professional singer were doing it. Sing it operatically.

7. Sing it as if extremely bashful. Sing it with confidence.

8. Sing it with only the primary vowel sound of your name.

9. Find ways of playing with it.

This inevitably produces laughter, but laughter is healing and cleansing. It breaks down the walls limiting the expression of our true essence.

Using the theme from the old Mickey Mouse Club is one that is effective, and one that the author uses. Instead of "M-I-C-K-E-Y M-O-U-S-E," I use "T-E-D A-N-D-R-E-W-S." Any name can be squeezed into that melody. It doesn't have to fit exactly. We are simply learning to use our name.

This will relieve stress and tension and facilitate the healing process of toning. Our name songs and tones can moderate our passions and shatter energy around us to whatever degree we desire. It is a way of cleansing the etheric band of energy surrounding us to allow greater manifestation of our spiritual energies into our physical environments. It is like cleaning the filter in a faucet so that the water runs full and clean into the glass we will be drinking from.

TECHNIQUE #2—Singing the Name Song

In the ancient mystery schools the students and the teachers sang to absorb their own sounds and vibrations. Once their thoughts and feelings were formulated, they needed to be grounded or focused into the physical realm. Singing enabled this to occur. They knew that the sounds were communicated to the throat by the energies of the soul, and by working with the sounds they could bring more light from the soul into the physical. They believed that light and darkness of the soul determined the quality of the voice. By working with sound and names and singing them for their healing qualities, they could overcome any darkness within the soul.

They worked to express themselves, and did not follow any tradition or imitate what they found pleasing. They knew it was possible for humans to escape the tensions and stresses of the physical through singing. They could balance themselves and thus not experience the detrimental effects of their environment and/or associations.

We are by nature complete. We are each a harmony, but we have learned to separate and create combinations of tones and energies that fight each other. The power of music and names can help us re-create the harmonies. They can enable us to experience the qualities of the energies of specific gods and goddesses within the universe, and more importantly, they can enable us to experience the energies of the Divine within ourselves!

1. Convert your first name to musical notes.

2. Beginning with the first letter, play it on your musical instrument or upon the pitch pipe, then sing your first name in that note.

3. Move to the next letter of your name and its appropriate note. Play it, and then sing your first name in that tone.

4. Continue until you have completed your first name. You may repeat each note and the name sung in that note several times. There are no hard and fast rules with this.

5. Repeat the singing of your name through the whole sequence. As you work with this you will begin to remember the melody of your name, and after several weeks you will not have to go through each note, although you can do so if you wish.

You have begun to awaken yourself to your name-song. This can be employed in various ways. Singing and humming it throughout the day keeps one balanced and energized. It can be used as a prelude to meditation, as it facilitates the induction of altered states of consciousness. It relieves stress, and it strengthens the aura, promoting healing on all levels.

Throughout the universe, and in almost every society since the beginning of time, there has been what the ancients called The Song of the Absolute or The Threefold Song. As we have mentioned, three in numerology is the great creative number. It is the number of the artist, the musician and the poet. The Song of the Absolute has three aspects, which reflect the manner in which musical tones and sound direct the energies of the universe:

1. Rhythm—from which all motion comes.

2. Melody—from which comes the manifestation of the Divine into the physical.

3. Harmony—from which comes individual power, which manifests throughout the universe and is reflected within us.

Our names are miniature forms of the Song of the Absolute. Each has a melody, comprised of its glyphs, sounds and musical notes. When all are put together and linked by the individual, we create a melody that bridges our physical with our spiritual essence. The rhythms of our name enable us to employ that melody, to raise and lower the bridge and to travel across it within this incarnation. When we employ all aspects, when we learn to blend the rhythms with the sounds and energies, we create a harmony of life. Giving life to our melodies through our rhythms creates harmony. We create a magickal, musical journey through our life. We recover our own innate divinity and begin to express it with a joy for living and for each other!

PART TWO

Sacred Seeds

*O pure of heart! thou need'st not ask of me
What this strong music in the soul may be!
What, and wherein it doth exist,
This light, this glory, this fair luminous mist,
This beautiful and beauty-making power.
Joy, virtuous Lady! Joy, that ne'er was given,
Save to the pure, and in their purest hour,
Life, and Life's effluence, cloud at once and shower,
Joy, Lady! is the spirit and the power,
Which wedding Nature to us gives in dower
A new Earth and new Heaven,
Undreamt of by the sensual and the proud—
Joy is the sweet voice, Joy the luminous cloud—
We in ourselves rejoice!
And thence flows all that charms or ear or sight,
All melodies the echoes of that voice,
All colors a suffusion from that light."*

—Samuel Taylor Coleridge
"Dejection: An Ode"

"In the Name of . . ."

Two roads diverged in a wood, and I—
I took the one less traveled by,
And that has made all the difference.
>   —Robert Frost ("Road Not Taken")

And if the world were black or white entirely
   And all the charts were plain
Instead of a mad weir of tigerish waters,
   A prism of delight and pain,
We might be surer where we wished to go
   Or again we might be merely
Bored but in brute reality there is no
   Road that is right entirely.
>   —Louis Mac Neice ("Entirely")

EVERYONE IS SEARCHING today for that path of fulfillment. Many enter into the metaphysical and spiritual fields, believing it to be a path that leads upward into some kind of blinding light in which all their troubles will be dissolved. The path is so much more than just a "path." It is a process of unfoldment, a process of unveiling, polishing and manifesting. It is the spiritualizing of matter, not escape from it. It is not what leads to a light that shines down upon us, but it is awakening the light within to shine out from us.

The Ancient Mystery Schools had but one precept—"Know thyself!" If we wish to become more than what we are now, if we wish to use our energies creatively, if we wish to become active in our lives, rather than allowing events to play upon us, we must discover the patterns and energies to do so. We must come to know what we are capable of manifesting. We must come to look beyond the immediate and the tangible. We must begin to understand that there are energies beyond what can be physically experienced. It is our name that can provide one of the safest and easiest means to do so.

Part of our responsibility in the growth process is learning to take what we have and build upon it, to re-synthesize teachings in the manner that best works for us as individuals. It requires that we ultimately must recognize that no one knows better for us than ourselves. It begins with reawakening and re-expressing the ancient reverence of naming ceremonies. It begins with recognizing that there are energies and forces active within the entire birthing process that can be used to bless our lives and manifest our greater potentials.

The Blessing Way is but one example of a naming ceremony. Loved ones gather and create and offer a blessing, an invocation or an expression of love to assist that child and open that new blessed soul to a greater manifestation of its own divinity. It proclaims the holiness of birth and the holiness of the child of birth.

This ceremony can be designed by the individual. Learning to do so again is important—we must learn to use our creative energies in honoring the creative process of birth. Rote ceremonies do not fulfill. Holding it upon the time of the waxing Moon prior to the actual delivery is often recommended. This is a time when the Moon is building its energies and opening up. The waxing Moon reflects life coming forth from the womb of the heavens.

It is at this time that the name chosen for the child should be announced among those loved ones present at the ceremony. It is a time to dedicate the child to the healing of the Earth, the strengthening of the family and the awakening of the Divine within all humanity.

We are living in a powerful and exciting time. We are at the cusp between two major ages in the evolution of humanity, and at the deepest level of our consciousness there is a spiritual transformation occurring. We are all being challenged to let go of the old and to create the new. Changes are blessings. They are signal flares of growth, but in order to appreciate the blessing of a change to the utmost degree, we must take responsibility for our individual lives. To do so means opening up to the infinite power that resides within each of us without exception.

Those who are serving as channels for new souls to come into the earth plane at this time need to recognize this even more so. If we are to take advantage of the opportunities available to us, we must expand our awarenesses of our own essences and of the world. As we increase our own awarenesses, we are in a better position to pass it on to those for whom we may be channels. For this to occur, we must break down the limitations we have imposed upon ourselves or allowed society and others to impose upon us, and we must open new doors and wonders to which we have rights.

In the infinity of God and Life, of which we are all manifestations, everything is possible. As we expand our awarenesses and break down old limitations, this becomes a reality for us and a blessing for our children. It begins with you and the amount of love that you are capable of extending to yourself.

The past cannot be changed, but the future is being shaped right now by our current thinking. We are here to transcend our limitations, no matter where they came from, and to recognize and utilize our own magnificence and divinity. The Universal Law of Energy states that "all energy follows thought." Where we focus our thoughts is where the energy goes.

We must begin looking for and dwelling upon the infinite possibilities, rewards and blessings within our lives, rather than on how limited we may be. "As a man thinketh, so he is."

There is only one Power in the universe. And that power is Perfect Fulfillment, Perfect Abundance, Perfect Prosperity and Perfect Love. Each and every one of us is a perfect manifestation of that Power. We each have the right and the ability to claim and manifest our own individual fulfillment, abundance, prosperity and love. It is the recognition of this and the utilization of it that lies within the creative magick and wonder of our names.

THE NAME ANALYSIS PROCESS

1. Work primarily with your first name.

2. Write out your full first name at birth, as it appeared upon your birth certificate. This will be used not only for analyzing the vowels, the sounds and your first name meaning, but also for providing clues to the basic life rhythms, as discussed in chapter 4.

3. Using your first name—your primary creative essence—determine its meaning and write it down in your name journal or underneath where you have written your full name in working out this analysis. Use the following dictionary of names to help. If your name is not listed, there is a list of name variations at the

end of the dictionary. Many names are simply variations of others, and they all hold approximately the same meaning. This list will refer you to the name which has a meaning similar or identical to your own. (If your name is not listed in either of these, consult your local library for other sources of names and their meanings. The bibliography also has several sources.)

4. Write down your name's meaning, and beside it construct an "I am . . ." affirmation using your name and its meaning as described in chapter 1. The dictionary of names provides sample affirmations, but you do not have to use them. It is often better if you make your own.

5. Examine your first name and determine the primary vowel. Write this vowel beneath your name.

6. Determine the element of your vowel as described in chapter 2 and write it down next to the vowel. Re-read the information on this element and its associations with your astrological element. Jot down major lessons and potentials associated with both, along with any incidents in life that you have had that seem to reinforce this.

7. Next, review the symbolism of the glyph of your primary vowel. List the major weaknesses and strengths, the positive and negative traits associated with the energies of the vowel glyph. This is your key to your primary lessons and inherent potentials. (Skip a space between each section so that you can go back and add more information as it unveils itself in future work and meditations.)

8. Now set up a section based upon the sound of this primary vowel. Review chapter 3 on the sounds of the vowels and the kinds of energies they activate within one's life. Which chakra have you come to work with most through the sound in your name? What are some of the positive and negative traits associated with that chakra? What are some imbalances that can manifest within this chakra, and what are some of the potentials? Are there incidents in your life that seem to reflect and reinforce this? Do these associations explain in any way some of the incidents of your life?

9. Determine the secondary vowels in your name. What elements

and energies do those elements activate in your life? How does the secondary element work with your primary vowel element? Are they compatible? Use the table of elemental combinations on page 29 to help. The interplay of elements does not refer only to the astrological elements and the name elements. They apply to any interplay of these elements in any part(s) of your life.

10. What are the secondary glyphs and the positive and negative traits that will be activated within your life by them? Are there any that seem to strengthen or enhance the traits of the primary vowel? Are there any that can hinder the traits and energies of the primary vowel?

11. What are the sounds of the secondary vowels? Which chakras will they be activating within your life? Are they the same or different from the primary vowel sounds? How do the chakras and their energies differ? How will they work together? Some meditation on this alone will elicit much insight.

12. Determine the rhythm of your birth name. How many syllables are there? Using chapter 4, what is the significance of this rhythm in your life? What are the potentials of this rhythm for unfolding capabilities and for learning specific lessons?

13. Determine the name you are going by currently. What is its basic rhythm? How is it different from your birth rhythm? Are the rhythms male or female (odd or even)? How does this compare with the masculine or feminine energies of your vowel sounds (long and short)?

14. Review your name's meaning. How does all this information about your vowels fit with learning to express the essence or meaning behind your name?

15. Refer to the dictionary of names, and read the meditation associated with your name or with the name that yours is a variation of. This will provide further insight into synthesizing the information and finding ways to activate the energies and soul purpose more fully.

16. At the end of your analysis, take time to list ways in which you can strive to manifest the power and potential of your name more fully. What are things that you can visualize yourself

doing, being, manifesting once your innate energies are fully activated? Remember: If you can imagine it, you can be it. Change your imaginings and you change the world!

Take time each day to at least affirm and visualize your essence in its fullest, brightest potential. Use the sounds and rhythms to heal and balance yourself when you feel yourself "coming down" with something, even if it is a negative attitude. Know that by working with your name you are realigning yourself with your highest essence. You begin the process of integrating the soul potential with the physical life. Use the song of your name like a magick wand, for it can turn any pumpkin into a golden carriage!

SAMPLE ANALYSIS SHEET

FULL NAME AT BIRTH:_____

I.   First name and its meaning
     Affirmation based upon first name and meaning.

II. Primary vowel and its element
     Major lessons and potentials of this element.
     Correspondences to your astrological element.
     Incidents in life which reinforce or affirm these energies.

III. Symbol/glyph of the vowel
     Major weaknesses and strengths associated with this glyph.
     Primary lessons, traits and incidents that confirm the energies
       of the glyph within your life to this point.

IV. Primary sound
     The chakra the sound of your name activates.
     Associations of the chakra in general.
     Incidents and ways in which this has been reflected in
       your life.

V.   Secondary vowels
     Major lessons and potentials of their elements.
     Relationships and energies of the elements working together
       (Refer to Table 2).
     Other chakras affected in your life and correspondences and
       relationships you can draw upon.

VI. Name rhythm
     Basic rhythm of full name at birth.
     Potentials and energies associated with that rhythm.
     Basic energy rhythm with your current name and its relation-
       ship to birth name rhythm.

VII. Further meditations and correspondences

Metaphysical Dictionary of Names

But you are a chosen race, a royal priesthood, a holy nation, a people of his acquisition, so that you may proclaim the perfections of Him who calls you out of darkness into the Light.
—I Peter 2:9

MANY NAMES ARE simply variations of other names. These variations (see Appendix A) are not dealt with separately. The meaning, the affirmation and the meditations will be the same. They differ only in vowels and lessons.

N. B. The Meditation information for each name is to be used in conjunction with the lessons and potentials associated with the vowel element and sounds within the name. It should be added to the information delineated in the first part of the book. Any lessons or abilities mentioned under specific names are to supplement and provide insight into the energies previously discussed (i.e., the element and the sounds and chakras of the vowels).

AARON

Meaning: "The Light Bringer"
Suggested Affirmation: "I am Aaron. I am the Bringer of Light!"
Primary Vowel/Element: A / Element of Ether or Akasha
Primary Sound/Chakra: "ay" / Heart Chakra
Other Vowels/Elements: O / Element of Water
Other Sounds/Chakras: "uh" / Throat Chakra

MEDITATION

Aaron is a name that reflects energies that many have come to manifest within the present time period. Its primary vowel is the *A*, and it corresponds to the ether element and heart chakra. The secondary vowel *O* is of the water element (spleen and solar plexus chakras) but manifesting through the throat, as denoted by its sound. During the Atlantean epoch, many individuals focused upon the power of the solar plexus chakra. That must be bridged into higher expression in our present time, which is the work of the heart chakra. The double *A* indicates that those with this name have chosen to double the effort to raise their energies from the solar plexus to the active heart and the expression of this new heart light through the throat chakra.

Aaron is also a name that has a rhythm of two, which signifies the feminine energies. It is the feminine that gives birth to the higher self, again a reflection of the task the soul is endeavoring to do—to give birth to the new energies and power of light on new levels, for themselves and for others.

ABNER

Meaning: "of the Light; trustworthy"
Suggested Affirmation: "I am Abner. I am the trustworthy light of God!"
Primary Vowel/Element: A / Element of Ether or Akasha
Primary Sound/Chakra: "ahh" / Throat Chakra
Other Vowels/Elements: E / Element of Air
Other Sounds/Chakras: "eh" / Throat Chakra

MEDITATION

Abner is a name that reflects working with all of the elements. It is a name that also reflects the lessons of learning to work with all things, especially learning to synthesize them in a new and creative manner, and to remain balanced (heart chakra) while expressing one's creative energies in a new manner (throat chakra). It is a name that gives the potential for great expressions of love and creativity. It reflects one who has the capability of bringing the light of love up and out of the heart area into increased expression in the physical life. This is an inherent ability to stimulate the same in others.

Its rhythm is two, the feminine energies. This reinforces the ability and the manifestation of opportunities within the life to give birth to new expressions of the love light. People will find it easy to communicate to those of this name, as its basic energy is "expressed love" that is felt by others, allowing them to open up and place their trust in you.

ABRAHAM

Meaning: "protector and father of many"
Suggested Affirmation: "I am Abraham. I am God's righteous
    protector!"
Primary Vowel/Element: A / Element of Ether or Akasha
Primary Sound/Chakra: "ay" / Heart Chakra
Other Vowels/Elements: A / Element of Ether or Akasha
Other Sounds/Chakras: "ahh" / Throat Chakra
                        "uh" / Throat Chakra

MEDITATION

Abraham is a very powerful name, often associated with the qualities of the archetypal father. It is comprised of three *A's*, which is an abundance of ether. This simply means that the person with this name has the potential of working abundantly with all things and from many levels. This is often what the good "father'" must also learn to do. It is also a name which has sounds associated with two chakras, the first *A* for the heart and the second and third *A's* for the throat. This indicates that there is a need to assert that heart energy with greater strength of will (throat). Fathers often have to show their love through strong control and work effort.

It has a rhythm of three, which is masculine in its force, but three is also the creative number, birth-giving. For the greatest balance, it is important for this individual to find creative ways of working with fatherhood and life, and asserting that creative energy with strength of will, often a lesson to be learned. Once learned it imbues one with great power.

ADA

Meaning: "one of happy, cheerful spirit"
Suggested Affirmation: "I am Ada. I am the happy child of God!"
Primary Vowel/Element: A / Element of Ether or Akasha
Primary Sound/Chakra: "ay" / Heart Chakra
Other Vowels/Elements: A / Element of Ether or Akasha
Other Sounds/Chakras: "uh" / Throat Chakra

MEDITATION

Ada is one who has come to learn to maintain a positive, cheerful balance under all circumstances. Those with this name often experience life situations that test their ability to be positive, while also drawing to them individuals that can help them awaken their own heart light and love in cheerful, happy ways.

Once she has learned to awaken the happy song within her heart and manifest it in all situations, there usually follows the opportunity to help others learn the same. This is the importance of the second *A* and its sound. There usually manifests situations and many opportunities to make others happy and to stimulate a rippling effect in their lives.

Ada has a rhythm of two—the feminine energy. In this case it is awakening the nurturing aspect within the heart and applying that nurturing to oneself. Learning to love and be happy with oneself is an important lesson, but once learned it unfolds opportunities to teach others about the power of positive thought.

ADAM

Meaning: "a man of the earth; God's creation"
Suggested Affirmation: "I am Adam. I am God's creation for the Earth."
Primary Vowel/Element: A / Element of Ether or Akasha
Primary Sound/Chakra: "ahh" / Throat Chakra
Other Vowels/Elements: A / Element of Ether or Akasha
Other Sounds/Chakras: "uh" / Throat Chakra

MEDITATION

The Earth has all elements within and upon it, everything necessary for fulfillment of any lesson to any degree. This reflects the essence of one with this name. He has the opportunity to manifest to any degree the assertion of his energies. This is why the *A* vowel of the ether element has sounds associated with the throat chakra. The throat chakra is sometimes known as the "cornucopia" center, as it can give one the ability to manifest anything to any degree. Learning to assert one's will and creative endeavors properly is what those of this name must learn. Manifestation—either positive or negative—is often quite easy for these individuals, according to where their thoughts are. Keeping focused on the positive and on the goals insures that the positive will manifest. Learning to handle lessons associated with abundance is often a part of it. "Be careful what you ask for, for it is what you will receive" should be taken to heart by all Adams.

ADELL

(variations of this name include Adeline, Adella, Adellia)

Meaning: "woman of noble esteem"
Suggested Affirmation: "I am Adell. I am God's woman of noble esteem!"
Primary Vowel/Element: A / Element of Ether or Akasha
Primary Sound/Chakra: "uh" / Throat Chakra
Other Vowels/Elements: E / Element of Air
Other Sounds/Chakras: "eh" / Throat Chakra

MEDITATION

Adell brings with it interesting lessons associated with the heart and the throat chakras. The energies of the heart—the intuition and healing sensitivities—have come to be expressed in a new manner. They have come to be discerned and understood from a "knowledge" perspective (the element of air) rather than from just a mere "feeling" perspective. Those of this name always have strong intuition, but it is often not understood. Part of the lesson is learning to understand how that intuitive aspect works and finding ways of practically applying it to one's life. Learning to assert one's control over those "feelings" is almost always a lesson for those of this name, in conjunction with those lessons and abilities associated with the elements and the sounds.

ADRIAN

Meaning: "of the black earth; the creative soil and heart"
Suggested Affirmation: "I am Adrian. I am the creative heart
    of God."
Primary Vowel/Element: A / The Element of Ether or Akasha
Primary Sound/Chakra: "ay" / Heart Chakra
Other Vowels/Elements: I / The Element of Fire
                             A / The Element of Ether
Other Sounds/Chakras: "ee" / Brow and Crown Chakras
                               "uh" / Throat Chakra

MEDITATION

This is a very powerful name, giving one great potential and valuable lessons. Its primary vowel and sound is the *A* for the heart chakra. Its next most important vowel is the *I*, associated with the energies of fire, and because of its sound within this name, it is also associated with the head. It also has a third sound, associated with the throat chakra. This indicates that individuals with this name have come to link the heart with the mind for greater creative expression and assertion of one's own unique energies. This may mean that the individual would have to overcome other impositions to express his or her own, or it could mean that he/she has come to unfold it by learning to balance the mind and the emotions. When they work together, it gives one tremendous power. This is also reflected in the rhythm of the name. Three is the creative number, its creativity the result of linking the male and female, heart and the mind. Black soil is rich and fertile, and this fertility is inherent in those of this name.

AGNES

Meaning: "purity or the pure one"

Suggested Affirmation: "I am Agnes. I am the pure child of God!"

Primary Vowel/Element: A / Element of Ether

Primary Sound/Chakra: "Ahh" / Throat Chakra

Other Vowels/Elements: E / Element of Air

Other Sounds/Chakras: "eh" / Throat Chakra

MEDITATION

Inherent within those of this name is an ability to express and communicate with individuals from all walks of life. Often in learning to do this, they are thrown into contact with a wide variety of people. This is reflected through the ether element working in the throat chakra. Learning to maintain mental balance with all these variants is often a lesson as well.

Because these individuals are often exposed to such a wide spectrum of individuals and energies, with an innate ability to have resonance or rapport with them, it is important that assertion of will be developed so that they remain pure and true to themselves. It is often reflected in the idea of being "holy even in unholy places."

There also exists a strong ability to synthesize teachings into a system of personal growth and expression in day-to-day life.

AL

Meaning: "cheerful; of good cheer"
Suggested Affirmation: "I am Al. I am the cheerful child of
    God!"
Primary Vowel/Element: A / Element of Ether
Primary Sound/Chakra: "ah" / Throat Chakra
Other Vowels/Elements: ——
Other Sounds/Chakras: ——

MEDITATION

Those of this name have a wonderful ability to find the positive
in all things. Sometimes their ability to be positive and cheerful in all
circumstances will bewilder others. The ether element gives them the
ability to see all sides to things, to look upon all situations from all
perspectives. For many, learning to do this actually becomes the
"philosopher's stone," the key to the alchemical process.

There is almost always an innate ability to communicate simply
and yet universally. They can make others feel comfortable about
themselves, having a knack for saying the right thing at the right time.
They can bring cheer to others' lives when they follow their instincts
and strong, intuitive healing insights. They make others feel good
about themselves!

ALAN
(variations include Allan, Allen)

Meaning: "of good cheer, harmonious, handsome"
Suggested Affirmation: "I am Alan. I live the harmony of God!"
Primary Vowel/Element: A / Element of Ether
Primary Sound/Chakra: "ah" / Throat Chakra
Other Vowels/Elements: A / Element of Ether
Other Sounds/Chakras: "ah" / Throat Chakra

MEDITATION

Those of this name have an innate ability to communicate with everyone. They have something of importance to say, and they should work to prevent any inhibition in speech. There is usually an ability to perceive and synthesize group energy, and they can be the key to true group harmony and group effort.

The secondary vowel and its sound—in all variations of this name—deals with the throat chakra, and reinforces those energies and lessons associated with it. Learning to assimilate knowledge and express it uniquely is important. Alans may not always be taken as intelligent as they truly are because they communicate in a light, cheerful manner. The somber, serious attitudes toward knowledge that are prevalent in society tend to cause misjudgments about these individuals, who manifest the lighter aspects of life, knowledge and life circumstances.

ALBERT
(variation: Bert)

Meaning: "noble, industrious; full of honor"
Suggested Affirmation: "I am Albert. I am filled with honor and nobility!"
Primary Vowel/Element: A / Element of Ether
Primary Sound/Chakra: "ah" / Throat Chakra
Other Vowels/Elements: E / Element of Air
Other Sounds/Chakras: "eh" / Throat Chakra

MEDITATION

Those of this name have a powerful sense of honor and truth, and they must take care to express it fully within their lives. Dishonor or shame is what hurts them the most deeply. They have an instinct for articulating the heart of issues, and they can reveal the honor of opposite sides of issues. They can be very circumspect in their view of life and world situations.

It is important for those of this energy to work, and work at something that produces effects. Learning to take pride in one's efforts, regardless of the task's status, is important. When this lesson is learned, they exhibit pride and are examples of the work ethic in its truest sense. The most menial task is revealed as one of honor. There is a wonderful ability to reveal and teach the nobility that resides within all life, all societies, and all individuals.

ALEXANDER
(variations: Alec, Alexis, Alexa)

Meaning: "the brave, protecting man; the secure soul"
Suggested Affirmation: "I am Alec. I am the brave protector of God!"
Primary Vowel/Element: A / Element of Ether
Primary Sound/Chakra: "ah" / Throat Chakra
Other Vowels/Elements: E / Element of Air
Other Sounds/Chakras: "eh" / Throat Chakra

MEDITATION
Working with, manifesting and utilizing proper courage is important to these individuals. They are very protective of their possessions, family and friends, but it is important for them to learn not to become overprotective. They have a power that manifests most dynamically when they come to the aid and/or protection of another, and there can be a tendency to not apply that same courage and energy to themselves. If the need arises, they can activate the energies of the throat chakra in a powerful manner, asserting a strength of will and might that can easily overpower. Learning to assert the will in a creative manner is an important lesson. Teaching others to stand strong for themselves is also a lesson that can manifest. It is important for them to heed the phrase, "Those whom we kill, we must bring back to life. Those whom we hurt, we must also heal. And those whom we protect, we must strengthen!" Developing a new sense of security in self and others will be a part of their life lesson.

ALICE
(variations: Alicia, Allison, Alyce, Alyssa)

Meaning: "truthful one"

Suggested Affirmation: "I am Alice. I am the truthful child of
    God." or "I am Alice. I am the bringer of truth!"

Primary Vowel/Element: A / Element of Ether

Primary Sound/Chakra: "ah" / Throat Chakra

Other Vowels/Elements: I / Element of Fire

    E / Element of Air

Other Sounds/Chakras: "ih" / Throat Chakra

    Silent E / Brow, Crown, and Throat
    Chakras

MEDITATION

This is a powerful name that activates the energies and lessons of
ether and fire in the individual's life. These lessons will manifest to a
great degree, as the sounds for both elements stimulate the throat
chakra, or center of will force and manifestation. The silent E tem-
pers the fires of the individual so that verbal expressions are not
too intense.

Individuals of this name must be cautious of their words, as the
ability to express themselves and have that expression responded to
is very great. The things said that are more lovingly will be felt more
lovingly by others. The things said more cuttingly will cut more
deeply. As these individuals grow and mature, there is a powerful
ability to utilize expression to strongly influence those in their life.
These individuals are often strong catalysts in the lives of others,
with great potential to heal and enlighten through their own manner
of expressiveness.

ALVIN

Meaning: "friend of all people; the noble friend"
Suggested Affirmation: "I am Alvin. I am the noble friend of all."
Primary Vowel/Element: A / Element of Ether
Primary Sound/Chakra: "ah" / Throat Chakra
Other Vowels/Elements: I / Element of Fire
Other Sounds/Chakras: "ih" / Throat Chakra

MEDITATION

Individuals of this name have a wonderful capacity to relate to others. Their persuasive skills, if developed, go almost unequaled. The sounds in the name activate the throat chakra, the center for expression. This expression can be filled with fire or it can adjust itself to every situation and individual, as reflected through the ether element.

Learning to speak from the heart and to stand strong in all relationships and friendships is most important for these individuals. Learning to develop clarity of thought in regard to personal situations that involve others is often a task for those of this name. Faithfulness and strength of character should be the keynotes for these individuals, and the lack of either, in themselves or in others, usually creates the greatest hurt within their lives. As they mature, their auras often assume a noble bearing, one of quiet and strong respect.

AMANDA
(variations: Amy, Ami)

Meaning: "worthy of being loved; beloved"
Suggested Affirmation: "I am Amanda. I am the beloved of
  God!"
Primary Vowel/Element: A / Element of Ether
Primary Sound/Chakra: "uh" / Throat Chakra
Other Vowels/Elements: A / Element of Ether
                         A / Element of Ether
Other Sounds/Chakras: "ah" / Throat Chakra
                        "uh" / Throat Chakra

MEDITATION

Lessons of the heart are predominant in the lives of those with this name. There is an abundance of *A*'s within the name—three to be exact. Three is the creative number, and thus those of this name have come to create a new expression of love and heart energies somewhere within their lives. For many it may mean learning to love themselves and being able to express and demonstrate that love through proper choice of activities and associations within their lives. It may also manifest with learning how to express love to a much wider variety of people, on a higher level than what has been done before, be it in this life or in breaking the pattern from previous lives. There is usually much healing ability with those of this name, which usually manifests first through learning to heal oneself and one's life experiences. For almost all, there will come a maturing and flowering of the heart chakra in dynamic ways, with many opportunities to express love to others and help them recognize that they too are "worthy of being loved."

AMOS

Meaning: "the bearer of burdens; the spirit of compassion"
Suggested Affirmation: "I am Amos. I bear the spirit of compassion!"
Primary Vowel/Element: A / Element of Ether
Primary Sound/Chakra: "ay" / Heart Chakra
Other Vowels/Elements: O / Element of Water
Other Sounds/Chakras: "uh" / Throat Chakra

MEDITATION

This is a powerful name, giving those with it the potential to raise their energies and the energies of others to new heights. The sounds and the elements of the vowels all are linked to the middle three chakras: heart, solar plexus and throat. This indicates that the soul has come to bridge its energies to a new level, to raise the energies and power of the solar plexus to new heights of expression. Bringing up the power from the lower levels and expressing it as a practical and positive power of love is what many of these individuals have come to do. There is an ability to see beyond the faults to feel the needs. Helping others to bear their burdens and learn the lessons of compassion is preeminent. The water element is very powerful, but when raised as a force of love to the heart level it brings new life. Expressing compassion for oneself and for all life must become a priority. Unless compassion is developed, bitterness can fill one's life. The gift of empathy is strong within these individuals, and they usually have a passion for life.

ANDREA

Meaning: "womanly; woman who is like a god"
Suggested Affirmation: "I am Andrea. I am the godly woman."
Primary Vowel/Element: A / Element of Ether
Primary Sound/Chakra: "ah" / Throat Chakra
Other Vowels/Elements: E / Element of Air
A / Element of Ether
Other Sounds/Chakras: "ee" / Brow and Crown Chakras
"uh" / Throat Chakra

MEDITATION

Those of this name have an energy that is often more "mature" than many believe. Even as a child there is a mature "knowing" of these individuals. They have an ability to absorb and assimilate information easily, and usually only have to be shown something once, especially if it interests them. They like knowledge and find it easy to tune into others for knowledge of it. They must be careful not to put on "airs," because the air element is strong within them, and they could get swept up in their own illusions. Keeping ther feet on the ground may have to be learned. Those of this name usually have an aura that draws at least one person who follows them around, almost worshipping the ground they walk on, but they usually are found at the heart of groups. Names of three syllables were always considered as wielding great power by the ancient societies. Most archangelic names have three syllables. With those of this name, there is always an ethereal quality to their energy that appeals to most people. There will be lessons, though, in balancing the ideal and the practical.

ANDREW
(variation: Andy)

Meaning: "the strong, manly one"

Suggested Affirmation: "I am Andrew. I am the strong child of God."

Primary Vowel/Element: A / Element of Ether

Primary Sound/Chakra: "ah" / Throat Chakra

Other Vowels/Elements: E / Element of Air

Other Sounds/Chakras: "oo" / Base Chakra

MEDITATION

This is a name that activates a unique interplay in the chakra energy. Those of this name have come to develop strength in some facet of their personality and life. As to where this strength lies, it will vary, but it could be in more than one facet, as the element of ether affects them all. Strength of will, control of the emotions, and physical strength are but some ways it may manifest. There is also a link between the throat and the base chakras, indicating that there will arise within the individual's life opportunity to draw greater energies from that center for our basic life force and express it in a beneficial manner. There is a lesson of learning to breathe new "air" into that strong life force that is prevalent in those of this name. Learning to express that life force in a creative manner will be tested. The kundalini has the opportunity to be raised by the individual to empower his or her life. Learning to do so will be important. For those upon the spiritual initiatory path, this will involve learning the esoteric aspects of the sexual energies and how to use them to trigger the alchemical process.

ANGELA
(variation: Angel)

Meaning: "messenger of truth; the angel"
Suggested Affirmation: "I am Angela. I am the angel of truth."
Primary Vowel/Element: A / Element of Ether
Primary Sound/Chakra: "ah" / Throat Chakra
Other Vowels/Elements: E / Element of Air
                           A / Element of Ether
Other Sounds/Chakras: "eh" / Throat Chakra
                               "uh" / Throat Chakra

MEDITATION

Those of this name have come to use the throat chakra to express themselves in new and powerful ways. All three vowels take the sound that activates this center. Learning to express with simplicity and truthfulness is very important. Speaking honestly is a key lesson. Along the same line, displays of dishonesty in communication is what hurts them the most. These individuals have a knack for saying the right thing at the right time, in the right manner. Learning to connect and mimic the activities of the Angelic hierarchy is the best that these individuals could do. Names of angels traditionally have three syllables (the creative rhythm), and this name, its rhythm and its meaning reflect those same qualities. Creative expression of some form is essential to the health and well-being of these individuals. They are natural healers with their voice and can make excellent counselors, which is why so many come to unload their problems on them. There is also a strong link to working with nature, be it flowers, herbs, stones, animals, etc.

ANNE
(variations: Ann, Anna, Annette, Anita)

Meaning: "graceful and gracious child"
Suggested Affirmation: "I am Anne. I am the gracious child of God!"
Primary Vowel/Element: A / Element of Ether
Primary Sound/Chakra: "ah" / Throat Chakra
Other Vowels/Elements: E / Element of Air
Other Sounds/Chakras: Silent / any of the Head Chakras

MEDITATION

Those of this name have come to bring to fruition the energies of love in some major area of their lives. They have come to learn the lessons of graciousness and mercy in all circumstances. Gracefulness can apply to the physical abilities as well as to the ability to work with people. It can involve gracefulness and agility of mind, particularly in those whose name has a secondary *E* within it.

Following one's heart is often difficult and can involve one in situations that are painful, but all situations help us to grow. It is important for all those of this name and its variations to follow the heart, to do what they know in their heart is right for them, and to temper all activities with love. In this way the heart can flower and the individual can create a beautiful healing experience and influence in the lives of those he or she touches. The healing intuition flowers with the heart.

ANTHONY
(variations: Tony, Antonio)

Meaning: "the priceless one; of inestimable value"
Suggested Affirmation: "I am Anthony. I am priceless in the
    eyes of God!"
Primary Vowel/Element: A / Element of Ether
Primary Sound/Chakra: "ah" / Throat Chakra
Other Vowels/Elements: O / Element of Water
                      Y / no specific element (combination
                          of Fire/Air)
Other Sounds/Chakras: "uh" / Throat Chakra
                      "ee" / Brow and Crown Chakras

MEDITATION

Those of this name are multifaceted. There are many abilities and energies capable of being manifested by them. They often undergo extensive testing and learning as well. "To them whom much is given, much is required" holds true for those of this name and its variations. The Anthonys have come to breathe fresh air into their hearts and emotions and the hearts and emotions of others, thus the unique combination of vowels. They have a gift for relating to others if they choose to develop it.

Regardless of the kind of work or life they choose to live, Anthonys will have a very subtle and powerful effect upon those within their lives. They feel what others feel—strong clairsentience—which must be learned to be balanced properly. Balancing the mind and the emotions is the key to fulfilling their hearts' desires. Most Anthonys have a capacity for being of tremendous value in the growth and maturing of those whose lives they touch, but it requires a growth and maturing of their own heart and mind first.

APRIL

Meaning: "the new opening; new birth; new in faith"
Suggested Affirmation: "I am April. I live in new faith!"
Primary Vowel/Element: A / Element of Ether
Primary Sound/Chakra: "ay" / Heart Chakra
Other Vowels/Elements: I / Element of Fire
Other Sounds/Chakras: "ih" / Throat Chakra

MEDITATION

April is a name that awakens during the incarnation opportunity to be reborn. It activates the energies to change the old patterns of incarnation and establish new ones according to the heart desires of the individuals. Usually those of this name have a wonderful capacity to manifest their hearts' desires. Learning to do so without it being at the expense of others must be learned.

April is the first full month of the spring season, a time of freshness and new beginnings. In esoteric Christianity it is the time of the resurrection of the soul. The "giving up of the ghost upon the cross" was the implanting of the Christ energy into the etheric plane of the Earth, so that in every incarnation thereafter, the divine spark within the heart chakra would come more to life. This is most reflected and activated in the lives of those with this name. There is a passion and fire to their hearts' expressions, but learning to express it in a balanced manner will be tested. These individuals have an ability to influence strongly those they touch. If they focus on positivity, that is what will manifest. If they focus on the negative, that also will manifest. They must learn that what they do affects others strongly.

ARLENE
(variation: Arland)

Meaning: "the promise; pledge; faithful one"
Suggested Affirmation: "I am Arlene. I am the promise of God!"
Primary Vowel/Element: A / Element of Ether
Primary Sound/Chakra: "aw" / Solar Plexus Chakra/
Other Vowels/Elements: E / Element of Air
                      E / Element of Air
Other Sounds/Chakras: "ee" / Brow and Crown Chakras
                      Silent / Head Chakras

MEDITATION

Those of this name have an innate strength and power to be faithful in every thought, word and deed. They are ones to be depended upon. They sometimes have difficulty handling others that are not as faithful, as it is such an intricate part of their own lives. The solar plexus chakra and the brow chakra have a wonderfully unique relationship. The solar plexus activates clairsentience, intuitive feelings within an individual. The brow chakra is the seat of higher clairvoyance, spiritual and intuitive sight. Those of this name have the ability to work from the feeling aspect or from the mental. They can even learn to unite them both, bringing the male and the female together to form a new unit of strength. "The two shall be as one" is a phrase that reaps much power and benefit in meditation for those of this name. Arlenes are often not given the credit they deserve for their mental abilities, which is reflected in the silent *E*. Learning to use that mental ability and to remain strong in their promises are major lessons for those of this name.

ARNOLD

Meaning: "brave and strong; strong like an eagle"
Suggested Affirmation: "I am Arnold. I am the strong eagle of life."
Primary Vowel/Element: A / Element of Ether
Primary Sound/Chakra: "aw" / Solar Plexus Chakra
Other Vowels/Elements: O / Element of Water
Other Sounds/Chakras: "uh" / Throat Chakra (sometimes pronounced "oh"—Solar Plexus Chakra)

MEDITATION

This is a name of great strength and stature, physical or otherwise. Even those who are not treated as though they have any stature at all find such treatment incomprehensible, for deep down they know there is a strength and an ability that someday will raise their stature. Learning to manifest that individual ability in some area of life will be the task of those with this name. Achieving some form of stature will be important, and finding stature in all tasks and efforts must be learned. There is always the lesson of recognizing that the only ones who determine our true strength and stature is ourselves. Thus learning not to be adversely influenced by the opinions of others will be important. Those of this name have great foresight. Just like the eagle, they can see for great distances. They can see where they are ultimately going—one year, ten years and even 30 years or more down the road. Keeping eyes focused upon that image and vision is what will move the individual through the mire of day-to-day life and open and unfold the true strength of soul so that the vision can be used for self and for others.

ARTHUR
(variation: Art)

Meaning: "the bear; the noble one; man of integrity"
Suggested Affirmation: "I am Arthur. I am the noble bear of integrity!"
Primary Vowel/Element: A / Element of Ether
Primary Sound/Chakra: "aw" / Solar Plexus Chakra
Other Vowels/Elements: U / Element of Earth
Other Sounds/Chakras: "uh" / Throat Chakra

MEDITATION

Those of this name have the task of developing a strong sense of honesty and integrity. For many, there will occur circumstances that reveal the opposite in those around them. For others, learning to overcome the opposite will be a priority. People trust those of this name. There is a down-to-earth quality about them (*U*) that resonates with other people. This trust can of course be acted upon beneficially or taken advantage of.

There is a great persuasiveness about these individuals, and because of the innate trust others seem to place in them, they can become excellent counselors or con men. Like their namesake, the bear, they can seem to just lumber along, but there is a power and strength that is overwhelming when set in motion. Bears are extremely fast and powerful beasts, and they hold true to their character and patterns. The bear was also a sacred totem in many societies, and those of this name could do no better than to assume it as their own. It is a totem of power, agility, strength and protection.

AUDREY
(variation: Audra)

Meaning: "of noble strength; strong nobility"
Suggested Affirmation: I am Audrey. I am of noble strength!"
Primary Vowel/Element: A / Element of Ether
Primary Sound/Chakra: "aw" / Solar Plexus Chakra
Other Vowels/Elements: U / Element of Earth
          E / Element of Air
Other Sounds/Chakras: Silent / grounding to heart energies
          "ee" / Brow and Crown Chakras

MEDITATION

Audrey is a name that resonates with the inner nobility that resides within the soul. Those of this name have come to learn to manifest that nobility within their lives and to teach others to awaken it as well. Regardless of their life task or occupation, those of this name must learn to see the nobility in doing a task—simply for the purpose of doing it well.

Those of this name also have an innate ability to see the lighter side of the everyday world, and they are capable of helping others to breathe fresh air into their own world. Thus some of the significance of the hidden earth element (*U*) within the name. Trying to develop a capacity to lighten the everyday world through new knowledge and new perspectives is essential. There is usually an aura around these individuals that speaks of hidden royalty. At some level of their consciousness, they know they are daughters of the Divine, and as such they must recognize that it requires certain behaviors, expressions and learnings for them and for those they touch.

BARBARA
(variations: Barb, Barbie)

Meaning: "stranger coming with joy; bringer of joy"
Suggested Affirmation: "I am Barbara. I am the bringer of joy!"
Primary Vowel/Element: A / Element of Ether
Primary Sound/Chakra: "aw" / Solar Plexus Chakra
Other Vowels/Elements: A / Element of Ether
                        A / Element of Ether
Other Sounds/Chakras: "aw" / Solar Plexus Chakra
                        "uh" / Throat Chakra

MEDITATION

This name has energies significant to the opening of the heart chakra. The sounds of the vowels correspond to the solar plexus and throat chakras, while the triple A element corresponds to the heart. The heart must bridge the lower emotions into higher expression. These individuals must take care not to do or say anything to consciously hurt another, as it is the antithesis to what they have come to learn. They have come to be a bringer of joy, and thus they must seek out that which brings joy to themselves. When this ability is unfolded it opens up the realms of the nature kingdom and those of the devic and angelic hierarchies. They too bring joy to their existence and to those of others, and they are drawn to those who also have that ability. Suffering is only good for the soul if it teaches us how not to suffer again. Those of this name have an energy that demands filling their lives with joy and creative expression.

BARRY

Meaning: "a pointed spear; courageous weapon"
Suggested Affirmation: "I am Barry. I am a spear of light!"
Primary Vowel/Element: A / Element of Ether
Primary Sound/Chakra: "ay" / Heart Chakra
Other Vowels/Elements: Y / Element of Air
Other Sounds/Chakras: "ee" / Brow and Crown Chakras

MEDITATION

Those of this name are linked to that energy that manifests in opportunities to bring light to areas of their heart. The heart is the seat of karma, and those of this name often have come to shed light upon the past and thus bring it out of the shadows to deal with it once and for all. Thus it is important for them to look upon every situation as significant and intrinsic to overall evolution. They must learn to take time at the end of the day to evaluate the day's situations in order to put it all into the proper perspective. Barrys have a strong sense of intuitive sight, which can be easily developed, but it also requires that it be balanced so that what is envisioned does not become an illusion. These individuals need to awaken the light within rather than searching for a light without. In this way they become a channel or spear of light for others.

BEATRICE
(variations: Bea, Beata)

Meaning: "she who makes others happy and brings joy;
   blessed and happy"
Suggested Affirmation: "I am Beatrice. I am the blessed bringer
   of joy!"
Primary Vowel/Element: E / Element of Air
Primary Sound/Chakra: "ee" / Brow and Crown Chakras
Other Vowels/Elements: A / Element of Ether
                        I / Element of Fire
                        E / Element of Air
Other Sounds/Chakras: "uh" / Throat Chakra
                       "ih" / Throat Chakra
                       Silent / Throat, Brow or
                          Crown Chakras

MEDITATION
This is a name that can activate the energies and opportunities to lift oneself from the earthly perspective. Its primary element is air, which rules mental activities. These individuals usually have a special field of knowing, or they are "knowing" enough to converse and synthesize a wide spectra of information. They usually know the proper thing to say and how to say it. They instinctively know how to relate to others. Sometimes in the growing stages they can be rather introverted. They receive so many signals—intuitive knowings about others—that they cannot synthesize them or express them. Thus it can become easy to withdraw. Learning to express themselves and their knowledge in whatever field is important. These individuals often make excellent teachers and find it easy to relate to children. They often go about their tasks in a competent manner that makes them a blessing to others.

BENJAMIN
(variation: Ben)

Meaning: "the favored son, son of the right hand"
Suggested Affirmation: "I am Benjamin. I am the favored son of God!"
Primary Vowel/Element: E / Element of Air
Primary Sound/Chakra: "eh" / Throat Chakra
Other Vowels/Elements: A / Element of Ether
                        I / Element of Fire
Other Sounds/Chakras: "uh" / Throat Chakra
                             "ih" / Throat Chakra

MEDITATION

If anyone can be considered lucky, it is often those of this name. The sounds and energies associated with this name tie the individual to the cornucopia of life. There is always abundance in some form. Whether it is good or bad abundance depends upon the individual and his or her outlook. All three sounds activate the throat chakra, the center of will force and manifestation. This is an indication that the thoughts and words must be watched carefully, as these individuals have a powerful and innate ability to set energy in motion according to their words or thoughts. There is an old saying about being careful of what you ask for, because it may be exactly what you get. This is a key to those of this name. There is also a natural ability to make others feel special and favored as well. Creative expression will always be important, whether in the field of business or in the arts. It is essential to the purpose of these souls. Any inhibition of it or wrong use will bring disfavor. If applied correctly, their energies can manifest the Midas touch, which can be passed on to others.

BERNARD
(variations: Bernie, Bernadette, Bernice)

Meaning: "brave as a bear; strong, mighty and powerful; victorious"

Suggested Affirmation: "I am Bernard. I am the powerful bear of God!"

Primary Vowel/Element: E / Element of Air

Primary Sound/Chakra: "eh" / Throat Chakra

Other Vowels/Elements: A / Element of Ether

Other Sounds/Chakras: "aw" / Solar Plexus

MEDITATION

The seven rays of light and energy that emanate from the Godhead upon all life on the Earth are filtered to us through the constellation known as the Great Bear. This holds much significance for those of this name or any of its variations. When we can align ourselves to our soul rays, we attain our true power and the expression of it within this lifetime.

This name has sounds that activate the throat and solar plexus chakras, two centers of great will force within our lives. These individuals have come to develop and manifest the proper use of strength of will, for themselves and for those within their lives. It also involves learning that the strength and power is also very gentle. These individuals are at their strongest when defending themselves or others. It is always foolish to back a bear into a corner, no matter how small. It is important for those of this name to assert their energies in something constructive, for it is then that the bear raises up to its full height and power.

BETH
(variations: Elizabeth, Betty, Betsy, Bessie)

Meaning: "house of God; consecrated to God"
Suggested Affirmation: "I am Beth. I am consecrated to God!"
Primary Vowel/Element: E / Element of Air
Primary Sound/Chakra: "eh" / Throat Chakra
Other Vowels/Elements: ——
Other Sounds/Chakras: ——

MEDITATION

Those of this name and its variations have an ancient thought-form of reverence associated with it. Learning to give proper reverence to all aspects of life—both physical and otherwise—is important and necessary for those of this name. In some form they have come to consecrate their lives to new expressions of spirituality. This may take traditionally religious forms or it may take the non-traditional. Often it is their example that awakens greater respect and reverence in others. Though quiet, their words should be heeded, as there is an innate wisdom that will come through. They have a unique ability to evaluate situations and get to the meat and potatoes of matters. Learning to heed those inner sights and words is important. Many are capable of developing clairaudience and hearing that strong inner voice. Many enter physical incarnation with those inner ears already connected, and thus efforts to "turn on the switch" may seem frustrating. They need to realize that the link to the higher is natural and quiet. It is that still voice within they must heed.

BEVERLY

Meaning: "diligent beaver; dweller at the meadow of the beaver"

Suggested Affirmation: "I am Beverly. I am the diligent worker of God!"

Primary Vowel/Element: E / Element of Air

Primary Sound/Chakra: "eh" / Throat Chakra

Other Vowels/Elements: E / Element of Air

Y / Element of Air or Fire

Other Sounds/Chakras: "eh" / Throat Chakra

"ee" / Brow or Crown Chakras

MEDITATION

The beaver, from which this name derives, is a diligent worker and builder. Beavers fashion a strong home, one that can stand up to and stop the flow of a stream or river. It can work in the water or upon the land. All the qualities of this animal are totem signs for those of this name.

Those of this name must learn to assert proper strength of will and balance. They must be able to swim in the emotional waters that may surround them, rather than being swept up in them. They must build a home—physical, emotional, mental and spiritual—for themselves.

If focused properly, the incarnation will set a new foundation and pattern for lifetimes to come. The law of cause and effect—either for good or for ill—is strong within their lives and has repercussions that extend beyond the immediate. Opening the perspective is essential to building that new home. Once done, it gives the vision of promise.

BONNIE
(variation: Bonita)

Meaning: "sweet and good; the good heart"
Suggested Affirmation: "I am Bonnie. My life is filled with the sweet and good!"
Primary Vowel/Element: O / Element of Water
Primary Sound/Chakra: "aw" / Solar Plexus Chakra
Other Vowels/Elements: I / Element of Fire
                         E / Element of Air
Other Sounds/Chakras: "ee" / Brow and Crown Chakras

MEDITATION

Those of this name have come to assert the mind over the emotions, and by doing so open themselves to spiritual vision rather than psychic sight. The solar plexus is a harbinger of strong feelings and emotions—the water element. Added to the water is fire from the vowel *I*—together they create steam, the generation of energy, part of the alchemical process. Steam rises in the air towards the heavens, thus the significance of the vowel *E*.

Controlling the emotions and using them in creative ways, as illumined by the fires of the mind, is a task that brings sweetness and light to one's life. When the mind is linked with the emotions, the power for creating wonders within one's life becomes manifest. If this is not done, these individuals will experience an emotional merry-go-round, replaying the same circumstances, only with different coverings. These individuals are very empathetic and must learn to discriminate between their own true feelings and those that they have picked up from others. When this occurs the waters of their life are filled with life-giving air, raising the energies and the soul consciousness to new visions.

BRADLEY
(variations: Brad, Bradford)

Meaning: "from the broad meadow; the good provider"
Suggested Affirmation: "I am Bradley. I provide abundance!"
Primary Vowel/Element: A / Element of Ether
Primary Sound/Chakra: "ah" / Throat Chakra
Other Vowels/Elements: E / Element of Air
Other Sounds/Chakras: "ee" / Brow and Crown Chakras

MEDITATION

Abundance and *providing* are the key words reflecting the energies of those with this name. These individuals have come to learn about abundance and providing for others. Sometimes, though, they must experience lack in order to appreciate abundance. Any lack there is within their lives should only be temporary, as they have a unique ability to manifest opportunities that can bring greater abundance into their lives. Whether they choose to do so is a matter of free will.

Meadows are places of peacefulness, security and fertile earth. These individuals are like a meadow. They have everything necessary to provide for their wants and needs during this incarnation if they use it. There is usually a strong drive to share this abundance with others. And there is often a lesson in recognizing that there are kinds of abundance other than physical, material abundance.

BRENDA

(variations: Brandon, Brant, Brendon, Brent)

Meaning: "from the fiery hill; the beacon; strong and en-
thusiastic"

Suggested Affirmation: "I am Brenda. I am a beacon unto
others!"

Primary Vowel/Element: E / Element of Air

Primary Sound/Chakra: "eh" / Throat Chakra

Other Vowels/Elements: A / Element of Ether

Other Sounds/Chakras: "uh" / Throat Chakra

MEDITATION

Those of this name or any of its variations have come in to fuel
the inner fires. Fires burn brighter when oxygen is available, and air is
the primary element. Sometimes these individuals must exercise
strength of will (throat chakra) to control their enthusiasm.

These individuals are usually passionate in their beliefs, and
when they speak of them, they can fire that same passion in others.
They can become fiery beacons upon a high hill, drawing others to
them. In fact, they usually draw a wide variety of individuals from a
wide spectrum of society. They can be attractive to all sorts of
individuals. Discrimination is important for them to develop, and
they often have an ability to serve as channels for spiritual communications, both conscious and unconscious. Their words should
be chosen carefully in life, as they have a much greater impact on
others than they often believe.

BRIAN
(variation: Bryan)

Meaning: "strength, virtue and honor"

Suggested Affirmation: "I am Brian. I am strong in virtue and honor!"

Primary Vowel/Element: I / Element of Fire

Primary Sound/Chakra: "eye" / Medulla Oblongata Chakra Point

Other Vowels/Elements: A / Element of Ether

Other Sounds/Chakras: "uh" / Throat Chakra

MEDITATION

Brian, as the name means, is a name that embodies the awakening of greater virtue and strength. The *I* is the primary element, indicating that the fires of virtue and honor are to be activated and developed within this life. The *A*, whose element is ether, is connected to the heart chakra. Thus those with this name have come to ignite new fires, raising the energies of the heart to new levels of expression (the throat chakra).

Most Brians find that their strength of will and honor is often tested, and it is important for them to stand strong, regardless of how others might respond. As long as they do what they know in their hearts is right, events will ultimately work out for them. Their life example can ignite fires of inspiration in others. Virtue is what they most cherish and is what they most need to express. By doing so, they unfold a wisdom and knowledge beyond the physical.

BRUCE

Meaning: "dweller in the thicket; secure"
Suggested Affirmation: "I am Bruce. I am secure in the thicket
   of divine life!"
Primary Vowel/Element: U / Element of Earth
Primary Sound/Chakra: "oo" / Base Chakra
Other Vowels/Elements: E / Element of Air
Other Sounds/Chakras: Silent

MEDITATION

Even the soil and earth require aeration for things to grow, and
the activity of air in the earth usually goes undetected. This reflects
much in the life and activities of those with this name. They may
seem very down to earth and practical, but there is much mental
activity and energy that silently works its influence (the silent *E*
influencing the *U*).

These individuals often keep their thoughts to themselves. They
often hope their actions speak for them. This is particularly true in
affairs of the heart. They often can fall into the trap of assuming that
since they provide for the home, their partner in life will know how
they feel. There is strength in silence, but it must be balanced as
well.

Those of this name usually have come to add new breath to their
life-force energies, to set new growth in motion that will extend far
beyond this incarnation. This is reflected in the base chakra and the
silent *E* activity. Often these individuals do not recognize just how
much new growth and energy they are setting in motion, and thus
extending perspectives is essential.

BURT

Meaning: "bright; abundant provider"
Suggested Affirmation: "I am Burt. I am the abundant provider of brightness."
Primary Vowel/Element: U / Element of Earth
Primary Sound/Chakra: "uh" / Throat Chakra
Other Vowels/Elements: ——
Other Sounds/Chakras: ——

MEDITATION

Those of this name have come to give new expression to their ability to provide. They often choose to take upon themselves lessons of providing with the proper attitude. Learning to see the light in all forms of provision is something they all must learn. Learning to provide for more than just earthly, physical needs is also part of their task. Thus the significance of the earth element operating through the throat chakra.

A true provider provides physical, emotional, mental and spiritual nourishment, and they do it with a brightness that lightens and heals those they touch. This is the lesson of those of this name. Learning to recognize that there is no eleventh commandment that states: "Thou shalt do without!" is essential. As these individuals recognize there is an infinite abundance available to them, the light shines upon the opportunities to manifest that abundance.

BYRON

Meaning: "bear; full of strength"

Suggested Affirmation: "I am Byron. I am the strong bear of God!"

Primary Vowel/Element: Y / Element of Fire

Primary Sound/Chakra: "eye" / Medulla Oblongata

Other Vowels/Elements: O / Element of Water

Other Sounds/Chakras: "uh" / Throat Chakra

MEDITATION

Those of this name have come to pursue that Quest for the Holy Grail, the search for our true spiritual essence and how to best manifest it in this lifetime. The Y glyph is a symbol for the chalice, and the name also has the element of water, the elixir of life that the chalice holds. When this elixir is ignited with fire (the Y sound) then it comes time to drink the charged liquid and cross into the Grail Castle of true spirituality.

Those of this name must learn to synthesize opposites. Learning to mix fire and water is only one example. It involves learning to work with the Hermetic principle of polarity, learning that hot and cold are simply different degrees of the same thing—temperature. Linking the mind and the emotions—Intelligence of the Heart—is essential. It is this that will be tested and will bring the greatest rewards.

"Everything is dual; everything has poles; everything has its pair of opposites; like and unlike are the same..." (The *Kybalion*) Balancing these concepts will give control over life.

CANDICE
(variations: Candy, Candi, Candace)

Meaning: "glittering white; woman of honor and light"
Suggested Affirmation: "I am Candice. I am God's glittering, white light!"
Primary Vowel/Element: A / Element of Ether
Primary Sound/Chakra: "ah" / Throat Chakra
Other Vowels/Elements: I / Element of Fire
                      E / Element of Air
Other Sounds/Chakras: "ih" / Throat Chakra
                      Silent

MEDITATION
There is a sound of lightness to this name. It is one of those names whose stereotypes often reflect the energy. Its abbreviated form "Candi" is often associated with those who are cute and light. Those who have this name will need to develop a lightness in their attitudes and perceptions. Overcoming the desire to take things too seriously can be oppressive to these individuals. Learning to treat the emotions more lightly is also part of their task. In this way, higher aspirations can evolve from the lower emotions, making them a light to others.

Doing something creative that involves short-term goals in which the results can be seen helps these individuals bring their lights to full force. These individuals have come to begin the process of merging the heart and the mind in a manner that is deeply joyful to them. At times this may seem self-centered, which must be guarded against, but it is important for these individuals to express themselves without worry over the response or possible response of others. In this way they become an example to others in expressing their inner light with joy.

CARL

Meaning: "farmer; strong and manly"
Suggested Affirmation: "I am Carl. I am the farmer of all life!"
Primary Vowel/Element: A / Element of Ether
Primary Sound/Chakra: "aw" / Solar Plexus Chakra
Other Vowels/Elements: ——
Other Sounds/Chakras: ——

MEDITATION

This is a name that can invest the individual who knows how to apply his or her energies with great power. The solar plexus chakra is a powerful center, whether used for good or for bad. When it is associated with the element of ether, it gives one the potential to activate power in all manners, affecting all peoples.

For many of this name, there are reflections of Atlantean incarnations in which the power may not have been used properly or at all. In this incarnation, many have come to re-express that power so as to benefit others in their lives.

A farmer needs all elements to make crops grow. He or she needs good soil, fresh water, oxygen and sunlight—all in the right combination. When that is present, there is the potential to produce a crop that will feed many. It must be remembered, though, that just because the elements are good does not insure the well-being of the crops. The farmer must tend to them at all times, keeping the balance to insure the best produce. The shaft of wheat—an ancient symbol of nourishment and abundance—is an excellent symbol for these individuals to meditate upon.

CARLA
(variation: Carrie)

Meaning: "little womanly one; strong"
Suggested Affirmation: "I am Carla. I am the strong woman of
the Divine!"
Primary Vowel/Element: A / Element of Ether
Primary Sound/Chakra: "aw" / Solar Plexus Chakra
Other Vowels/Elements: A / Element of Ether
Other Sounds/Chakras: "uh" / Throat Chakra

MEDITATION
Those of this name or its variation have come to develop greater
strength in their feminine energies. It is the feminine energies of the
universe that represent the enlightened or illumined soul, the only
kind of soul capable of giving birth to the Divine within. For illumination to occur, greater strength of will must be activated and fused
with the heart energies of love and light. Then the individual will
have the capability of becoming a dynamic healing force. They
become living proof that being feminine and being weak are not syn-
onymous. Giving birth to new energies on all levels is the task of these
souls—new emotional birth (solar plexus chakra), new healing birth
(heart chakra) and new birth in creative expression (throat chakra).
Birth always has a gestation period and a labor period prior to it, thus
the individual must develop patience and strength and not give in
to dismay.

CAROL
(variations: Caroline, Carolyn, Carrie)

Meaning: "womanly; song; song of joy."
Suggested Affirmation: "I am Carol. I am a song of joy!"
Primary Vowel/Element: A / Element of Ether
Primary Sound/Chakra: "ay" / Heart Chakra
Other Vowels/Elements: O / Element of Water
Other Sounds/Chakras: "uh" / Throat Chakra

MEDITATION
Those of this name and its variations have a unique gift for awakening the inner song of joy in others if they desire. The "name song" exists within the heart chakra, the primary center for those individuals of this name. They must learn to take that song and express it in the lives of others and themselves by fulfilling their life obligations and tasks with joy and proper attitude.

These individuals have an ability to relate to others' emotional needs and problems, and will often find others coming to them for help and assistance. It is important for these individuals to give that assistance with joy. This does not mean that they must sacrifice themselves constantly for others. Sometimes the best way of helping others is by not helping them. In this manner they are forced to take responsibility for themselves. Those of this name have the ability to make others see this most easily. Their ability to keep their own emotions balanced will be tested, but that is how the song within the heart can sing most clearly.

CATHERINE
(variations: Kathryn, Cathy, Kathy, Kathleen,
Katie, Kay, Cathi, Kathi)

Meaning: "one of purity"
Suggested Affirmation: "I am Catherine. I am the pure child
of God!"
Primary Vowel/Element: A / Element of Ether
Primary Sound/Chakra: "ah" / Throat Chakra
Other Vowels/Elements: E / Element of Air
                          I / Element of Fire
Other Sounds/Chakras: "eh" / Throat Chakra
                         "ih" / Throat Chakra

MEDITATION

Those of this name and its variations have a simplicity about them that eases their life and the lives of those they touch. All of the energies are focused above the heart chakra, which is usually the case of those who have balanced most of the negative traits of the lower chakras. Now they have come to give expression and concentration to the upper. These upper chakra energies are just as powerful as the lower, but they play upon the individual much more subtly. It is important that those of this name "be ever watchful," as circumstances are much more significant than what may be initially discerned. These individuals have come to awaken to the underlying significance of life experiences. Thus purity of perception is important. These individuals usually have strong intuitions, although they frequently do not trust them. They are too busy being rational about it. Learning to connect with their own strong and pure intuition is part of their life task, whether to help fulfill life's obligations or to accelerate spiritual growth. Purity is the keynote in all things—physical, emotional, mental and spiritual—and effort must be maintained for it.

CHARLES
(variations: Chuck, Charlie, Charlene; Charlotte)

Meaning: "strong; manly / womanly"
Suggested Affirmation: "I am Charles. I am strong in life!"
Primary Vowel/Element: A / Element of Ether
Primary Sound/Chakra: "aw" / Solar Plexus Chakra
Other Vowels/Elements: E / Element of Air
Other Sounds/Chakras: Silent

MEDITATION

Those of this name have come to breathe new air into personal power and its expression within their life. The element of air (*E*) is silent, and air is silent in its operations. It is what it connects with that gives it its sound and visibility. Those of this name will be judged not by their mental capabilities, but by how they use them. They will be judged according to what business and tasks they employ it in. These individuals have come to assert their energies outwardly, demonstrating their competence and abilities in whatever field they have chosen. Learning to express outwardly will be essential. This means overcoming any form of introversion and false humility.

These individuals have come to breathe new life into those endeavors of power within the world. Charles has a stereotype of being associated with bloodlines and the rich and powerful. Learning to breathe new power and life into all endeavors for all people is the activity of the ether element in and through this name. Doing so without losing oneself in that power is the task. Power does not have to corrupt, but it takes great control and inner strength of will (the activity of the silent *E* working through the throat chakra).

CHERYL

(variations: Cheri, Cherise, Sheryl, Sheri, Sherry, Sherri)

Meaning: "beloved and cherished one"
Suggested Affirmation: "I am Cheryl. I am the cherished child of God!"
Primary Vowel/Element: E / Element of Air
Primary Sound/Chakra: "eh" / Throat Chakra
Other Vowels/Elements: Y / Element of Fire
Other Sounds/Chakras: "ih" / Throat Chakra

MEDITATION

This is a name that activates the expression of the divine feminine element within the individual's life. It is through the feminine energy, the symbol of the illumined and enlightened soul, that one can give birth to new expressions (throat chakra). Those with the Y vowel most reflect this energy. Those whose name has the I vowel in it have come to give fire to the feminine energies, to learn to assert them more fully within their lives. The two predominant gifts of the feminine principle are those of intuition and imagination. Learning to trust and use the intuitive side will be a part of the individual's life. Controlling and focusing the imagination properly and realistically, as opposed to letting it run wild and uncontrolled, will also be tested. Lessons of asserting strength of will and individual expression, regardless of outside influence, is what enables these individuals to most fully awaken the higher intuition and imagination.

CHRISTINE
(variations: Christopher, Christine, Chris, Chrissie, Kristine)

Meaning: "the follower of Christ; The bearer of the Christ"
Suggested Affirmation: "I am Christine. I am at one with the Christ!"
Primary Vowel/Element: I / Element of Fire
Primary Sound/Chakra: "ih" / Throat Chakra
Other Vowels/Elements: I / Element of Fire
                        E / Element of Air
Other Sounds/Chakras: "e" / Brow and Crown Chakras
                        Silent

MEDITATION

All names tie the individual to certain archetypal energies within the universe. This name and its variations tie one to the Teacher and Educator for all life within this solar system. In occult Christianity, one learns that the Christ is the highest of the Archangels. Those of this name and its variations are tied strongly to that archangelic energy which serves to influence humanity most strongly through the astral and etheric planes. Balancing the emotions and living the healing and loving life will open the angelic hierarchy to those of this name.

This is a name of spiritual fire, which is given expression within the physical life. These individuals usually have strong beliefs in something and must learn to express them in the most creative and beneficial manner possible. Keeping the emotions balanced will be most important for the realization of the highest capability.

CLAUDE
(variations: Claudette, Claudia, Claudine)

Meaning: "of humble heart; humility"
Suggested Affirmation: "I am Claude. I am filled with the humility of God!"
Primary Vowel/Element: A / Element of Ether
Primary Sound/Chakra: "aw" / Solar Plexus Chakra
Other Vowels/Elements: U / Element of Earth
  E / Element of Air
Other Sounds/Chakras: Silent

MEDITATION

Those of this name and its variations have come to learn and to express humility. They usually are very talented in some area, so they must learn to work at it with humility. This name can reflect a past life in which the individual received great acclaim in some area of proficiency and as a result developed lack of humility. This proficiency may even have been expressed in a manner to gain power over others.

This name has several silent vowels, indicating a lesson of significance in humility: Let others do your praising, rather than yourself. The solar plexus chakra is activated as well. This is a power center that is influenced by the element of ether. This may make the individual talented in many areas—both practical (*U* and the element of earth) and creative (*E* and the creative expression of element of air). These individuals have the ability to fit in with most any crowd. They can be down-to-earth and intellectual, as is fitting the occasion.

CLIFFORD
(variation: Cliff)

Meaning: "From the cliff; vigilant"
Suggested Affirmation: "I am Clifford. I am the vigilant child!"
Primary Vowel/Element: I / Element of Fire
Primary Sound/Chakra: "ih" / Throat Chakra
Other Vowels/Elements: O / Element of Water
Other Sounds/Chakras: "eh" / Throat Chakra

MEDITATION
From a cliff a person can see much of what approaches. Learning to see the patterns of events that are about to unfold is an important lesson for those of this name—learning to look to the future, rather than dwelling in the past. The two elements are water and fire. Water is the element of emotions and fire is the element of spiritual aspiration. Desire can be turned into aspiration only when the future is focused upon. Learning not to dwell upon and live in the past is important for these individuals. By doing so, the past (water) and the future (fire) can meet in the present. The individual can learn to control life's events rather than being controlled by them. The significance of all events and people must be discerned by those of this name if revelations of the future are to manifest. Dreams are important to these individuals, and dreamwork should be utilized in the self-realization process.

CLYDE

Meaning: "heard from far away; of good heart"
Suggested Affirmation: "I am Clyde. My heart is felt near and far!"
Primary Vowel/Element: Y / Element of Fire
Primary Sound/Chakra: "eye" / Medulla Oblongata
Other Vowels/Elements: E / Element of Air
Other Sounds/Chakras: Silent

MEDITATION

Those of this name have come to join the heart and the mind for greater expression and activation of the spiritual quest. The Y is the Grail Fire, the fire of the alchemical process. The expression of the spiritual fire must be balanced with the spiritual mind, otherwise the expression of the love and the heart is likely to be split, creating inner turmoil. This can result in physical, mental or emotional imbalances. Just as the Y joins two diverse factions in its glyph, those of this name often expend great energy trying to link and bind what may not need to be bound in this incarnation. Learning to recognize that all are bound and tied together, regardless of outer, physical circumstances, is a lesson for those of this name. This requires farsightedness, something that those of this name can activate. Looking into the Grail cup, one can see the pattern of events extending beyond this incarnation. Learning to do so while in this incarnation will ease the trials and keep the heart strong, enabling the love to radiate with health and light for all surrounding these individuals.

CONNIE
(variation: Constance)

Meaning: "firmness, constancy; earnest devotion"
Suggested Affirmation: "I am Connie. I am constant in all
   endeavors!"
Primary Vowel/Element: O / Element of Water
Primary Sound/Chakra: "aw" / Solar Plexus Chakra
Other Vowels/Elements: I / Element of Fire
                        E / Element of Air
Other Sounds/Chakras: "ee" / Brow and Crown Chakras

MEDITATION

Those of this name have come to build a new bridge in dealing
with their emotions. They have come to balance them with greater
mental activity. It is important for these individuals to learn to
express their emotions, or the buildup of inner fires can result in
imbalances. Learning not to get enmeshed in emotions of the past,
learning to release the past for the future, and learning to fill their
lives with refreshing activities on a regular basis is necessary for the
greatest growth.

These individuals have excellent psychic and creative abilities.
Their emotional nature makes them very empathetic to others. If
hurt occurs in their early years, this psychic empathy may be expressed in later years through imbalance. On the other hand, if past
situations are put in their proper perspective, these individuals make
excellent psychic healers, clairvoyants and mediums.

CRAIG

Meaning: "strong, enduring; dwells at the crag"
Suggested Affirmation: "I am Craig. I am strong in all things!"
Primary Vowel/Element: A / Element of Ether
Primary Sound/Chakra: "ay" / Heart Chakra
Other Vowels/Elements: I / Element of Fire
Other Sounds/Chakras: Silent

MEDITATION

Those of this name have come to develop strength in all endeavors. Learning to stick to something, to play it all out, is part of their life task. Learning to put their hearts into all activities, no matter how trivial or insignificant they may seem, can be difficult, but once accomplished, it strengthens the entire energy system of the individual—physically, emotionally, mentally and spiritually. Many times in order to learn these lessons, they seem to be battered by a variety of life situations. Just like a crag overlooking the sea that is battered by all the elements, it always stands strong and impressive. This is how those of this name must come to see themselves. In this manner, they become a stabilizing force in their world, assisting others and enabling those less strong to build new foundations for their lives. This is the essence of love and the heart chakra, and it prepares one for the intense tasks of discipleship in lives to come.

CYNTHIA
(variation: Cindy)

Meaning: "goddess of the Moon; reflector of light"
Suggested Affirmation: "I am Cynthia. I am the Goddess reflecting light for all!"
Primary Vowel/Element: Y / Element of Fire
Primary Sound/Chakra: "ih" / Throat Chakra
Other Vowels/Elements: I / Element of Fire
                          A / Element of Ether
Other Sounds/Chakras: "ee" / Brow and Crown Chakras
                         "uh" / Throat Chakra

MEDITATION

The Grail Chalice (associated with the Y) is a feminine symbol. It is the cup of life, the womb, the moon that reflects the sun. Those of this name or its variation have a unique talent for enabling others to see their talents. They reflect the energies of those they are around. They are chameleon-like in their behavior, resonating with the energy of whatever environment they may be in. Caution must be exercised in choosing right friends and environments.

Being a shapeshifter is difficult. One must be able to manifest and control many emotions, attitudes, etc. Those of this name have come to learn to shift their energies more assertively and creatively, in order to bring out the light within themselves and others. They have excellent clairvoyant and mediumistic capabilities, but they must learn to control them at all times. Once done, they become the moon in the nights of all those they touch, bringing light into the darkness.

DALE

Meaning: "one who dwells in the valley; courageous"
Suggested Affirmation: "I am Dale. I am courageous in life!"
Primary Vowel/Element: A / Element of Ether
Primary Sound/Chakra: "ay" / Heart Chakra
Other Vowels/Elements: E / Element of Air
Other Sounds/Chakras: Silent

MEDITATION

Those of this name have come to express their courage in new environments. Often there is a lesson associated with relating to people from a new perspective. One who moves into a dale or valley must make new acquaintances and associations. This is an energy that reflects the spiritual lesson in varying degrees to those of this name. They have come to breathe new life and air into their hearts. They have come to experience that there is much more out there in the world than what exists around them. They have come to open their hearts to new experiences that will ultimately enable the expression of the heart in all endeavors. Learning to discriminate as to which activities to involve themselves in will be part of the lesson. Learning to love with a courage and a committedness will bring rewards and all the fruits of the valley into their lives.

DANIEL
(variations: Dan, Danny, Danni)

Meaning: "God is my judge"
Suggested Affirmation: "I am Daniel and God is my judge!"
Primary Vowel/Element: A / Element of Ether
Primary Sound/Chakra: "ah" / Throat Chakra
Other Vowels/Elements: I / Element of Fire
  E / Element of Air
Other Sounds/Chakras: "ee" / Brow and Crown Chakras

MEDITATION
There is a lot of fire deep within those of this name. This fire can interfere with judgment, the predominant lesson of those who have this name and its variations. At some point within their lives, discernment and discrimination—critical judgment—is tested. Learning to accept others as they are without being judgmental will be important. When this is done, higher psychic and spiritual discernment can unfold. These individuals have the ability to look beyond the faults to see the needs of others, which is true loving discernment. Giving expression to what is seen must always be tempered so as to heal and nurture rather than hurt. When this occurs, the individual becomes a major force in the lives of others. Clairvoyance is natural with most of this name, although it frequently is not recognized as such.

DARLENE
(variation: Darla)

Meaning: "dear little one; tender love"
Suggested Affirmation: "I am Darlene. I am filled with tender love."
Primary Vowel/Element: A / Element of Ether
Primary Sound/Chakra: "aw" / Solar Plexus Chakra
Other Vowels/Elements: E / Element of Air
Other Sounds/Chakras: "ee" / Brow and Crown Chakras

MEDITATION

Those of this name have a capacity for expressing great tenderness in love. The predominant vowel sounds are associated with the solar plexus, a seat of great emotion and power, and the head centers, new life and new air. These individuals have come to give new air to old emotions, expressing them from a higher level through the heart and head rather than from the lower desire centers. Those of this name have a tremendous sensitivity that must be balanced at all times to avoid emotional manipulation and power struggles. The mind over the emotion becomes the lesson. When this is accomplished, the tenderness of expression that emanates is one of great nurturing. The child within unfolds to nurture and love the child in others. Softness and tenderness are keynotes for these individuals, but they must remember that there is great strength in both of those qualities.

DARREN
(variations: Darius, Dario, Darryl, Derryl)

Meaning: "bountiful; great one who is beloved"
Suggested Affirmation: "I am Darren. I am bountiful in all
   things!"
Primary Vowel/Element: A / Element of Ether
Primary Sound/Chakra: "ay" / Heart Chakra
Other Vowels/Elements: E / Element of Air
Other Sounds/Chakras: "eh" / Throat Chakra

MEDITATION

Learning the lessons associated with bounty and true "blessedness" will be in store for those of this name. For many it may have
to do with realizing that bounty is not measured in material objects or
wealth. For others it may revolve around recognizing that there is a
bounty out there in the world to be taken advantage of. In either case,
though, those of this name and its variations must learn to recognize
the bounty of ability they have, the bounty of love they must manifest
for themselves, and the bounty of creative ability. The heart and
throat chakras are centers of tremendous healing and abundance. As
we heal ourselves of limiting ideas and perceptions we open ourselves to the abundance that is ours by right.

Those of this name and its variations must come to understand
they are part of abundance; they are not separate from it. In this manner it then only becomes a matter of opening the appropriate cup-
board of life and choosing what is wanted or needed.

DAVID
(variations: Dave, Davey)

Meaning: "beloved one"

Suggested Affirmation: "I am David. I am the beloved child of God!"

Primary Vowel/Element: A / Element of Ether

Primary Sound/Chakra: "ay" / Heart Chakra

Other Vowels/Elements: I / Element of Fire

Other Sounds/Chakras: "ih" / Throat Chakra

MEDITATION

Those of this name have a powerful and ancient thoughtform to which they have access. David was beloved within the Biblical scripture. He slew the giant Goliath. His heart was so strong and true that he held no fear in the face of this giant. At the same time the heart was so pure that he sang and wrote many of the psalms. Both indicate the creativity and the strength of the fire within those of this name. Many actually live lives that parallel many of the activities of the David within scripture. Davids must learn to trust in the fact that they are "sons of God," as all men and women are "sons and daughters of God." Learning to express the love in all things to all people is what most benefits these individuals. There is usually always one thing or person to which they hold a great passion and love. Most Davids have great healing and intuitive energies as well.

DAWN

Meaning: "new day; joy and praise"
Suggested Affirmation: "I am Dawn. I sing for the new day!"
Primary Vowel/Element: A / Element of Ether
Primary Sound/Chakra: "aw" / Solar Plexus Chakra
Other Vowels/Elements: ——
Other Sounds/Chakras: ——

MEDITATION

The solar plexus chakra was called the "manger" by the esoteric group known as the Ancient Essenes. It was the point in the body that gave birth to the lower self so that it could be raised up to the highest possible expression. Those of this name have come to give birth to their energies. This is a birth that involves joy and praise, and should include much meditation upon the idea that everything in the physical is a miracle, as we are all essentially Spirit. Each day we have the opportunity to give birth to new endeavors and to new expressions of our energies. Those of this name need to keep this in mind, for they have a wonderful ability to enable others to see the glory in a new day, in spite of the past. They have come to uplift those they touch and to awaken the song of new birth in them.

DEBORAH
(variations: Debbie, Deb, Debra, Debby)

Meaning: "the bee; seeker"
Suggested Affirmation: "I am Deborah. I am the bee seeking the honey of life!"
Primary Vowel/Element: E / Element of Air
Primary Sound/Chakra: "eh" / Throat Chakra
Other Vowels/Elements: O / Element of Water
A / Element of Air
Other Sounds/Chakras: "uh" / Throat Chakra

MEDITATION
The bee is an ancient symbol for fertility. It has the stinger and it collects the honey of life, or the male and female energies that "pollinate" our lives. Learning to balance them is part of what these individuals have come to do. They have a tremendous capacity for influencing others, and enable them to find their honey in life. These individuals instinctively handle many of their life tasks.

Those of this name or its variations need to model themselves after the bee. The bee is an insect that aerodynamically should not be able to fly. They defy engineering, physics and the natural laws. Nothing is too impossible or far out for these individuals. They can make almost anything succeed, if worked at in the proper manner of making anything manifest in their lives. It may take some time, but they can do the impossible, and they do it *naturally*.

DENISE
(variation: Dennis)

Meaning: "follower of Dionysius; discerner"
Suggested Affirmation: "I am Denise. I am the wise discerner!"
Primary Vowel/Element: E / Element of Air
Primary Sound/Chakra: "eh" / Throat Chakra
Other Vowels/Elements: I / Element of Fire
E / Element of Air
Other Sounds/Chakras: "ee" / Brow and Crown Chakras

MEDITATION

The Dionysian Mysteries are very ancient. Strongly connected to nature and the grape, there was much mystical symbolism associated with them. Before they degenerated into the bacchanalia that they are now associated with, tremendous initiation and heightened consciousness occurred through alignment with the forces of nature. Those of this name or its male variation have a wonderful ability to link with nature and the kingdoms of nature as a whole. The predominant lesson is one of discrimination and discernment. Too much wine causes one to lose his or her judgment, thus maintaining proper judgment is always tested in these individuals.

The grape and the grape vine were symbols of the Dionysian Mysteries and the true Christian Mysteries. The grape vine bears fruit. That fruit can become a sweet wine or vinegar, depending on how it is harvested. Meditating upon these symbols will reveal much about their life purpose.

DIANA
(variations: Diane, Dianne)

Meaning: "divine one; living in glory"
Suggested Affirmation: "I am Diana. I am the divine child living
   in glory."
Primary Vowel/Element: I / Element of Fire
Primary Sound/Chakra: "eye" / Medulla Oblongata
Other Vowels/Elements: A / Element of Ether
Other Sounds/Chakras: "ah" / Throat Chakra
                           "uh" / Throat Chakra

MEDITATION

Those of this name have come to rediscover the glory in their lives. This does not imply that they have come to do anything of great magnificence, although that can be the case. It does mean that they have to find the glory of themselves. They must learn to be fulfilled in and through themselves, not through others or not through outside activities. It is important for these individuals to discover that they are complete and creative beings unto themselves, regardless of who knows it.

One must first recognize the inner divinity before one can ever begin to express it. Learning to be at peace with themselves and life is what will awaken them most to that realization. When this occurs, then and only then do they begin to shine with that glory in the lives of others, regardless of environment. Then they become examples, teaching others that *all* life's conditions reflect God's operation and glory, if we learn to look for it.

DONALD
(variation: Don)

Meaning: "mighty world ruler; overcomer"
Suggested Affirmation: "I am Donald. I am mighty in overcoming the world!"
Primary Vowel/Element: O / Element of Water
Primary Sound/Chakra: "aw" / Solar Plexus Chakra
Other Vowels/Elements: A / Element of Ether
Other Sounds/Chakras: "uh" / Throat Chakra

MEDITATION

Those of this name have come to work with the lesson of strength of will. Learning to assert proper strength of will and when to be flexible are all part of this lesson. The solar plexus chakra works with the energies of the lower sensory will, while the throat chakra is the center for the higher divine will. Finding ways of bridging them is important for those of this name. Learning to assert one's will without becoming dogmatic and without overriding the wills of others is often tested.

This name gives one a tremendous ability to be strong enough to overcome anything within the physical world. These individuals know what must be done in their life pursuits and must continue forward to accomplish it. They may not lead what appear to be glamorous lives, but they often epitomize the precept of "no greater love hath man than he give his life for another." These individuals usually have given up an incarnation of focusing on themselves so that others around them may be able to do what they need to do.

DONNA

Meaning: "lady; dignity of character"
Suggested Affirmation: "I am Donna. I am dignified through God."
Primary Vowel/Element: O / Element of Water
Primary Sound/Chakra: "aw" / Solar Plexus Chakra
Other Vowels/Elements: A / Element of Ether
Other Sounds/Chakras: "uh" / Throat Chakra

MEDITATION

Those of this name have come to demonstrate dignity of character through the example of their lives. Demonstrating the quality of being a lady is important. A true lady embodies the qualities of strength, nurturing, humility, humor, understanding and self-pride. Discipline oversees all of them. Learning to assert all these qualities is part of life's lesson for them. These individuals have all these qualities, but they may need to learn to synthesize them for their own benefit and for the benefit of those closest to them.

Just as knightship had its code of ethics, ladyship does as well. Truth and honesty above all else should be the guide words for those of this name. Usually those of this name have a past-life association with medieval times, when chivalry and ladyship were preeminent. For some, it may reflect that they have come to express those same qualities in the 20th century. For others it may indicate that they never got to achieve that "state" and thus have set that energy in motion for themselves in this incarnation through their name.

DOROTHY
(variations: Dora, Theodora, Doris)

Meaning: "gift of God"
Suggested Affirmation: "I am Dorothy. I am the gift of God!"
Primary Vowel/Element: O / Element of Water
Primary Sound/Chakra: "oh" / Spleen Chakra
Other Vowels/Elements: O / Element of Water
                                  Y / Element of Air
Other Sounds/Chakras: "uh" / Throat Chakra
                                  "ee" / Brow and Crown Chakras

MEDITATION

One that learns to raise his or her energies—following the path of the kundalini—can then manifest those energies in a multitude of forms for others as gifts. Out of the waters of life came all gifts and all energy expressions. This same water element is prominent in the lives of those with this name. They have an ability to express themselves with most people. They can work in a variety of fields; they are not limited in their scope.

One who is a gift of God touches the lives of others in subtle ways. The influence, although not always as acknowledged as it should be, is very great. These individuals bring joy into the lives of others, and they should take care not to do or say anything to hurt others, as this is the antithesis of their purpose. They have a capability of manifesting any of the "metaphysical" gifts within their lives: clairvoyance, healing, manifestations, etc.

DOUGLAS
(variation: Doug)

Meaning: "from the black or dark water; seeker of light"
Suggested Affirmation: "I am Douglas. I seek and find the light
    in all things!"
Primary Vowel/Element: O / Element of Water
Primary Sound/Chakra: "uh" / Throat Chakra
Other Vowels/Elements: U / Element of Earth
                    A / Element of Ether
Other Sounds/Chakras: "uh" / Throat Chakra

MEDITATION

This name literally means "from the dark water." This is significant in the lives of those with this name. These individuals have lessons that involve seeing the light in all situations, which means learning to find the "silver lining." Black, just like white, has the full color spectrum within it, but it must be searched out.

The dark waters is an ancient symbol or metaphor for the womb and waters of life. Out of the darkness of the womb came new life. These individuals have come to give new meaning and significance to their life and their life expressions. This also can indicate past lifetimes when energy was not focused upon the light, and thus they have come to focus it more strongly in this one. Nothing is entirely without light, and thus these individuals always have a knack for finding the light. Someone comes into their lives at the appropriate time, etc. For this reason, they often seem to be lucky. In essence they are learning that there is always a light in the world for them.

DUANE

Meaning: "song; of cheerful heart"
Suggested Affirmation: "I am Duane. I am the song of the cheerful heart."
Primary Vowel/Element: A / Element of Ether
Primary Sound/Chakra: "ay" / Heart Chakra
Other Vowels/Elements: U / Element of Earth
　　　　　　　　　　　　E / Element of Air
Other Sounds/Chakras: Silent

MEDITATION

Just as there are silent vowels within this name, allowing the predominant vowel for the heart to ring out stronger, so is the life of those with this name. These individuals must learn to silence the mind and withdraw occasionally from the physical world to hear the song within the heart. It has been said that the angels sing for us each day, but to hear the song of the angels one must first hear the song within his or her own heart.

Those of this name have come to awaken the song of "cheerfulness" in the lives of others. They have an ability to lift the spirits of others if they choose to develop it. They can touch the hearts of both the most earthy individuals and the most intellectual. Music has no boundaries, and neither do those of this name. Understanding this and employing it to their benefit is what will unfold in the course of their lives.

EDWARD
(variations: Ed, Eddie, Edgar, Edwin, Edith, Edmund, Edna)

Meaning: "prosperous, cheerful and friendly guardian"
Suggested Affirmation: "I am Edward. I am the prosperous guardian of all."
Primary Vowel/Element: E / Element of Air
Primary Sound/Chakra: "eh" / Throat Chakra
Other Vowels/Elements: A / Element of Ether
Other Sounds/Chakras: "uh" / Throat Chakra

MEDITATION

Those of this name and its variations have a tremendous ability to bring fresh, calming air into the lives of others. They have a knack for prosperous opportunities, if they develop it. The east winds (element of air) bring new life, prosperity and abundance with them.

Learning to tap that abundance and to use it to share and protect others is part of the lesson for those of this name. Finding the courage to assert one's energies for abundance will be tested. This is throat chakra energy—assertion of will for the manifestation of cornucopia. One who serves to guard and protect others needs a certain amount of prosperity in order to do it to the fullest. This may be material prosperity or it may be an abundance of love that must be manifested. Learning to recognize that to those whom much is given, much will be expected is important for all of these individuals.

EILEEN
(variations: Elinore, Eleanor)

Meaning: "light"
Suggested Affirmation: "I am Eileen. I am the Light of God!"
Primary Vowel/Element: I / Element of Fire
Primary Sound/Chakra: "eye" / Medulla Oblongata
Other Vowels/Elements: E / Element of Air
Other Sounds/Chakras: "ee" / Brow and Head Chakras

MEDITATION

The element of fire is the predominant element. Fire provides warmth, light and comfort. It burns away the dross. It drives back the shadows. It guides us and illuminates our paths so we can see where we are going. It needs air in the form of oxygen to burn strong. All these aspects are important to keep in mind if one has this name or any of its variations.

These individuals need to fire the mind. They need to be involved in some form of education, or they will find themselves feeling their way through life with no direction. These individuals also have strong intuitions which if nourished can give birth to dynamic spiritual illumination.

ELAINE

Meaning: "the lily maid; the bright one"
Suggested Affirmation: "I am Elaine. I am the bright lily of God!"
Primary Vowel/Element: E / Element of Air
Primary Sound/Chakra: "ee" / Brow and Crown Chakras
Other Vowels/Elements: A / Element of Ether
I / Element of Fire
E / Element of Air
Other Sounds/Chakras: "ay" / Heart Chakra

MEDITATION

This is a very powerful name. It is associated with the lily, a very ancient and mystical symbol. The lily is associated with the archangel Gabriel, the Mother Mary and the Christian Mysteries of the Winter Solstice. Through purification, one opens oneself to the celestial realms and those beings that serve to initiate humankind—the angelic hierarchy.

There are two kinds of birth: first, the birth of the lower "manger" where the beasts feed and which ultimately can lead to birth of the second, the higher manger. The higher manger is the bridging of the pineal and the pituitary (brow and crown chakras) to give birth to the Holy Child within. This is only accomplished by purifying the mind (element of air) and the heart (element of ether). This is the task of those of this name. Feminine Christian Mysteries would serve these individuals well.

ELLEN
(variation: Ella)

Meaning: "bright one"
Suggested Affirmation: "I am Ellen. I am the bright one of
    God!"
Primary Vowel/Element: E / Element of Air
Primary Sound/Chakra: "eh" / Throat Chakra
Other Vowels/Elements: E / Element of Air
Other Sounds/Chakras: "eh" / Throat Chakra

MEDITATION
Those of this name usually have major decisions to make in their
lives as to how best express their energies. The two *E*'s are separated
by two *L*'s, almost as if forming a wall between the higher expression
of creative energy and the lower. Learning to assert one's will properly, without intruding upon the will of others and without allowing
others to assert theirs over you, will be part of the life lesson. Also
involved with this will be learning to scale some new heights, out of
the shadows of the walls, for one's own light to manifest strongly. It is
thus important for these individuals to find their own unique creative outlet. As this is worked upon, other gifts will manifest, clairaudience and the "hearing" of spirit being but one. Sound carries
through the air unless obstructed. Learning to keep the mind calm so
that the sound of the inner voice can be heard will open great creative expression.

EMILY
(variations: Em, Emma, Emil, Ema)

Meaning: "industrious, diligent and caring"

Suggested Affirmation: "I am Emily. I am the industrious and caring child of God!"

Primary Vowel/Element: E / Element of Air

Primary Sound/Chakra: "eh" / Throat Chakra

Other Vowels/Elements: I / Element of Fire

                           Y / Element of Air

Other Sounds/Chakras: "ih" / Throat Chakra

                           "ee" / Brow and Crown Chakras

MEDITATION

Those of this name or its variations have a quiet, caring quality about them. Others feel secure around them and will find it easy to talk and work with them. There may be a tendency in others to depend too strongly upon them because they are so diligent in their efforts. Strong, solid counsel is a forte with many of them, but they all have a knack for saying the right thing at the right time.

These individuals respond well to the spoken word of others. Things said lovingly to them are felt more lovingly. A voice raised can tear at their heart. The throat chakra is active within them, and thus the "word" has great impact and import. They must learn to develop reticence in speech, and they do have a gift for written or spoken expression, no matter how rough. Theirs is the poetic heart and soul with all of the inherent sensitivities.

ERIC
(variation: Ericka)

Meaning: "ever powerful; godly power; ever the ruler"
Suggested Affirmation: "I am Eric. I am ever powerful in life!"
Primary Vowel/Element: E / Element of Air
Primary Sound/Chakra: "ay" / Heart Chakra
Other Vowels/Elements: I / Element of Fire
Other Sounds/Chakras: "ih" / Throat Chakra

MEDITATION

This is the name of one who has a strong auric energy, one who will be noticed on some level. These individuals are almost always receiving attention in some vein, either positive or negative. Finding the right expression is, of course, the task. Learning not to give into life conditions is what will often be tested. These individuals have come upon the Earth to learn they have a power that can be expressed in all aspects of life.

These individuals are capable of linking mind and heart for greater manifestation of fulfillment, abundance, prosperity and love within their lives. Finding the best way of doing so usually creates a kind of forward and back motion through the early years. As greater individual focus crystallizes, so do their paths in life. They must learn to do what they know in their heart is right for them. Then they manifest their true power and rule over their life circumstances.

EVELYN
(variations: Eve, Eva, Evan)

Meaning: "light; life or full of life"

Suggested Affirmation: "I am Evelyn. I am full of the light of life!"

Primary Vowel/Element: E / Element of Air

Primary Sound/Chakra: "eh" / Throat Chakra

Other Vowels/Elements: E / Element of Air
Y / Element of Fire

Other Sounds/Chakras: "eh" / Throat Chakra
"ih" / Throat Chakra

MEDITATION

Those of this name and its variations have come into the physical to stimulate the inner light to greater intensity. This is to be done through education. Learning, both formal and informal, must never cease for these individuals. Education provides the light in our modern world. It enables us to see who we are and just where we fit within the entire scheme.

This is the name for the accumulation of new knowledge and the assimulation of the old. In the Hebrew Qabala, knowledge is the invisible level of consciousness that influences all levels of consciousness. As we grow in knowledge in any field, it opens up more avenues and opportunities. Learning to apply one's knowledge to the benefit of self and others will be tested at some point. This means one may have to learn to assert one's will, even if it goes against the thinking or ways of those in authority. By not withholding, you learn to fill your life with light and set new fires of light and inspiration for others as well.

FAITH
(variation: Fay)

Meaning: "belief in God; loyalty; trustful"
Suggested Affirmation: "I am Faith. I am loyal in all things!"
Primary Vowel/Element: A / Element of Ether
Primary Sound/Chakra: "ay" / Heart Chakra
Other Vowels/Elements: I / Element of Fire
Other Sounds/Chakras: Silent

MEDITATION

Those of this name or its variation have come to instill greater fire within their hearts and express it in their lives. The *A* is the heart chakra energy, but it is tied to the *I*, the silent fires in the heart. These individuals have come to learn lessons associated with the proper expression of passions and aspirations. They have the task of learning to be loyal to their hearts, doing what they know in their heart is right for them. This is often difficult, as they easily sense what others "feel" and thus may need to assert greater strength so as not to sacrifice themselves in order not to hurt others' feelings. When they work and live according to their hearts, they make excellent empathetic healers, and they become loyal to the energies of the heart rather than to the lower emotions. The heart is the seat of much karma, and these individuals have come to learn to stand by their beliefs and thus cleanse the heart and the soul for newer and higher expressions.

FERN

Meaning: "abundant life and growth"
Suggested Affirmation: "I am Fern. I grow abundantly day
    by day!"
Primary Vowel/Element: E / Element of Air
Primary Sound/Chakra: "eh" / Throat Chakra
Other Vowels/Elements: ——
Other Sounds/Chakras: ——

MEDITATION

Those of this name have come into the physical to learn about
growing in greater abundance. They have a knack for drawing abundance to them in any area of life in which they are focused. There is
also the ability to similarly influence others, stimulating abundance
and growth in them as well. These individuals must remember that
abundance is not a quantity; it is a quality. It is a realization that there
is no lack or shortage in the world. Learning to share the abundance of
their lives will serve to increase the abundance within it—physically,
emotionally, mentally and/or spiritually. Just as we would not tell
another not to breathe because we wanted a breath of air, those of
this name must recognize that there is plenty for all. The throat
chakra is the center of will force, the cornucopia, so those of this
name must learn to assert their wills to manifest the abundance that
is their divine right.

FLORENCE
(variations: Flo, Flora)

Meaning: "blooming; a flower; the fragrant spirit; flourishing"
Suggested Affirmation: "I am Florence. I am the flower of
   God!"
Primary Vowel/Element: O / Element of Water
Primary Sound/Chakra: "oh" / Spleen Chakra
Other Vowels/Elements: E / Element of Air
Other Sounds/Chakras: "eh" / Throat Chakra

MEDITATION

Just like a flower, these individuals must learn to blossom within
this life. Using a flower, any flower, as a symbol for personal meditation and unfoldment would be beneficial. They are the flowers, and a
flower has its roots in the earth and its stem lifts its head to the sky. A
flower needs fresh water in the right amount (balanced emotions),
and it needs fresh air of the right temperature or it can become sickly.
Most individuals of this name or its variations lead lives that parallel
the growth cycle of perennial flowers. Learning to recognize and
work with their personal cycles will facilitate their growth. All these
stages are significant for those of this name: seed germination,
development of roots, growth of the stem upward through the soil,
budding and blossoming, etc.

Flowers are gifts of light and beauty from the angelic hierarchy
to humankind. They are not only beautiful and inspiring to the
emotions (water element) but they also help produce oxygen (air element). In this analogy lies much significance for those of this name
and their individual purposes in this present incarnation.

FRANCES
(variations: Francis, Fran, Frank)

Meaning: "living in freedom; the free individual"

Suggested Affirmation: "I am Frances. I am free to live to my fullest!"

Primary Vowel/Element: A / Element of Ether

Primary Sound/Chakra: "ah" / Throat Chakra

Other Vowels/Elements: E / Element of Air

Other Sounds/Chakras: "eh" / Throat Chakra

MEDITATION

These individuals have come into life to learn the lessons associated with freedom. Learning to be free in the truest sense becomes the task. To be truly free, one must learn to focus and not scatter. Life will present many opportunities to involve oneself in a myriad of activities, both positive and negative, and asserting proper discrimination and self-control will be tested (throat chakra energy). These individuals learn to experience people and life in beautiful ways, and they have all the necessary tools to work with in life. This name endows them with ideas and great energy, which must be disciplined. These individuals have the capability of literally injecting new life into other people and their surroundings. This name has an energy of adventure, enthusiasm and versatility that can easily have an effect in the lives of others. Learning not to abuse one's own inherent freedoms or the freedoms of others is often the life task of those with this name.

FREDERIC
(variations: Frederick, Fred)

Meaning: "the peaceful ruler; one who is at peace"

Suggested Affirmation: "I am Frederic. I am the peaceful ruler of my life!"

Primary Vowel/Element: E / Element of Air

Primary Sound/Chakra: "eh" / Throat Chakra

Other Vowels/Elements: E / Element of Air

                   I / Element of Fire

Other Sounds/Chakras: "eh" / Throat Chakra

                   "ih" / Throat Chakra

MEDITATION

Those of this name have a wonderful wit about them if they permit themselves to express it. This is throat chakra energy at its best. To these individuals, education and their being able to come to terms with life and life pressures is most important. These individuals have a unique perspective and can take old knowledge and data and synthesize it in a manner that breathes new life into it. Their simple charm is generally a calming influence that eases the minds and emotions of others. Learning not to become dogmatic in beliefs will be important for their balance. Flexibility of mind and attitude is most essential. Communication of any sort will be a priority and a power. These individuals can make excellent counselors and salespersons when they open themselves to listening and expressing that inner voice which is always strong within them. When they maintain their own peace of mind, that voice will ring out for them.

GABRIEL
(variation: Gabe)

Meaning: "man of God"
Suggested Affirmation: "I am Gabriel. I am the man of God!"
Primary Vowel/Element: A / Element of Ether
Primary Sound/Chakra: "ay" / Heart Chakra
Other Vowels/Elements: I / Element of Fire
                        E / Element of Air
Other Sounds/Chakras: "ee" / Brow and Crown Chakras
                       "eh" / Throat Chakra

MEDITATION
Those of this name have as their namesake the great Archangel Gabriel. Gabriel is the archangel of the western quarter of the Earth and the overseer of the winter season and energies associated with it. The Winter Solstice triggers a time when the feminine energies of love and nurturing can be manifested. It is the time for awakening to greater illumination, intuition and imagination. Those of this name have come to do this within this lifetime. All the archangelic names have three syllables, the creative number, the number associated with the birth of the Holy Child within us.

This is a name that requires that one give birth to greater love, tenderness and compassion. It requires purity of expression. When these are achieved, then the celestial realms open up and contact is established with the angelic hierarchy who will oversee much of humanity's initiation in the age to come. Balancing the emotions and finding joy in all life will be the major tasks.

GAIL
(variation: Gayle)

Meaning: "gay; lively; a source of joy and cheer"
Suggested Affirmation: "I am Gail. I am a source of joy for others!"
Primary Vowel/Element: A / Element of Ether
Primary Sound/Chakra: "ay" / Heart Chakra
Other Vowels/Elements: I / Element of Fire
Other Sounds/Chakras: Silent

MEDITATION

Those of this name have big hearts, which they share easily with others. Because of their bigheartedness, they may find themselves getting hurt in the process. It will be important for them not to allow such circumstances to prevent them from giving their hearts again. These individuals have come to learn to instill new fires within the heart—for themselves and for others. They have a wonderful intuition about the needs of others and can use it to bring aid and joy to them. Their ability to discriminate and discern is what will most often be tested. Learning to not rush in to "affairs of the heart" will be important. Learning to allow the heart to unfold like a flower will awaken great healing energy and unfold heart chakra potentials, which will set a course of evolvement affecting lifetimes to come.

GARY

Meaning: "the spear; spear carrier; loyalty"
Suggested Affirmation: "I am Gary. I carry the spear of loyalty to all!"
Primary Vowel/Element: A / Element of Ether
Primary Sound/Chakra: "ay" / Heart Chakra
Other Vowels/Elements: Y / Element of Fire
Other Sounds/Chakras: "ee" / Brow and Crown Chakras

MEDITATION

Those of this name have come to express the heart chakra energy as an actual spear of light in the lives of others. They have a tenacity and loyalty unparalleled in relationships. Many have come to awaken the love aspect on more than just a physical or emotional level. The *Y* is the glyph for the Holy Grail—the Chalice. These individuals often come into life to discover it as a loving cup that involves much more than just one person or idea. Learning the lessons of loyalty will be preeminent, and this may mean they will learn that one can be loyal to both spiritual principles and physical life experiences and energies simultaneously. It involves learning that we don't always have to sacrifice one for the other. There are ways of being loyal and strong in spiritual *and* physical endeavors. This only occurs when the love is strong and true. Developing such a love for all life will be the task of these individuals.

GENE
(variations: Eugene, Geneva)

Meaning: "one who is well-born; noble and pure"
Suggested Affirmation: "I am Gene. I am the noble and pure child of God!"
Primary Vowel/Element: E / Element of Air
Primary Sound/Chakra: "ee" / Brow and Crown Chakras
Other Vowels/Elements: E / Element of Air
Other Sounds/Chakras: Silent

MEDITATION

Those who are noble and well born carry themselves in a manner that reflects it, but the carriage is not a result of birth. It is the result of the proper mental attitude. Purity and nobility are not in the blood; they are in the mind. This is the lesson for those of this name. They must develop the mindset of nobility and purity, carrying themselves as such. It must be remembered, though, that it also requires a sense of humility. One does not flaunt one's state in life. Thus we can see the significance of the silent *E* within the name. Overcoming negative self-images and a tendency toward daydreaminess and self-illusion will be important for these individuals. Once accomplished, they will be awakened to the realization that they are the sons and daughters of God—nobly born. This opens up the creative imagination and the power of transformation that can be applied to any area of their lives. It re-instills a contagious sense of wonder at the world, and a farsightedness occurs, unfolding a realization of hidden abilities.

GEORGE
(variation: Georgia)

Meaning: "industrious; worker or farmer"
Suggested Affirmation: "I am George. I am the worker of God!"
Primary Vowel/Element: O / Element of Water
Primary Sound/Chakra: "oh" / Spleen Chakra
Other Vowels/Elements: E / Element of Air
Other Sounds/Chakras: Silent

MEDITATION

Those of this name have come to build new foundations in their evolvement. For anything to grow, there must be proper aeration of the soil and water, the elements associated with this name. These individuals have brought in the soil and the tools to work the soil. They must learn to water and aerate as well. Bringing the mind and the emotions together will be but part of the task. Keeping the emotions balanced and steady, rather than allowing them to fluctuate from one moment to the next with whatever wind blows will be the other part. Once this is accomplished the energy and industriousness will astound many. Whatever the life task, there must be an emotional and mental link to it for this individual to succeed. Routines are difficult for these individuals to handle unless there is some emotional and mental variety and stimulation. When this occurs, there is nothing that can prevent success. They have the capability of making anything grow within their lives, as long as they have the proper motivation.

GERALD
(variations: Geraldine, Gerard, Gertrude)

Meaning: "spear; the mighty warrior; courageous"
Suggested Affirmation: "I am Gerald. I am God's courageous warrior!"
Primary Vowel/Element: E / Element of Air
Primary Sound/Chakra: "eh" / Throat Chakra
Other Vowels/Elements: A / Element of Ether
Other Sounds/Chakras: "uh" / Throat Chakra

MEDITATION

Those of this name have to learn to express their greater strength of will and courage. They often find themselves in a position of having no choice but to stand strong, take the responsibility and do whatever is necessary. They often find themselves having to stand alone in different periods of their life in order to learn how to draw more fully upon the inner strength and courage, to which they have great access. They are at their strongest when it is in defense of others. They must take care not to bully others, as this is the antithesis of what they have come to do in this lifetime. These individuals usually allow their actions to speak for them. Learning to develop discipline in thought, words and deeds will allow that inner strength and courage to manifest in the most balanced manner. Until it is developed, bullying, sarcasm, timidity and a weak will may dominate. Learning that real strength and courage is gentle in all expressions will be important.

GLEN
(variations: Glenn, Glenda, Glenna)

Meaning: "dweller in the valley; prosperous one"
Suggested Affirmation: "I am Glen. I share in the prosperous valley!"
Primary Vowel/Element: E / Element of Air
Primary Sound/Chakra: "eh" / Throat Chakra
Other Vowels/Elements: ──
Other Sounds/Chakras: ──

MEDITATION

Those of this name have come to learn that they have all they need to succeed and prosper in life. Learning to recognize this can take time and involve strong learning circumstances, but once accomplished the full cornucopia of life spills out for them. Often these individuals must first learn to recognize their own talents and abilities before they can share in the prosperity and fulfillment they so strongly desire. Learning to recognize that they are complete in themselves, regardless of what physical circumstances reflect, is the task. As this attitude develops, their life becomes like a valley filled with people and benefits to supplement and enhance their own individual lives. Every little thing is just a "bonus," since they have everything already within them. Developing this sense of abundance, realizing there are no limits except those that are self-imposed, is the start. Once learned, these individuals have a unique ability to assert their energies in any direction and succeed.

GLORIA

Meaning: "glory; glorious one"
Suggested Affirmation: "I am Gloria. I am the glorious child of God!"
Primary Vowel/Element: O / Element of Water
Primary Sound/Chakra: "oh" / Spleen Chakra
Other Vowels/Elements: I / Element of Fire
                A / Element of Ether
Other Sounds/Chakras: "ee" / Brow and Crown Chakras
                "uh" / Throat Chakra

MEDITATION

Those of this name have come to live a life that embodies the glories of life. The predominant elements are fire and water. They do not cancel each other; together they generate steam, a powerful source of energy. These individuals have come to express their energies. They have strong emotions to which they can give powerful expression, using them as a creative source of power in their own life. These individuals have come to learn about the Creative Word. Learning to use the Word as a creative tool—either for healing or for manifestation—will be the task. There is a strong fire in these individuals that must be given expression. They are naturally intuitive, especially in discerning the moods and emotions of others, and they have the ability to be a catalyst in the lives of those they touch. They have the ability to work and to play in a myriad of activities and by their examples, they show others the glory of life experiences.

GRACE

Meaning: "thanks; graciousness; the thankful spirit"
Suggested Affirmation: "I am Grace. I am the gracious and thankful spirit!"
Primary Vowel/Element: A / Element of Ether
Primary Sound/Chakra: "ay" / Heart Chakra
Other Vowels/Elements: E / Element of Air
Other Sounds/Chakras: Silent

MEDITATION

Those of this name have a true sense of graciousness and gracefulness. Gracefulness does not involve only physical gracefulness. It involves a mental and emotional sense of balance. Those of this name have come to learn new ways of maintaining balance in all situations. Learning to relate to all people and all situations will be part of the task. Once accomplished, there is the ability to make others feel at home and at peace with themselves. This is heart chakra expression. The heart chakra is the balancing center, and thus balancing the mind and emotions, the rational and the intuitive, the physical and the spiritual will be part of life's lesson. Once accomplished, the healing touch that can manifest through such individuals is magnificent, whether that touch is through a word, a thought, a look or a hand.

GREGORY
(variation: Greg)

Meaning: "watchman; the watchful one; observant"
Suggested Affirmation: "I am Gregory. I am the observant child of God!"
Primary Vowel/Element: E / Element of Air
Primary Sound/Chakra: "eh" / Throat Chakra
Other Vowels/Elements: O / Element of Water
$\qquad\qquad\qquad\qquad$ Y / Element of Fire
Other Sounds/Chakras: "oh" / Spleen Chakra
$\qquad\qquad\qquad\qquad$ "ee" / Brow and Crown Chakras

MEDITATION

Those of this name learn much by observation. They are very receptive to the influences of their environments. Although the primary vowel is the *E,* the *Y* at the end has a strong influence. The *Y* is the Cup of the Grail; it holds the experiences of life that will shape and mold the growth. Those individuals of this name or its variations hold onto all experiences. They have an excellent memory, and a way of shaping that memory into a personal expression. Their feeling nature is strongly shaped by outer experiences. Control of the environment and the psychic atmosphere, especially in childhood, strongly determine the creative expression of the soul throughout the rest of life. These individuals have a wonderfully creative way of expressing themselves. This may take form through conversation, through artistic endeavor or through a variety of ways. Their task is to observe and synthesize life experiences so as to draw new conclusions and realizations for themselves and for those they touch. They have a capacity for instilling in others the wonder of seeing the world anew.

HAROLD
(variations: Harry, Harriet, Harvey, Harley, Harlan)

Meaning: "ruler in the army; strong leader"

Suggested Affirmation: "I am Harold. I am a strong leader in life!"

Primary Vowel/Element: A / Element of Ether

Primary Sound/Chakra: "ay" / Heart Chakra

Other Vowels/Elements: O / Element of Water

Other Sounds/Chakras: "uh" / Throat Chakra

MEDITATION

Those of this name have come to strengthen the expressions of the heart—be it in a physical, emotional or spiritual manner. These individuals have a capacity to direct and control their lives, but they must learn to assert their energies and their authority more strongly. Thus the significance of the throat chakra influence. Leaders must be balanced and keep their emotions from getting out of control. In the army, one who is out of balance could cause others to get hurt. Those of this name in any position of authority must learn to balance them as well for the benefit of all. Overcoming any tendency toward being weak-willed, self-deluded and secretive must be overcome. Generosity and tolerance will strengthen the heart and the life of these individuals, giving rise to a strong inner voice, greater openness and true strength of will.

HEATHER

Meaning: "heather flower or shrub; joyful spirit"
Suggested Affirmation: "I am Heather. I am the flower of joy!"
Primary Vowel/Element: E / Element of Air
Primary Sound/Chakra: "eh" / Throat Chakra
Other Vowels/Elements: A / Element of Ether
       E / Element of Air
Other Sounds/Chakras: Silent
       "eh" / Throat Chakra

MEDITATION

Those of this name have the gift of gab, and if they are not expressing it, there is usually plenty they wish they could or would say. There is a lightness to this name, a simplicity and beauty just like the heather flower. Heather is a name that should call forth the joy in the heart, giving greater expression to it as one grows older. In childhood many of this name are very fairylike in appearance and activity. There is a natural tie to those of the nature kingdom, those we know of as the fairies and elves, by anyone whose name rings of nature and its plants. Learning to quiet the mind will be the greatest task of these individuals. They are constantly thinking, rethinking, putting it down and picking it up again, the mental wheels constantly turning. By learning to quiet the mind, the inner voice can come out and the expressions have greater impact. Counseling is natural to those of this name. Others find it easy to talk with them. Learning to express in the most creative and beneficial manner will be important. This involves lessons in strength of will as well as when to speak and when not to.

HELEN

Meaning: "light; torch; the bright one"
Suggested Affirmation: "I am Helen. I am the bright torch of
    God!"
Primary Vowel/Element: E / Element of Air
Primary Sound/Chakra: "eh" / Throat Chakra
Other Vowels/Elements: E / Element of Air
Other Sounds/Chakras: "eh" / Throat Chakra

MEDITATION

Those of this name have come to learn to bring out the inner
light. They must learn the lesson of not looking for an outer light.
They must often learn that the path of spirituality is not one that
leads to a divine light in which all of our problems are dissolved.
These individuals must learn to find the light within and learn to let it
shine, rather than looking for a light from without to shine down
upon them.

Learning to assert one's own strength of will will be part of the
task. These individuals often find that other people, because of their
strong wills, may have a tendency to dominate and control them.
This may get to the point where they are constantly giving in or
vacillating. Deciding what is right in the situation and sticking to it
must become a daily process. In this way their own inner light can
shine forth and carry over any outer walls to light the lives of others
as well. Involvement in any creative activity will best facilitate
that process.

HENRY
(variations: Henrietta, Hank)

Meaning: "ruler of a home or estate; industrious"
Suggested Affirmation: "I am Henry. I am the ruler of my life!"
Primary Vowel/Element: E / Element of Air
Primary Sound/Chakra: "eh" / Throat Chakra
Other Vowels/Elements: Y / Elements of Fire and Air
Other Sounds/Chakras: "ee" / Brow and Crown Chakras

MEDITATION

These individuals have come to learn to work heartily and industriously in some endeavor(s). This, of course, involves lessons in discipline and strength of will. To learn to take control of their lives, with full responsibility, is the task. Often these individuals have come over into this incarnation to learn a new aspect of responsibility. Maybe they did not fully take it in the past or did not learn all there was about it. Learning to make decisions and stand by them, regardless of consequences, will be important, and it is how they will most effectively learn. To assist with this they have an innate mental capability for focus and concentration. As they learn to sustain that focus on endeavors they enjoy and find creative, they are no longer at the mercy of life circumstances. They control life, rather than life controlling them. As this unfolds, the inner sense of "not truly belonging anywhere" will dissipate, and they will find that they can belong anywhere and develop rapport with anyone. Following their own inner fires and urges—the intuitive aspect that is strong within them—facilitates this process.

HOWARD
(variation: Howie)

Meaning: "chief; guardian; reasonable one"
Suggested Affirmation: "I am Howard. I am the guardian of life!"
Primary Vowel/Element: O / Element of Water
Primary Sound/Chakra: "ow" / Spleen and Solar Plexus Chakras
Other Vowels/Elements: A / Element of Ether
Other Sounds/Chakras: "uh" / Throat Chakra

MEDITATION

Those of this name have an energy that requires they develop balance in dealing with emotions and basic life energies. These individuals have a gift for seeing the practical side of all things, and they can assist others in this as well. Learning to express this practical and reasonable side is essential to their growth. Unless the practical side is balanced with the emotional, without overriding it, emotional and/or mental conflicts can arise. Learning to be secure in themselves without self-delusion is essential. When this is accomplished, these individuals have the capacity to express endurance in all things, along with courage, faith and true self-awareness. There is kindled a fighting spirit with the ability to change their fortune and future to any degree they wish. These individuals are at their best when they have someone to watch over.

HUGH

Meaning: "one of the mind and of reason"
Suggested Affirmation: "I am Hugh. I live the reason of God!"
Primary Vowel/Element: U / Element of Earth
Primary Sound/Chakra: "oo" / Base Chakra
Other Vowels/Elements: ——
Other Sounds/Chakras: ——

MEDITATION

Individuals of this name have come to express the basic life force through reasonable living and balance. These individuals have a naturally strong zest for life. The life force pulses strongly within them. In the present period of humanity's evolution, they have come to express it in a reasonable and mindful manner. Ensuring that all thoughts, words and deeds serve a purpose is essential for these individuals, otherwise there is likely to be great mental agitation through periods of their lives. Recklessness and over-reactiveness must be guarded against. The development of discrimination and discernment in all things is essential to their well-being. In this manner prosperity and self-confidence exudes from them in a way that puts others at ease. These individuals are extremely instinctual and intuitive. They exhibit great spontaneity and can discover much about themselves and their lives through their very vivid dream activities. There is a strong psychic energy about them.

IAN

Meaning: "God's gracious gift"
Suggested Affirmation: "I am Ian. I am God's gracious gift."
Primary Vowel/Element: I / Element of Fire
Primary Sound/Chakra: "ee" / Brow and Crown Chakras
Other Vowels/Elements: A / Element of Ether
Other Sounds/Chakras: "uh" / Throat Chakra

MEDITATION

These individuals have come to give greater expression to the heart energies in their day-to-day lives. They have come to learn to balance heart and mind, giving greater expression of that balance. Whenever the *I* and the *A* come together within the name, there is a tremendous fertility and creativity within the individual. This can express itself in either the physical or the spiritual. They have come to awaken greater fires in the heart. This means there are lessons in overcoming insecurity and self-doubt, along with false pride. When this occurs, they exhibit and manifest a security that allows them to be a nurturing force in the lives of others. They give birth to great compassion and healing, focused through a strong idealism and true devotion.

IRENE

Meaning: "peace; peaceful spirit"
Suggested Affirmation: "I am Irene. I am a peaceful spirit!"
Primary Vowel/Element: I / Element of Fire
Primary Sound/Chakra: "eye" / Medulla Oblongata
Other Vowels/Elements: E / Element of Air
Other Sounds/Chakras: "ee" / Brow and Crown Chakras

MEDITATION

Irene is a name that activates those archetypal energies which enable one to manifest a greater sense of peacefulness. The medulla oblongata is a brain center that brings clarity to thought. When our emotions are balanced with clear thinking, worry and doubts dissipate, leaving peace of mind. Failure to recognize one's abilities can be the greatest obstacle for those of this name. It is almost as if they have a blocked vision. This can manifest as a restlessness, or an unwillingness to take advantage of growth opportunities, or even an unbalanced emotionalism. At its highest level, it can release energies of nourishment, wisdom and higher forms of understanding. True recognition of potential can manifest along with dynamic, artistic energy, enhanced by expanded intelligence.

IRIS

Meaning: "the rainbow; divine promise"
Suggested Affirmation: "I am Iris. I am the divine rainbow of promise!"
Primary Vowel/Element: I / Element of Fire
Primary Sound/Chakra: "eye" / Medulla Oblongata
Other Vowels/Elements: I / Element of Fire
Other Sounds/Chakras: "ih" / Throat Chakra

MEDITATION

This is a name that ties one to the healing forces of light and life. The rainbow has the full color spectrum within it, and thus these individuals may encounter a full spectrum of life experiences that must be synthesized for the greatest individual expression to manifest. In essence, many of them have come to round out their life experiences so that they can later assist others who go through similar ones. Learning to keep situations in their proper perspective and to discern the underlying lessons in external events is essential to their peace of mind and future growth. Fire is the element of this name, and while it can burn, it can also provide heat, warmth, and light to soothe, nurture and inspire the soul.

ISAAC

Meaning: "laughter; cheerful and strong faith"
Suggested Affirmation: "I am Isaac. I am filled with laughter and faith."
Primary Vowel/Element: I / Element of Fire
Primary Sound/Chakra: "eye" / Medulla Oblongata
Other Vowels/Elements: A / Element of Ether
Other Sounds/Chakras: "uh" / Throat Chakra

MEDITATION

Those of this name have come to learn to see life and its events from a new perspective. Learning to raise the shroud of doom from one's life is difficult, but it is here that the healing medicine of laughter can best reveal itself. Not taking oneself too seriously enables one to keep life and its surprising elements in proper perspective. Those individuals of this name must learn this process. There is much fire and much to stimulate this fire within the lives of these individuals. Learning to control and direct the inner flames and fires so that they express themselves in life like a warm fireside is difficult, but once accomplished, it provides opportunities to heal the soul and to light the spiritual path anew. These individuals will also encounter a wider variety of life circumstances. "If it can happen to anyone," it will be said that it can happen to these people. This is not bad, for there is the potential then to interact with a greater number of others and thus become a catalyst, stirring the inner embers into flames.

JACOB
(variations: Jack, Jackie, Jacqueline,
Jake, James, Jamie)

Meaning: "the supplanter; truthful; noble in truth"
Suggested Affirmation: "I am Jacob. I am noble in truth!"
Primary Vowel/Element: A / Element of Ether
Primary Sound/Chakra: "ay" / Heart Chakra
Other Vowels/Elements: O / Element of Water
Other Sounds/Chakras: "uh" / Throat Chakra

MEDITATION

This is a very ancient Hebrew name from which came many derivations. In Biblical scripture, Jacob was molded into character from the love of God's heart. Individuals of this name or its variations have come to mold their lives anew. The heart chakra energy gives them strong aspirations to create their lives in accordance with love. Discovering what that love is, is often the most difficult part of life for these individuals. They enjoy many things, but it is as if these things are simply reflections of a greater love or activity that has not yet been given birth to. *Yet* is the key word. As long as these individuals hold true to their hearts and aspirations, they will give birth to new aspects of their lives. This often requires that they step out of old patterns and into something that may not seem practical to others, but if the love for it is there, the success and abundance will follow. This then serves to teach others and fire heartfelt inspirations in them.

JANET

(variations: Jan, Jane, Janell, Janice, Jean,
Jeanette, Joan, Joanne, Joanna)

Meaning: "God is gracious; God's gracious gift"
Suggested Affirmation: "I am Janet. I am God's gracious gift!"
Primary Vowel/Element: A / Element of Ether
Primary Sound/Chakra: "ah" / Throat Chakra
Other Vowels/Elements: E / Element of Air
Other Sounds/Chakras: "eh" / Throat Chakra

MEDITATION

These individuals embody the concept of true gifts. Like any surprise present or gift, it is usually wrapped so as not to disclose its contents. Then like a box within a box, each layer unfolds new surprises and wonders. These individuals reflect this aspect. As they grow and mature, they unfold even more wonders and abilities. And what makes these individuals most enjoyable is that they are equally surprised at what they are capable of unfolding. Every layer and experience of life brings more of their true essence out, an essence that is healing and nurturing to all those touched. Learning to express the inner abilities and gifts—from intuition and clairvoyance to a marvelous way of expressing themselves (vocally and in writing)—will be important. They may need the occasional nudge to embark on new activities, but it is important that they constantly expand their horizons, because it is then that they are most capable of living the life of one who is a gracious gift from God.

JASON

Meaning: "the healer; one who heals"
Suggested Affirmation: "I am Jason. I am the healer!"
Primary Vowel/Element: A / Element of Ether
Primary Sound/Chakra: "ay" / Throat Chakra
Other Vowels/Elements: O / Element of Water
Other Sounds/Chakras: "uh" / Throat Chakra

MEDITATION

There are many forms of healing—physical, emotional, mental and spiritual—and there are techniques for working with each of these. There are also ways in which we can be a healing influence in the lives of others through the things we say and do and by living a positive and creative existence. Those of this name will be healing in the lives of those they touch in some manner, whether they are conscious of it or not. These individuals have a natural ability for empathic associations with others. This is the water element within them. Water adjusts itself to whatever contains it, and thus the healing energies and its manifestations will adjust its expression to the individual's life circumstances. Learning to balance their own emotions will be part of the task, especially in distinguishing between their own feelings and the feelings of others. Once done, the capacity to influence and heal large numbers grows tremendously.

JEFFREY
(variations: Geoffrey, Jeff)

Meaning: "divinely peaceful; one who is at peace"
Suggested Affirmation: "I am Jeffrey. I am at peace with all!"
Primary Vowel/Element: E / Element of Air
Primary Sound/Chakra: "eh" / Throat Chakra
Other Vowels/Elements: E / Element of Air
Other Sounds/Chakras: "ee" / Brow and Crown Chakras

MEDITATION
Those of this name have a very strong mental energy. Their minds are constantly whirling about. This has both advantages and disadvantages. If there is proper discipline, especially in the areas of strength of will, the mental energy can stimulate a powerful ability to see life and its circumstances in a balanced perspective. To assist in this, it is important for those of this name to expand the mind through some form of philosophical or metaphysical study. If there is not proper strength of will, there can manifest an overly active imagination that cannot be practically applied. This can create mental turmoil and can hinder these individuals in their ability to manifest what they need within their lives. The chakra centers of the head have the capability of manifesting great insight and physical abundance if balanced. Learning to do so will be the task and the reward for those of this name.

JENNIFER
(variation: Jenny)

Meaning: "white wave or phantom; the fair lady"
Suggested Affirmation: "I am Jennifer. I am the fair lady of
    life!"
Primary Vowel/Element: E / Element of Air
Primary Sound/Chakra: "eh" / Throat Chakra
Other Vowels/Elements: I / Element of Fire
                            E / Element of Air
Other Sounds/Chakras: "ih" / Throat Chakra
                            "eh" / Throat Chakra

MEDITATION

    This is a name that ties one to the energies and thoughtforms of
Welsh legends and myths, especially those of the little people and the
nature kingdom. There is often a fairylike aspect to these individuals,
whether in looks or mannerisms. These individuals are also connected—
or have been in previous lives—to those known as the White Ladies.
The White Ladies of lore are what we now refer to as fairy god-
mothers. They are beings of great antiquity and light, and they be-
stow many blessings. Those of this name have an ability to open up
communication with the beings of light from the nature kingdom,
but caution is advised. There is a strong need for those of this name to
first develop a good foundation and proper strength of will, otherwise they leave themselves to being "fairy charmed" and somewhat
deluded. Holding to the words: "Test all things and hold fast to that
which is true" is necessary for proper balance and growth, especially
in relation to psychic, metaphysical and spiritual teachings and
unfoldment.

JEREMY
(variations: Jerome, Jerry, Jerold)

Meaning: "appointed by God; of devout heart; consecrated
   and mighty heart"
Suggested Affirmation: "I am Jeremy. I am appointed by God!"
Primary Vowel/Element: E / Element of Air
Primary Sound/Chakra: "eh" / Throat Chakra
Other Vowels/Elements: Y / Fire and Air
                                       E / Element of Air
Other Sounds/Chakras: "ee" / Brow and Crown Chakras
                                      "eh" / Throat Chakra

MEDITATION
   Those of this name have come to unfold a new life purpose. As a
result, they often have periods within their lives when they seem to
bounce around, not quite knowing that to do or how to go about finding what would be best to do. Deep down within all of them is a feeling that there must be something out there for them. Education is
where it all begins, where the fires of revelation become ignited. The
chakra centers of the head are activated very strongly in those of this
name. This implies the need for mental activity and expression. Being
open to all kinds of educational opportunities, both formal and informal, will be important. The fires of imagination are strong within
these individuals, which when applied to something they can put
their hearts into, will manifest a product, activity or life that will spur
others on and enable them to become spears of light and life as well.
Patience and *imagination* are key words. Together they manifest a
vision applicable to all aspects of life.

JESSICA
(variations: Jessie, Jesse)

Meaning: "wealthy and blessed one; God exists"
Suggested Affirmation: "I am Jessica. The blessedness of God
    lives in me!"
Primary Vowel/Element: E / Element of Air
Primary Sound/Chakra: "eh" / Throat Chakra
Other Vowels/Elements: I / Element of Fire
                        A / Element of Ether
Other Sounds/Chakras: "ih" / Throat Chakra
                        "uh" / Throat Chakra

MEDITATION

Those of this name and its variations have a knack for manifesting what they need when they need it, be it in the form of people,
money, etc. They have come to learn that there is an abundance of
wealth and prosperity to be had, but it will require asserting one's
will in a manner that lets the universe know that they are the heirs to
all within it. Throat chakra energy is the energy of asserting strength
of will and creative energy to tap the cornucopia of life. In the name
Jessica there are also three vowels, three being the creative and birth-
giving number. Those of this name have come to give new birth to the
creative desires within themselves. Learning not to allow others to
dominate and control or inhibit their creative expression will be most
important. Those of this name have much to express to the world or
to those within their part of the world. This expression must not be
inhibited but be allowed to grow, resulting in a manifestation of
physical and spiritual wealth.

JILL

Meaning: "the youthful one; the youthful heart"
Suggested Affirmation: "I am Jill. I am of youthful heart!"
Primary Vowel/Element: I / Element of Fire
Primary Sound/Chakra: "ih" / Throat Chakra
Other Vowels/Elements: ——
Other Sounds/Chakras: ——

MEDITATION

Those of this name have come to learn to express the child within them in all situations. This is not immaturity, although this may be something that has to be overcome by these individuals. Rather, it reflects an emergence into mature youthfulness. This is the ability to see all life, situations and people with the fresh and adventurous eyes of youth. These individuals have a fire and zest for life which if expressed properly instills new fires of life within those they touch. The fires of their inner passions, if kindled properly, will rise to any occasion, overcoming walls and obstacles and instilling illumination and great inner realization. If kept at purely an emotional level, it can reflect a tempestuous nature that creates fires which scorch those around them.

JODI
(variations: Jodie, Jody)

Meaning: "praised of God"
Suggested Affirmation: "I am Jodi. I am the praised child of God!"
Primary Vowel/Element: O / Element of Water
Primary Sound/Chakra: "oh" / Spleen Chakra
Other Vowels/Elements: I / Element of Fire
Other Sounds/Chakras: "ee" / Chakras of the Head

MEDITATION

Those of this name have come to give new fire and expression to their emotions. The elements involved are water and fire, and anytime water and fire come together there are lessons in the transmutation of energy, the alchemical process. This involves learning to recognize all of life's situations and happenings as polishing elements for the soul. Learning to raise the emotions to a higher form of aspiration through creative processes will be important. When water is heated by fire, steam rises (element of air), and thus education will come to these individuals most strongly in the emotional responses to and from others within their lives. If examined within the proper perspectives, life becomes an exciting adventure of aspiration and creativity.

JOEL

Meaning: "the Lord is God; declarer of God"
Suggested Affirmation: "I am Joel. I am the proclaimer of God in all life!"
Primary Vowel/Element: O / Element of Water
Primary Sound/Chakra: "oh" / Spleen Chakra
Other Vowels/Elements: E / Element of Air
Other Sounds/Chakras: "eh" / Throat Chakra

MEDITATION

These individuals have come to link and use two of the creative centers of energy, the spleen and the throat chakras. These are centers of great creative force that manifest most strongly through the development of two characteristics—purity and self-discipline. Strength of will is what enables one to consciously activate creative expression within the physical world, whether through the procreative process or through artistic endeavors. At its highest level, the energies of this name can make one a great light of creative force within the world, a light that will be noticed by all. On the other hand, misuse of the creative energies can deplete the individual's life force, diminishing the effects within the world with time. These individuals have a potential to work with and alter the waters of life in others through esoteric practices involving the purifying of the blood. The secrets of the blood of life can be unveiled, teaching the "raising of the serpent fire" of spirituality.

JOHN
(variations: Jon, Jonathan, Johan, Jonetta, Juanita)

Meaning: "God's gracious gift"
Suggested Affirmation: "I am John. I am God's gracious gift!"
Primary Vowel/Element: O / Element of Water
Primary Sound/Chakra: "aw" / Solar Plexus Chakra
Other Vowels/Elements: ——
Other Sounds/Chakras:——

MEDITATION

Those of this name in some way have come to give new birth to the potential within them. This name has ties to ancient energies and past masters. John the Baptist and John the Beloved are but two. Both are associated with the energies of initiation and the expression of energies and potentials in the physical world. Both breathed new life into their environments. Although this work does not deal with the consonants, the *H* comes from the Hebrew letter *Heh*. It is the energy of the life breath being breathed anew. When in a name, it reflects lessons in learning to breathe new life into old circumstances. The ancient Essenes called the solar plexus chakra the "manger." This is the point of lower birth into which we all must be born until such time as we can give birth to our higher faculties. The feminine qualities of intuition and imagination have come to be expressed anew with these individuals.

JOSEPH
(variations: Joe, Joey, Josephine)

Meaning: "one who adds; increasing in faithfulness"
Suggested Affirmation: "I am Joseph. I add increasing faithfulness to the world!"
Primary Vowel/Element: O / Element of Water
Primary Sound/Chakra: "oh" / Spleen Chakra
Other Vowels/Elements: E / Element of Air
Other Sounds/Chakras: "eh" / Throat Chakra

MEDITATION

These individuals have come to add to their life experiences by opening to greater perceptions of the divine interplaying within the physical. In more ancient times, nature was the way God spoke to humankind. Learning to interpret the rhythms of nature was part of the teaching of the mystery temples. This meant teaching that we have both a physical side and a spiritual side, reflected through waking consciousness and sleeping consciousness. Just as Joseph of Biblical fame integrated dreams with real life, those of this name must also learn to do so. Recognizing that there are reflections of subtle spiritual energies at play within one's life increases faith in the divine. These individuals have strong, vivid dreams and should learn to work with them. Both chakra centers are associated with dream activity, and the dream states of these individuals reflect accurately what is occurring on other levels around them—emotionally, mentally and spiritually. Learning to discern this facilitates the life process for these individuals.

JOSHUA
(variation: Josh)

Meaning: "God of salvation; the salvation"

Suggested Affirmation: "I am Joshua. I am the salvation of my life!"

Primary Vowel/Element: O / Element of Water

Primary Sound/Chakra: "aw" / Solar Plexus Chakra

Other Vowels/Elements: U / Element of Earth

A / Element of Ether

Other Sounds/Chakras: "oo" / Base Chakra

"uh" / Throat Chakra

MEDITATION

This is a name of tremendous harmony. It rings with music, creating a chord of balance within one's life. These individuals usually are a balancing factor in the lives of others. The first, third and fifth chakras are activated by this name. In the musical scale this triad makes a chord, a harmonic of balance. The predominant chakra is the solar plexus, which in the earlier evolution of humanity was the power center and balancing center of the seven major chakras. It is associated with the water element, linking the Earth and the heavens. The rains from Heaven fall upon the Earth to nurture and bring growth. It is this raining aspect that predominates in the vibration of this name. Water is salvation. It quenches the thirsty and parched land, enabling us to raise our outlook. It is important for these individuals to create and live in harmony. Their task is to find a way of synthesizing and linking the heavens and the Earth, the spiritual and the physical. Emotional aspiration will provide the best means. Asserting proper emotional control instills harmony that has an effect on all who surround these individuals.

JOY
(variations: Joyce, Joylynn)

Meaning: "joyful; the joyful one"
Suggested Affirmation: "I am Joy. I am the joyful child of God!"
Primary Vowel/Element: O / Element of Water
Primary Sound/Chakra: "oh" (actually a dipthong) / Solar Plexus Chakra
Other Vowels/Elements: Y / Element of Fire
Other Sounds/Chakras: Silent / Medulla Oblongata and Crown Chakra

MEDITATION

This is a name of great power, but it must be remembered that to them whom much is given, much is expected. This is actually a dipthong name in which the elements of water and fire are blended. This is the alchemical process, finding and discovering joy in all situations. On another level it is the linking of the female (O) and the male (Y) energies to give new birth. Finding a balance between the expressions of both will be tested in some way with these individuals. The O is the water element, the feminine being brought into expression within this incarnation. The chalice (Y) is often a female symbol—the shaping and molding of the feminine energies of intuition and creative imagination for greater expression in life. This name also reflects the birth process of initiation. The solar plexus is the manger, the place where the lower self is born so that we can follow the inner star to a new birth within the head, the point in esoteric Christianity of the higher manger. When we can give birth and find joy in the lower and the higher, we can share the cup of life and light with others. This is the essence of the life task of those with this name—sharing!

JUDITH
(variations: Judi, Judy)

Meaning: "praised of God"
Suggested Affirmation: "I am Judith. I am praised of God!"
Primary Vowel/Element: U / Element of Earth
Primary Sound/Chakra: "oo" / Base Chakra
Other Vowels/Elements: I / Element of Fire
Other Sounds/Chakras: "ih" / Throat Chakra

MEDITATION

This is the name of a teacher. The elements are earth and fire—the practical and the ideal, the spiritual and the physical. The chakras are the base and the throat, the creative life force united with the will force. Those of this name have come to give expression to basic life energies with new fire. In whatever environment, these individuals have come to take their high ideals and aspirations and find practical application within their lives. They have a great capacity for spiritual aspiration, but it must be balanced. A tendency can arise to ground and ignore the imaginative and the inspirational or to become so ensconced within it that there is no practicality at all. These individuals have a great capacity for expression of the ideal and the practical; they can synthesize both with practice and effort, and they can help others in synthesizing concepts into reality as well. A teacher is one who can see and experience the ideal and the concept, and at the same time translate it so that others can work with it within their own lives, in their own unique manner. This is both the lesson and the reward of those with this name.

JULIA
(variations: Julian, Julie, Julianne, Juliet, Julius)

Meaning: "youthful one; young in heart and spirit"
Suggested Affirmation: "I am Julia. I am young in heart and spirit!"
Primary Vowel/Element: U / Element of Earth
Primary Sound/Chakra: "oo" / Base Chakra
Other Vowels/Elements: I / Element of Fire
A / Element of Ether
Other Sounds/Chakras: "ee" / Brow and Crown Chakras
"uh" / Throat Chakra

MEDITATION
Youthfulness is in the mind and in the spirit. These individuals have come to learn the lessons associated with developing a fresh youthful perspective of life. This has nothing to do with maturity in a biological sense, but rather it has to do with developing an outlook on life that is one of wonder and childlike innocence. Although the Earth goes through cycles of aging in the course of a year, it re-attains its fresh growth and expression of new life with each spring. This is the significance of the element of earth in this name. Learning to bring new life from all circumstances is part of true youthfulness. This requires proper mindset—brow and crown chakras working with the base chakra life force energy for eternal expressions of new life and energy. These expressions in the outer life circumstances are the work of the throat chakra. This is the task of those with this name, and once accomplished these individuals become a continual breath of fresh air and spring sunshine in the lives of others.

JUNE

Meaning: "benevolent heart; born in June"
Suggested Affirmation: "I am June. I am of giving heart!"
Primary Vowel/Element: U / Element of Earth
Primary Sound/Chakra: "oo" / Base Chakra
Other Vowels/Elements: E / Element of Air
Other Sounds/Chakras: Silent

MEDITATION

Those of this name must learn not to allow their thinking to interfere with what they instinctively know how to do. Too much thinking can prevent a person from responding and acting when necessary. These individuals have come to listen and respond to that strong inner voice and intuition. They can translate things into practical expression. Others may not be able to discern their motives and reasonings, but they will usually work out well. These individuals seem to know instinctively what is important in grounding their energies and in providing a balanced grounding for others. Care must be taken, though, not to allow this to interfere with or override the free will expression of others. This would indicate that the silent *E* was not being silent. These individuals give with their heart, but in practical ways that cut through emotional and mental clouding. They have a capacity for putting situations in proper perspective and helping others to do so. Love without practical down-to-earth manifestation and expression does not assist the growth of others. The love of these individuals expresses itself through real life actions, giving from the heart but in the real world.

KARA

(variations: Cara, Karen, Kari, Karin)

Meaning: "dear beloved one; purity; the pure one"
Suggested Affirmation: "I am Kara. I am the beloved child of God!"
Primary Vowel/Element: A / Element of Ether
Primary Sound/Chakra: "ay" / Heart Chakra
Other Vowels/Elements: A / Element of Ether
Other Sounds/Chakras: "uh" / Throat Chakra

MEDITATION

This is a name whose energies influence the unfolding of the heart to greater expression within the individual's life. Situations will arise that will require the individual to make an effort to love in spite of outer circumstances. These individuals have a great capacity to express love, but guidance must be taken in learning to express it in the proper fashion. They know instinctively how to empathize with others in ways that are not demeaning, but rather that build the energies of others. Anyone of this name or its variations will touch the hearts of others. Purity—in thought, word and deed—shines forth from these individuals and should be the key word in their lives. As they learn to purify the heart and the expressions of the heart, they can open to the ministrations of the angelic hierarchy in all facets of their lives. With their assistance they truly become the beloved ones in the lives of others!

KEITH

Meaning: "from the battle place; secure and safe"
Suggested Affirmation: "I am Keith. I am secure and safe in all things!"
Primary Vowel/Element: E / Element of Air
Primary Sound/Chakra: "ee" / Brow and Crown Chakras
Other Vowels/Elements: I / Element of Fire
Other Sounds/Chakras: Silent

MEDITATION

This is a name that stimulates the energies, lessons and potentials of winning the battles of the mind. The imagination is strong for these individuals. Learning to balance it and not let it run over any cliffs will be the task. Once there is a mindset, the fires burn strong. These individuals will need to find something strong in which they can believe. In doing so, they have a great capacity for tapping the universal energies of faith and manifesting them within their lives. As they develop a faith and strength in the power of their ability to visualize goals, and recognize that they can manifest what they can visualize, they become secure in all life activities. Lessons of security and insecurity are predominant in the lives of these individuals, but when they become sure of themselves, outer circumstances adjust accordingly. It is then that they understand the significance of the words: "Faith can move mountains."

KELLEY
(variation: Kelly)

Meaning: "warrior; excellent virtue"
Suggested Affirmation: "I am Kelley. I am the spiritual warrior!"
Primary Vowel/Element: E / Element of Air
Primary Sound/Chakra: "eh" / Throat Chakra
Other Vowels/Elements: E / Element of Air
                     Y / Element of Fire
Other Sounds/Chakras: "ee" / Brow and Crown Chakras
                     Silent

MEDITATION
This is a name of great strength, which implies the kinds of lessons and potentials for individuals with it. A true warrior must be disciplined and of excellent virtue, and they must believe in what they fight for. The strength of will must be strong to assert itself over the battleground of life. For this reason the throat chakra is strongly activated (will force), as are the chakras for the head (proper mindset and belief). When these two come together, held within the cup of the Grail (the glyph of the Y), there is potential for great power. Learning to assert one's self-control and not allow others to dominate will be part of the life task of any individual with this name. Once accomplished, once asserted with proper vision, the individual's life becomes the spiritual quest that unveils the spiritual essence within and the means to express that essence.

KENNETH
(variation: Ken)

Meaning: "handsome; manly; gracious"
Suggested Affirmation: "I am Kenneth. I am the gracious one of God!"
Primary Vowel/Element: E / Element of Air
Primary Sound/Chakra: "eh" / Throat Chakra
Other Vowels/Elements: E / Element of Air
Other Sounds/Chakras: "eh" / Throat Chakra

MEDITATION

These individuals have come to assert the strong will-force to which they have great access. Learning not to say or do things that hurt others will be part of their task, which, especially in childhood, will not always be easy to do. Their words have great strength and are felt by others more strongly than is often recognized. These individuals have a great inner strength that if brought out into physical expression often manifests in an ability to counsel and advise in ways that strengthen others. An old adage tells us that those whom we protect, we must also strengthen. Those of this name have a graciousness in response to others that is strengthening to them. Their own strength of will will also be tested, but as long as the mind is focused on the high and ideal, such tests will be passed easily. There may also arise learning about asserting one's will at the expense of others; though infrequent, these lessons can be intense and almost always signal new changes in energy about to manifest within their lives.

KEVIN

Meaning: "gentle; loveable; kind"
Suggested Affirmation: "I am Kevin. I am the gentle and kind child of God!"
Primary Vowel/Element: E / Element of Air
Primary Sound/Chakra: "eh" / Throat Chakra
Other Vowels/Elements: I / Element of Fire
Other Sounds/Chakras: "ih" / Throat Chakra

MEDITATION

These individuals have an ability to discern the emotions and attitudes of others, which enables them to respond to people in a manner that is most beneficial. Their still, inner voice is heard, providing clues, inspiration and insight into others, even if not recognized for what it is. Learning not to take advantage of such insights or manipulating others with this insight will be an important lesson. The energy of this name is such that it gives these individuals the capacity to relate and get along with almost everyone. Because they are likeable, they must guard against others taking advantage of or manipulating them. Learning not to force, but to move gently in all circumstances will need to be developed to greater degrees. Once accomplished, like a gentle flowing stream, they will touch many shores and move easily around all obstacles, flowing through life freely and touching lives with kindness that inspires.

KIM
(variations: Kimball, Kimberly)

Meaning: "from the royal fortress; warrior chief; strong and noble"
Suggested Affirmation: "I am Kim. I am the noble warrior!"
Primary Vowel/Element: I / Element of Fire
Primary Sound/Chakra: "ih" / Throat Chakra
Other Vowels/Elements: ——
Other Sounds/Chakras: ——

MEDITATION

Those of this name have come to unfold the dignity within themselves that they often do not recognize. Others see this noble strength, whether the individual does or not. There is a quiet, dignified bearing to these individuals. They know what must be done, even if they don't want to do it. For many of them, they must learn to do what they have to do, in spite of the responses of others. A ruler and a warrior often must stand alone and remain strong, in spite of outer circumstances. Although not easy, it builds a nobility into their energy that grows with each passing day. It stimulates others, who unconsciously use them as role models. These individuals have come first to learn that they can be strong as a warrior and yet embody nobility. Once learned, they teach it to others through example. Many of these individuals exemplify the high character and discipline of the Grail Knights, and many were part of that training in previous lives. They are the true spiritual warriors.

KURT

Meaning: "bold counselor; strong in counsel; able to counsel"
Suggested Affirmation: "I am Kurt. I am strong in counsel!"
Primary Vowel/Element: U / Element of Earth
Primary Sound/Chakra: "uh" / Throat Chakra
Other Vowels/Elements: ——
Other Sounds/Chakras: ——

MEDITATION

This is one of those names whose meaning, energies and chakras so strongly reinforce each other that the effects are dynamic. The element of earth is a reflection of the ability of these individuals to put life and its circumstances into a down-to-earth perspective. They have come to do what is necessary, and help others to do the same without getting lost in concepts and ideas. Throat chakra energy can produce a coarseness of speech in these individuals, which they must learn to control, but at the same time they have a knack for bringing situations into perspective through their speech. There is often very little pretense in these individuals. They are straightforward, sometimes bluntly so, but they say what needs to be said in a manner that can be understood. They have a tremendously expressive ability that can be applied in a variety of ways, one of which is counseling (formal or informal). Straight talk and straight life are what brings the greatest rewards for these individuals.

LAURA
(variations: Laurel, Lauretta, Laurie, Lawrence,
Larry, Lora, Lori, Loren, Lorna)

Meaning: "crowned with laurel leaves; victorious spirit"
Suggested Affirmation: "I am Laura. I am the victorious spirit!"
Primary Vowel/Element: A / Element of Ether
Primary Sound/Chakra: "aw" / Solar Plexus Chakra
Other Vowels/Elements: U / Element of Earth
                        A / Element of Ether
Other Sounds/Chakras: Silent
                        "uh" / Throat Chakra

MEDITATION
Those of this name have come to become victorious, if only in spirit, over the energies and circumstances of earthly life. These individuals will encounter a wide range of life experiences that must be kept in their proper perspective. Learning to discern the underlying lessons, spiritual aand otherwise, in all life circumstances and situations is what will most enable them to develop a field of energy that resonates with victory. Those whose name is of the *AU* variations will encounter their strongest lessons through physical life situations. Those of the *O* variations will have their strongest battles with the emotions. In either case, victory is forthcoming as long as one persists. These individuals have come into physical life to learn that they can become victorious and can wear the crown of laurel leaves, no matter what the life circumstances. For many this is a lifetime to be healed, and healing is what brings true victory. Developing a spiritual outlook or positive manner of living ensures the victory and prevents the physical realms and all of its lessons from overcoming them.

LEO
(variations: Leon, Leonard, Leona)

Meaning: "the courageous lion"

Suggested Affirmation: "I am Leo. I am the courageous lion of God!"

Primary Vowel/Element: E / Element of Air

Primary Sound/Chakra: "ee" / Brow and Crown Chakras

Other Vowels/Elements: O / Element of Water

Other Sounds/Chakras: "oh" / Spleen Chakra

MEDITATION

These individuals have come to learn to express their courage in new ways. Tests and lessons of strength and courage will predominate in this life, be they physical, emotional mental or spiritual. The lion is an ancient and powerful symbol of strength and should become a personal mandala for these individuals. In astrology the lion in the sign of Leo is representative of the life-giving Father, and it is a sign through which one must learn to express the true personality. Although the chakras are those of the head and those of the spleen and lower stomach, the two are bridged through the heart. We need a heart and its dynamic love activity to animate our life and our life energies. Awakening the eternal flame within the heart to bridge the mind and the emotions will be the key. Air without water is dry and lifeless, and water with no oxygen is stagnant. It is the fire element that is essential to mixing the two through evaporation and condensation. The energies of love must be employed to balance the mind and emotions, and this is when one begins to become a powerful force or lion of God.

LESLEY
(variation: Leslie)

Meaning: "dweller at the gray fortress; the calm spirit"
Suggested Affirmation: "I am Lesley. I am the calm spirit!"
Primary Vowel/Element: E / Element of Air
Primary Sound/Chakra: "eh"/ Throat Chakra
Other Vowels/Elements: E / Element of Air
Other Sounds/Chakras: "ee" / Brow and Crown Chakras

MEDITATION

This is one of those names that is androgynous. This is significant, especially when examining its meaning and the chakras associated with it. All the chakras involve the head—mental energy. The mind is neither male nor female. The sounds of the name involve three chakras, and three is the creative, birth-giving number. New birth occurs only when there is union between the male and the female. Learning to bring the male and the female energies into balance and into new expression is part of the task of these individuals. Properly united male and female creates a home-fortress. When our energies—our home—become strengthened and united, there is calm and security. Learning to become secure in oneself—recognizing that within you are all that you need or require to give birth to any endeavor in life—is the lesson of these individuals. This is the creative process in action.

LINDA
(variations: Lin, Lynda, Lynn, Lynette)

Meaning: "pretty one; beauty; inner beauty; refreshing"
Suggested Affirmation: "I am Linda. I am the beautiful child of God!"
Primary Vowel/Element: I / Element of Fire
Primary Sound/Chakra: "ih" / Throat Chakra
Other Vowels/Elements: A / Element of Ether
Other Sounds/Chakras: "uh" / Throat Chakra

MEDITATION
Bringing the heart and mind together is part of the task of these individuals. The *I* is a vowel connected to the medulla oblongata, a minor chakra point necessary to linking the energies of the heart to the energies of the mind. It is also associated with the element of fire. The *I* was a vowel that at one time would have been associated with the heart, but vowels and the sounds and energies associated with them also change and grow. These individuals have come to give new expression to the heart energies, to discover the beauty that lies within the hearts of all people, especially themselves. Inherent within this discovery are lessons in self-esteem. Inherent also are lessons in healing the heart of the past and rising above it. The heart is the seat of karma. As it unfolds, so does much of our past-life karmic connections. These individuals have come to work with this and to learn that all situations are growing and learning situations. It is the recognizing of this that most unfolds the beauty that burns within them.

LISA
(variation: Elisa)

Meaning: "consecrated one"
Suggested Affirmation: "I am Lisa. I am the consecrated child of
     God!"
Primary Vowel/Element: I / Element of Fire
Primary Sound/Chakra: "ee" / Brow and Crown Chakras
Other Vowels/Elements: A / Element of Ether
Other Sounds/Chakras: "uh" / Throat Chakra

MEDITATION
   This is a name of great healing tenderness. These individuals
have a fire within them that must be given expression in some creative activity, be that in healing or the creative arts. With most of these
individuals the intuitive fires are very strong and so naturally active
that there is really no need to try and wait for the "lights to click on."
These individuals came in with the lights already on. They are almost
always a blessing in the lives of those they touch, having great creative imagination and intuition, both of which have come to be
expressed more dynamically in this lifetime (throat chakra influence).
They make tremendous healers with their voice. The inner fires
emanate strongly through what they say and how they say it. The
words said more lovingly are felt by others more lovingly. Those that
cut, cut more deeply. At its highest level, these individuals have come
to learn about and use the Creative Word—to give manifestation to
their hopes, dreams and wishes and thus be an even greater blessing
in the lives of others.

LOIS
(variations: Louis, Louise)

Meaning: "warrior-maid; victorious"
Suggested Affirmation: "I am Lois. I am the warrior-maid of
    God!"
Primary Vowel/Element: O / Element of Water
Primary Sound/Chakra: "oh" / Spleen Chakra
Other Vowels/Elements: I / Element of Fire
Other Sounds/Chakras: "ih" / Throat Chakra

MEDITATION

Those of this name and its variations have come to learn to assert
the male and female energies. They have come into life to work the
alchemical process through their life circumstances. Water is the
feminine energy and fire the male; when both are employed, one can
be victorious in all things, all endeavors. Learning to balance the
feminine and the masculine, learning to recognize that there is the
need for both within life and within life circumstances is the task of
these individuals. Therein lies the significance of the "warrior-maid."
There are times when it is important to be more assertive, to respond
to life like a disciplined warrior, and there are times when it is
necessary to be the nurturing handmaiden. There are times to be cool
and there are times to be fiery. There are also times to generate new
energy (fire and water combining to create steam). Learning to use
the strong intuition will assist these individuals in learning to apply
the alchemical and shapeshifting process to all life circumstances.

LUKE

(variations: Luci, Lucille, Lucy)

Meaning: "enlightened; the bringer of light and knowledge"
Suggested Affirmation: "I am Luke. I am the bringer of light!"
Primary Vowel/Element: U / Element of Earth
Primary Sound/Chakra: "oo" / Base Chakra
Other Vowels/Elements: E / Element of Air
Other Sounds/Chakras: Silent

MEDITATION

Those of this name are a true light to those they touch within their lives. Regardless of life circumstances, they have a capacity for assisting others in seeing their way clear in day-to-day life situations, regardless how muddled they are. Knowledge helps us to chase away our fears and doubts and to overcome the miasma of superstitions and limitations, whether imposed upon us or by us. For this reason knowledge and education are essential to these individuals. The more knowledge they acquire, the more understanding and wisdom is brought into their lives. These individuals have a unique capacity for bringing revelations to normal circumstances, for seeing the spiritual light shining in all physical life happenings. Humility must become a part of their lives—the knowledge silent (silent *E*)—in order for their light to shine the brightest. These individuals have come to begin to unfold the process of involution (the spirit manifesting and condensing into the physical) to give greater propulsion to evolution (the raising from the physical into the spiritual). It is the mystery of life—birth, death and rebirth—that they have come to share and inspire.

MARDELL

Meaning: "the bittersweet delight; delightful myrrh"
Suggested Affirmation: "I am Mardell. I am the delightful myrrh."
Primary Vowel/Element: A / Element of Ether
Primary Sound/Chakra: "aw" / Solar Plexus Chakra
Other Vowels/Elements: E / Element of Air
Other Sounds/Chakras: "eh" / Throat Chakra

MEDITATION

Myrrh has a fragrance that is bittersweet, but it is a fragrance whose energy vibration can be delighted in. In many of the ancient mystery schools it was used to break down blockages of energy that accumulated within the body so that the spiritual could fully integrate with the physical. Its fragrance is purifying and protecting. Individuals of this name must come to understand that they are protected, that the fragrance of God surrounds them at all times, no matter how bitter circumstances may become, for it will be balanced by the sweet. To make this happen more easily, there must be balance between the mind and the emotions. The solar plexus center is one of great power but one that holds in and stores strong emotions. These emotions need to be given new air, new fragrance, new expression (throat chakra) for the greatest balance to occur. Learning to control the emotions (not to ignore them) will be part of the task. This will require assertion of strength of will. This is best manifested by remembering that we should delight in the way the Divine expresses through us, that we are the myrrh—the gift of fragrance—to our world.

MARGARET

(variations: Margie, Meg, Peg, Peggy, Marguerite)

Meaning: "the pearl"
Suggested Affirmation: "I am Margaret. I am the pearl of God!"
Primary Vowel/Element: A / Element of Ether
Primary Sound/Chakra: "aw" / Solar Plexus Chakra
Other Vowels/Elements: A / Element of Ether
                        E / Element of Air
Other Sounds/Chakras: "aw" / Solar Plexus Chakra
                        "eh" / Throat Chakra

MEDITATION

These individuals are, more often than not, true pearls in the lives of those they touch. As they get older and mature, they grow stronger and shine with even greater luster. Life, no matter how difficult, does not tear them down. Life and all its circumstances become polishing agents in them. A pearl begins as a grain of sand, an irritant in an oyster, but as time passes, so does the irritation. The sand is no longer just a grain of sand, but rather it is a pearl of great value. Life is the polishing agent, cutting and faceting the individual until the roughness is gone and the brilliance shines forth. This is the energy of this name and the inherent potential in all that bear it. Many tales exist around the world reflecting this same idea—the "ugly duckling" that grows to become the beautiful swan is but one. It is the long-range goal, not the immediate one, that must be focused on. These individuals must learn to look, not at what they think they are at the moment, but what they *will* beome in the future!

MARK
(variations: Marc, Marcia, Marcy, Marsha)

Meaning: "warlike; mighty warrior; brave heart, loyal one"
Suggested Affirmation: "I am Mark. I am the mighty warrior
   of God!"
Primary Vowel/Element: A / Element of Ether
Primary Sound/Chakra: "aw" / Solar Plexus Chakra
Other Vowels/Elements: ——
Other Sounds/Chakras: ——

MEDITATION

Those of this name and its variations have strong ties to the myths of the ancient war gods, particularly Mars and Ares. Examining the astrological chart for Mars placement will reveal much about the lessons of "war" that must be learned by these individuals. This is a name that can manifest lessons in anger, self-doubt, and fear. There may be a need to overcome self-confirmation, recognition and cowardice in some form, but it is also a name that manifests an energy of great strength, a strength to overcome the dragons of life no matter how they manifest. It can create the unfoldment of generosity and compassion, courage, devotion and idealism that can override outer circumstances. In the Persian mystery temples the "warrior" was one who took the occult teaching back out into the world, teachings that would not be readily accepted, and for this reason it was often like going to war. Standing strong in one's beliefs will always be part of the lesson for those of this name, a task they are more than capable of handling.

MARTHA

Meaning: "the lady of discretion"

Suggested Affirmation: "I am Martha. I am the lady of discretion."

Primary Vowel/Element: A / Element of Ether

Primary Sound/Chakra: "aw" / Solar Plexus Chakra

Other Vowels/Elements: A / Element of Ether

Other Sounds/Chakras: "uh" / Throat Chakra

MEDITATION

During medieval times, a true lady was knowledgeable about many things. This included knowledge of the outer world and the inner spiritual worlds as well. In many ancient traditions, the women were the keepers of the ancient traditions and wisdoms. It is this capacity that resonates strongly with individuals of this name. For one to be discreet and discerning, there must be knowledge. Learning when to speak and when not to speak is difficult but is necessary for true discretion. Discretion is not knowing and keeping secrets, it is knowing what to reveal, to whom and to what degree at all times. This must be based on outer circumstances and inner sight, thus for many of these individuals the task will be learning to balance what they see and experience outwardly with what they know to be true inwardly. Once accomplished, the individual becomes the true mystic Lady—the Lady of Wisdom and Understanding.

MARY
(variations: Marie, Marian, Maria,
Marietta, Marilyn, Marlene, Miriam)

Meaning: "myrrh; bitterness; from the sea; the living fragrance"
Suggested Affirmation: "I am Mary. I am the fragrance from the
    sea of life!"
Primary Vowel/Element: A / Element of Ether
Primary Sound/Chakra: "ay" / Heart Chakra
Other Vowels/Elements: Y / Element of Fire / Air
Other Sounds/Chakras: "ee" / Brow and Crown Chakras

MEDITATION

There is great significance in the meaning of this name and its variations and the life energies of those who have taken this name. It has an ancient thoughtform associated with the blessed one known as Mary in Christianity. In Hebrew the name translates as "god-bearer," which is appropriate to the Christian ethic. Beyond this, though, is even greater significance: It has roots in "mara," or the "sea," as well as strong associations with the fragrance myrrh. Tales and scriptures from all over the world abound about life coming from the living waters. Out of the waters of life, no mattter how turbulent, comes new being. It is the name of birth, and the fragrance of purity in the birth process is myrrh. No matter what the conditions of life are, no matter how murky and turbulent the waters, there is an ability within these individuals to give new birth to themselves and others. They have come to be their own god-bearer to find the Divine within. How this manifests for each individual will vary according to the vowel elements and chakras, but all are healers of the past, so that the new can be borne in them and through them.

MATTHEW
(variation: Matt)

Meaning "Gift of Jehovah; Gift of the Lord"
Suggested Affirmation: "I am Matthew. I am the gift of the Lord!"
Primary Vowel/Element: A / Element of Ether
Primary Sound/Chakra: "ah" / Throat Chakra
Other Vowels/Elements: E / Element of Air
Other Sounds/Chakras: "oo" / Base Chakra

MEDITATION

These individuals have come into life to learn how to be a true gift to all they touch. This does not imply that they must martyr themselves, but rather that there is an energy of abundance that can be shared with others. The predominant chakra is the throat, the center of cornucopia, which shows that there will be an abundance of something within the individual's makeup that can be shared with others. For some this may be a physical or material abundance, for others it may be a specific quality such as humor that can be shared, a gift to ease the life of others. This is an abundance that must be searched out; it lies within all of those with this name. It is reflected in the energies of the base chakra and the element of air. The base chakra is the center of our basic life force, our tie to the abundance of life energy within the universe. The element of air also reflects this. We do not worry about others breathing up our oxygen, and thus those of this name must not worry about depleting their own source of energy. Learning to activate it and express it as a gift will be the task, keeping in mind that gifts are gifts only when given in love.

MICHAEL
(variations: Mike, Michelle, Michaelina)

Meaning: "one who is like God; Godliness"
Suggested Affirmation: "I am Michael. I am like God!"
Primary Vowel/Element: I / Element of Fire
Primary Sound/Chakra: "eye" / Medulla Oblongata
Other Vowels/Elements: A / Element of Ether
E / Element of Air
Other Sounds/Chakras: "uh" / Throat Chakra
Silent

MEDITATION

Those of this name and its variations have come to work with powerful energies and powerful life experiences. These are not to be compared to the life experiences of others, but rather they will be powerful in relation to their previous life experiences. The predominant element is fire, and thus for many, new fires must be set within their lives. These individuals will have lessons involving the flames of the ego. Their affirmation is "I am like God," not "I am God." Their task is to live life as they know God would live life upon Earth. Michael the Archangel is second only to the Christ within the hierarchy of archangelic beings, and thus this association amplifies the energies of those with this name. These individuals must learn to overcome dishonesty (self- or otherwise) criticalness, coldness and aloofness. They have an inherent ability to manifest patience and prosperity through knowledge. Theirs is the ability to employ and gain knowledge of magic—the act of becoming more than human, of unfolding one's highest potentials. Precision and practicality must be developed in whatever endeavors are undertaken. This is the key to manifesting a life of new and perpetual fire.

NANCY
(variation: Nan)

Meaning: "grace; gracious one"

Suggested Affirmation: "I am Nancy. I am the gracious child of God!"

Primary Vowel/Element: A / Element of Ether

Primary Sound/Chakra: "ah" / Throat Chakra

Other Vowels/Elements: Y / Element of Fire / Air

Other Sounds/Chakras: "ee" / Brow and Crown Chakras

MEDITATION

Those of this name have come to unfold their ability to be gracious and graceful under all circumstances. This graciousness is what will accelerate the process of "drinking from the Grail Cup" (reflected by the *Y*). If necessary, these individuals can communicate and relate to people from all walks of life. They will come into contact with individuals from all sprectra of society and thus must learn to be gracious and graceful in dealing with them. This is the influence of the *A*. What is active in their life is the principle of Correspondence—"As above, so below. As below, so above." As they learn and unfold their ability to be graceful and gracious in the physical, the agility in the use of more ethereal energies also unfolds. These two words always integrate, and this must be realized. The heart is strong in these individuals, and they follow their hearts strongly, and yet even when their hearts are hurt, they emanate a grace and graciousness. They always have the Cup of the Grail to sustain them. If only seen once, either in the past or the present, it provides the energies of sustenance and protection in all circumstances. It is this vision that resides in the hearts of these individuals.

NATHAN
(variations: Nathaniel, Nate, Natalie

Meaning: "a gift; given of God"
Suggested Affirmation: "I am Nathan. I am the gift of God!"
Primary Vowel/Element: A / Element of Ether
Primary Sound/Chakra: "ay" / Heart Chakra
Other Vowels/Elements: A / Element of Ether
Other Sounds/Chakras: "uh" / Throat Chakra

MEDITATION
Those of this name have come to unfold the gift of life and heal-ing within themselves. This is a gift that will be shared with others. The energies of healing are strong within these individuals, and they often manifest this ability early in life. Effort must be taken to sustain that ability. These individuals can see into the hearts of others—they feel what others feel and they can see what others see. Because of this, care must be taken to keep themselves balanced and objective, or the emotions will create problems. They will resonate with their environments, and like a chameleon, can adjust to whatever energy is around them. Developing strength of will will be part of the task for these individuals. As this is developed, the gift of healing unfolds even more greatly. This healing may take many forms, depending upon the individual, such as simply being able to say the right thing at the right time. These individuals more often than others can easily live up to the vibrations and energies of their name. They have earned that right, but to them whom much is given, much is expected.

NEAL
(variations: Neil, Nelson)

Meaning: "champion"
Suggested Affirmation: "I am Neal. I am the champion of life!"
Primary Vowel/Element: E / Element of Air
Primary Sound/Chakra: "ee" / Brow and Crown Chakras
Other Vowels/Elements: A / Element of Ether
Other Sounds/Chakras: Silent

MEDITATION

Those of this name have come to learn lessons associated with winning and losing. Competition is usually strong within these individuals, but it must be balanced or it will become one-upmanship. They must also learn to understand that to be a champion in life does not involve doing a particular job or earning a certain amount of money. Being a champion has to do with maintaining the proper attitude toward who you are and enjoying what you do—finding fulfillment in your tasks whatever they may be. Keeping the proper perspective will be tested. This is the energy associated with the brow and crown chakras. Fears, lack of discipline, inefficient efforts and envy will deter them from their goals. If these are overcome, they will manifest great initiative and intuition that will be almost visionary. The ability to refine ideas and apply them practically will manifest, creating great success in their lives.

NICHOLAS
(variations: Nick, Nicole)

Meaning: "victory; the victorious spirit; the victorious heart"
Suggested Affirmation: "I am Nicholas. I am of victorious heart!"
Primary Vowel/Element: I / Element of Fire
Primary Sound/Chakra: "ih" / Throat Chakra
Other Vowels/Elements: O / Element of Water
                        A / Element of Ether
Other Sounds/Chakras: "uh" / Throat Chakra
                        "uh" / Throat Chakra

MEDITATION
Those of this name have come to learn to express strength of will in all situations, to learn that persistence will bring victory on some level, if only in spirit. The predominant elements are fire and water—elements of opposition. Whenever there is opposition, there is also a kind of battle. Victory is not where one element overpowers or controls the other. True victory arises by blending and synthesizing, by compromising. This kind of compromise is slow but powerful— the alchemical process of turning lead into gold. This takes great self-control and strength of will, persisting in what you know in your heart is true and right. The lesson for these individuals is in balancing the elements of their lives while keeping the inner fires strong and vibrant. It often involves much trial and error to find the proper balance, but once achieved, it manifests a strength and victory over all life circumstances that can never again be lost.

NORMA
(variations: Norman, Norm)

Meaning: "the pattern; the example; from the north; strong"
Suggested Affirmation: "I am Norma. I live the strong example of life!"
Primary Vowel/Element: O / Element of Water
Primary Sound/Chakra: "oh" / Spleen Chakra
Other Vowels/Elements: A / Element of Ether
Other Sounds/Chakras: "uh" / Throat Chakra

MEDITATION

In this name or any of its variations the predominant element is water. From the waters of life come many experiences and emotions, and these individuals have come to live in the manner that will enable them to best deal with these experiences. The north has always been the direction of teaching and experience as applied to the physical and material worlds. The best teaching is done by example, but before one can be an example by which others can live, he or she must be experienced. For this reason these individuals go through a wide variety of experiences, but they have an inherent flexibility and tenacity that prevents them from being overrun or overcome by any of them. They have an inner strength and resiliency that manifests itself whenever needed. It is this that they have come to live and teach to others. It is this that they have come to give greater expression to within this life.

OLIVIA
(variations: Olive, Oliver)

Meaning: "the olive branch; peaceful spirit"
Suggested Affirmation: "I am Olivia. I am of peaceful spirit!"
Primary Vowel/Element: O / Element of Water
Primary Sound/Chakra: "uh" / Throat Chakra
Other Vowels/Elements: I / Element of Fire
                          A / Element of Ether
Other Sounds/Chakras: "ih" / Throat Chakra
                        "uh" / Throat Chakra

MEDITATION

In this name or any of its variations, the key word to focus on in life is *peace*. Peace and maintaining it are both the task and the reward of these individuals. There is the potential to maintain an inner peace in spite of outer circumstances. This involves the development of strength of will—throat chakra energy and activation. This self-control and strength of will will be tested, particularly in regard to the emotions. Once achieved it will have a rippling effect, touching and kindling peace of mind and emotion within others as well. The olive branch is a powerful symbol of esoteric and exoteric Christianity, and it will yield much in meditation for those of this name, bringing enlightenment to life purpose and understanding of past life situations. Learning to maintain peace in all situations is difficult but attainable by those of this name.

OSCAR

Meaning: "spirit of the divine; blessed through service"
Suggested Affirmation: "I am Oscar. I am the spirit of the Divine!"
Primary Vowel/Element: O / Element of Water
Primary Sound/Chakra: "aw" / Solar Plexus Chakra
Other Vowels/Elements: A / Element of Ether
Other Sounds/Chakras: "uh" / Throat Chakra

MEDITATION

Those of this name have come to learn that they can be of service to anyone. It will be their task to realize they have something of significance to offer to others, regardless of who the others may be. The predominant element is water, and water flows within all people and is necessary for all life. These individuals are at their highest when they are involved in some kind of service to others. Service-oriented work situations bring great success. On the path to higher evolution, it is the purpose of all training and unfoldment to render ourselves more useful to humanity. The probationary path of discipleship involves going through what the ancients called the Doorway of Service to Humanity. This does not occur through artificially contrived situations, but through the normal day-to-day life circumstances. Service with a smile is the key, keeping in mind that one must also be of service to oneself!

PAIGE

Meaning: "attendant; obedient spirit"
Suggested Affirmation: "I am Paige. I am the obedient atten-
   dant of God!"
Primary Vowel/Element: A / Element of Ether
Primary Sound/Chakra: "ay" / Heart Chakra
Other Vowels/Elements: I / Element of Fire
                    E / Element of Air
Other Sounds/Chakras: Silent

MEDITATION

Those of this name have come to raise the energies of the heart
into greater expression. To help develop this, they will encounter a
myriad of life experiences, covering the whole spectrum. Part of this
involves re-stimulating the fires of the heart into greater, more creative expression. It is for this reason that the *I* and the *E* are silent. The
extra fire and air creates a greater stimulation of heart energies,
which acts subtly, so the individual must be extra discerning and
watchful of heart expressions. This always involves tests of balancing the mind and the emotions. The key word is *obedience.* There are
both physical and spiritual laws to obey. They do not fight each
other, and by obeying one, we are not disobeying the other. Finding a
way to work with both within one's life is the task. The heart is the
balancing chakra—it integrates the higher with the lower, the spiritual
with the physical. It is not easy, as it brings a confrontation with
insecurities, fears, self-doubts and irreverence at times; but as one
learns to balance, it manifests security, compassion, idealism and
healing of great magnitude—of self and others.

PAMELA
(variation: Pam)

Meaning: "honey; sweet spirit"

Suggested Affirmation: "I am Pamela. I am the sweet honey of God!"

Primary Vowel/Element: A / Element of Ether

Primary Sound/Chakra: "ah" / Throat Chakra

Other Vowels/Elements: E / Element of Air

         A / Element of Ether

Other Sounds/Chakras: "eh" / Throat Chakra

         "uh" / Throat Chakra

MEDITATION

Those of this name have an inherent sweetness about them that adds to the lives of those they touch. Their greatest tasks in life will revolve around discovering that same sweetness in others, regardless of how the others may present themselves. Honey is rich in nutrients and was a treasured delight, and it is this same kind of inner value that must be nurtured in others. Honey is the sweetness of flowers, the sweetness within the heart of flowers. There is a sweetness in the heart of all individuals, and those of this name have a capacity of seeing it or of stimulating it into expression. The primary chakra is that of the throat, and thus care must be taken to choose words carefully. The words of these individuals have a great penetrating strength that can touch the hearts of others more deeply than may ever be realized. That which is said more lovingly is felt more lovingly; that which is said to cut, cuts more deeply. This is the sweetness and power of the Creative Word which these individuals have come to uncover.

PAT
(variations: Patricia, Patrick, Trisha)

Meaning: "noble; full of honor"
Suggested Affirmation: "I am Pat. I am noble and full of honor!"
Primary Vowel/Element: A / Element of Ether
Primary Sound/Chakra: "ah" / Throat Chakra
Other Vowels/Elements: ——
Other Sounds/Chakras: ——

MEDITATION

Those of this name have an energy that is subtly noble. The Roman aristocracy was known as the patrician class. They were trained in all the arts, and honor was the code of living. Although this way of life declined with Rome, the spirit lives on. Various societies throughout the world have held codes of great honor and nobility that had nothing to do with birth but with how one lived his or her life. It is that eternal principle that these individuals have come to exemplify. They have come to give expression to that nobility, regardless of life circumstances. Nobility is of the heart, and it is honor in all things that gives life and expression to that nobility. Truth and honor are the watchwords, especially to oneself. These individuals have a code of honor which, though often unspoken, is truly lived and which touches those around them. It is what lifts them above the ordinary individual and enables them to achieve that which they most desire and need within their lives.

PAUL
(variations: Paula, Pauline)

Meaning: "little; dependent on God; follower of God"
Suggested Affirmation: "I am Paul. I am the follower of God!"
Primary Vowel/Element: A / Element of Ether
Primary Sound/Chakra: "aw" / Solar Plexus Chakra
Other Vowels/Elements: U / Element of Earth
Other Sounds/Chakras: Silent

MEDITATION

This is a name with hidden significances, thus the silent *U*. Although it means literally "little," this is not to be confused with "less than." It implies that even the little things—in the ways of thoughts, words and actions—have significance. It is through the little things of life that we demonstrate we are followers of God. This name activates an energy within one's life that creates an opportunity to give new birth to the old perceptions of earth activities. The *A* and the *U* are joining—creating a sound vibration associated with the solar plexus chakra. This center, once known as the "manger," was a place of birth. We are born to the lower self first so that we can ultimately give birth to the higher. This name activates an energy that manifests opportunities for new birth in many areas of life. These births operate in set cycles and rhythms (the silent earth element of *U*). Learning to recognize and follow those rhythms and then relaxing and allowing them to unfold will ease the struggle and facilitate the manifestation of opportunities.

PETER
(variation: Pete)

Meaning: "rock; strong in spirit"
Suggested Affirmation: "I am Peter. I am the rock of spirit!"
Primary Vowel/Element: E / Element of Air
Primary Sound/Chakra: "ee" / Brow and Crown Chakras
Other Vowels/Elements: E / Element of Air
Other Sounds/Chakras: "eh" / Throat Chakra

MEDITATION

Those of this name have an energy that ties them to the lesson of building strength and new foundations. They have come to be anchored in their beliefs like a rock. The predominant element is air, and unless one is anchored strongly upon a solid foundation, they will be blown hither and yon with every wind, gust and breeze. It is their task to strengthen the mind through knowledge. Dabbling in affairs and activities, especially metaphysical and psychic things, will create problems. A solid knowledge of the basic foundation of esoteric schooling processes is what will sustain them the most. There will be lessons in confronting fears, lack of discipline, impatience and superstitiousness. There may also be inefficiency and envy to overcome. Once accomplished, though, there is inherent a visionary quality and intuition beyond psychic perception. There manifests the ability to tune into inner world rhythms and a faith in these rhythms as they apply to the physical world. It is then that these individuals become the "rock."

PHILLIP
(variations: Phil, Philip)

Meaning: "lover of horses; strong in spirit"
Suggested Affirmation: "I am Phillip. I am strong in spirit!"
Primary Vowel/Element: I / Element of Fire
Primary Sound/Chakra: "ih" / Throat Chakra
Other Vowels/Elements: I / Element of Fire
Other Sounds/Chakras: "ih" / Throat Chakra

MEDITATION

Those of this name have strong fires of inspiration within them. These fires must be tempered with proper judgment—balanced mental ability. Implied within the "lover of horses" is the idea that such a person is able to make sound judgments about the strengths and weaknesses of the horses. They would be able to discern the strength of spirit within the horses. The horse is an ancient symbol of the Sun, and those of this name can find much significance in old tales and myths of the Sun gods. They must keep in mind that the tales of the Sun gods are the same as the tale of the Son of God. Often horses play a keen role in periodic dreams by these individuals, and special significance should be given to them. It is through the strength of the horse that humankind was once able to travel great distances, and it is through the strength of the spirit (symbolized by the horse) that these individuals can make tremendous progress within this life.

PHYLLIS
(variation: Phillis)

Meaning: "the leaf; the tender hearted"
Suggested Affirmation: "I am Phyllis. I am a leaf on the plant of God!"
Primary Vowel/Element: Y / Element of Fire
Primary Sound/Chakra: "ih" / Throat Chakra
Other Vowels/Elements: I / Element of Fire
Other Sounds/Chakras: "ih" / Throat Chakra

MEDITATION

Those of this name have come to work with the strong fires of the spiritual quest, either as an active member in the spiritual and metaphysical fields of study or through living the spiritual life in normal day-to-day circumstances. In either case, particularly those with the Y, there comes a point of major decision within their lives, in which they split strongly from the old way to a new lifestyle. A leaf is an outshoot of the plant, an indication of growth. The leaf may not be physically in touch with the roots or even with other leaves, but that does not mean the Divine is not operating within it. This is the lesson of those with this name. Comparisons must not be made, for the Divine operates uniquely in us each. Every leaf of every plant is different, and yet the life force is strong within them all. Learning to express the individual energies and to drink from the Grail of Life offered to you is the task. The grail may be a golden chalice, a tin cup or a cauldron. It may even be the womb within, but the divine elixir of fire and light is equally strong regardless of the container. Seeing oneself as the Cup of Life facilitates this in these individuals.

RACHEL
(variation: Rachael)

Meaning: "little lamb"
Suggested Affirmation: "I am Rachel. I am the little lamb of God!"
Primary Vowel/Element: A / Element of Ether
Primary Sound/Chakra: "ay" / Heart Chakra
Other Vowels/Elements: E / Element of Air
Other Sounds/Chakras: "eh" / Throat Chakra

MEDITATION

The lamb is a very ancient symbol, especially in Hebraic and Christian traditions. The lamb was sacrificed at Passover and its blood smeared upon the lintel posts to protect homes from death. Jesus was also known as the Lamb of God who was sacrificed for humanity. Those of this name have extremely large hearts to the degree that they may occasionally find themselves sacrificing themselves. This sacrificial aspect must be overcome. Learning to assert their love without martyrdom is difficult, but it can be accomplished. It simply requires recognizing that one cannot always take responsibility for others. Individuals with this name have great healing capabilities, but they must be asserted properly. They must keep in mind that the quickening comes from without, while the healing must come from within. All they can do is provide a quickening, and then it is up to the individual being healed. These individuals will give their hearts easily, and once given will do anything to maintain that love. They have a capability of sowing seeds of peace in their environments. Their energies are calming to others.

RAYMOND
(variation: Ray)

Meaning: "counsel and protection; mighty and wise protector"
Suggested Affirmation: "I am Raymond. I am the mighty and
   wise protector!"
Primary Vowel/Element: A / Element of Ether
Primary Sound/Chakra: "ay" / Heart Chakra
Other Vowels/Elements: O / Element of Water
                         Y / Element of Fire
Other Sounds/Chakras: "uh" / Throat Chakra
                        Silent

MEDITATION

Those of this name have a great inherent strength within them.
Usually as they grow older, this strength naturally unfolds itself. The
hearts of these individuals must be completely involved in whatever
work or endeavors they pursue. They have a capacity for discerning
others' hearts, needs and desires. Using this discernment in a positive
manner will be the test. They also have a capacity for making themselves understood when necessary. There may be insecurities and
self-doubts to overcome in the early years, but learning not to compare themselves to others will assist. These individuals usually have
a vision of success, and once their devotion is given, it remains strong.
Whether ostensible or not, the spiritual quest is usually strong within
them. There is a great curiosity and need for understanding spiritual
concepts in relation to their everyday life. Learning that the material
does not preclude the spiritual will bring them much peace of mind
and great intuitive insight into their own life quest.

REBECCA
(variations: Rebekah, Becky)

Meaning: "yoke; earnestly devoted or the devoted one"
Suggested Affirmation: "I am Rebecca. I am the devoted child
    of God!"
Primary Vowel/Element: E / Element of Air
Primary Sound/Chakra: "eh" / Throat Chakra
Other Vowels/Elements: E / Element of Air
                     A / Element of Ether
Other Sounds/Chakras: "eh" / Throat Chakra
                     "uh" / Throat Chakra

MEDITATION

Those of this name have come to learn to assert their strength of will in life, to take upon the yoke of life and follow through with what is set in motion. A farmer who yokes his horse to plow the fields does not stop plowing or attempting to plow simply because the horse may not want to do the work. Doing our tasks, fulfilling our responsibilities whether we like it or not, is part of the growing and learning process. It develops strength of will and true devotion. These individuals must learn to put their hearts and minds together and link them to physical endeavors—body, mind and soul in harmony. This builds true spiritual devotion and reveals the rewards of such within one's life. It opens to one who is willing to look knowledge of underlying purposes and energies, whether it is simple comprehension or the knowledge written in the ethers of Akasha. Knowing that there is a reason for everyone and everything within their lives is the first step to true revelation for these individuals.

RHONDA
(variation: Ronda)

Meaning: "grand strength of character"
Suggested Affirmation: "I am Rhonda. I am of great strength
  of character."
Primary Vowel/Element: O / Element of Water
Primary Sound/Chakra: "aw" / Solar Plexus Chakra
Other Vowels/Elements: A / Element of Ether
Other Sounds/Chakras: "uh" / Throat Chakra

MEDITATION

Those of this name have experienced the turbulent waters of life
in previous times and incarnations. In this incarnation they will have
ample opportunity to demonstrate to others how one can assert
strength of will over any conditions of life so as not to be drowned.
For them to do this, there must be a balancing of the emotions. Often
with these individuals the life circumstances are such that whether
there is tangible evidence of success or not, they do succeed. They
embody the hidden principle of the Quest for the Holy Grail. This
principle is one that says that *all* who set out upon the quest will
achieve it. Unfortunately, not everyone has the wisdom to recognize
this. We are primed for success, not failure, and it is the energy of this
name that activates the teaching of this to others. These individuals
demonstrate through their life that there is no failure, for these
individuals have come to make leaps and bounds in their own evolution and show others that it can be done simply by living one's life in a
positive and creative manner.

RICHARD
(variations: Rich, Rick, Ricky)

Meaning: "powerful ruler; brave one"
Suggested Affirmation: "I am Richard. I am the powerful ruler."
Primary Vowel/Element: I / Element of Fire
Primary Sound/Chakra: "ih" / Throat Chakra
Other Vowels/Elements: A / Element of Ether
Other Sounds/Chakras: "uh" / Throat Chakra

MEDITATION

Those of this name have an energy that can manifest within their lives as greater strength and courage. The fires of the heart and the fires of the mind when joined give great expression (throat chakra) to this energy. Thus it is important for these individuals to do what they know in their heart is right, regardless of others. There may be lessons in overcoming fears, self-doubts or even lessons in learning not to bully or be belligerent. They may encounter situations of aggression and impulsiveness, whether in themselves or others. As they mature and follow their strong inner promptings, they come into their true power regardless of outside pressure. This manifests as greater courage and strength, more confidence, critical judgment and the ability to deal with discord and enemies from a variety of perspectives. They manifest the ability to overcome discord in their own lives and in the lives of others. They then have the capability to institute any changes they deem important to their own life.

RITA

Meaning: "the pearl"

Suggested Affirmation: "I am Rita. I am the great pearl of God!"

Primary Vowel/Element: I / Element of Fire

Primary Sound/Chakra: "ee" / Brow and Crown Chakras

Other Vowels/Elements: A / Element of Ether

Other Sounds/Chakras: "uh" / Throat Chakra

MEDITATION

Those of this name have come to give new life to the fires of the mind. This is the vowel *I* operating through the brow and crown chakras. This gives these individuals great intuition and imagination, which must be expressed in a balanced manner. Finding pearls of wisdom by which to live one's life will be part of the task of these individuals. Pearls come from a very unlikely source—a grain of sand, an irritant in the oyster. This indicates that these individuals must look for and find their pearls in unusual places. The ordinary and the extraordinary all hold great pearls, and neither should be overlooked. Everything and everyone helps to mold the pearl. Learning to overcome subconscious fears, a lack of discipline, superstitiousness and envy will enable these individuals to manifest the great energy associated with this name. That energy is of intuition, imagination, inspiration, and understanding of the birth and death processes.

ROBERT

(variations: Bob, Bobbie, Roberta, Robin, Robyn)

Meaning: "shining with fame and excellent worth; **strength** of character"

Suggested Affirmation: "I am Robert. I shine with excellent worth!"

Primary Vowel/Element: O / Element of Water

Primary Sound/Chakra: "aw" / Solar Plexus

Other Vowels/Elements: E / Element of Air

Other Sounds/Chakras: "eh" / Throat Chakra

MEDITATION

Those of this name have an energy that will manifest two important tasks for them during this incarnation. The first is the development of strength of will and character, and the second is that of turning emotions into higher aspirations. It is the throat and solar plexus chakras that are most active within these individuals, and both are centers of great strength and power. They are bridged by the heart, and thus following one's heart is what will most facilitate the manifestation of light. Dealing with emotions and lessons of proper use of strength of will will be a part of their life, particularly in the early years, but it will intensify as long as the lessons are not dealt with properly. The solar plexus chakra holds on to energies, thus those not cleansed, dealt with, etc. may have a tendency to accumulate until there is no choice but to deal with them. These energies of both chakras at their highest can manifest reverence, compassion, idealism and healing that affect all within range, strongly influencing the lives of others.

ROGER

Meaning: "famous spear carrier; God's warrior"
Suggested Affirmation: "I am Roger. I am God's spear of light!"
Primary Vowel/Element: O / Element of Water
Primary Sound/Chakra: "aw" / Solar Plexus Chakra
Other Vowels/Elements: E / Element of Air
Other Sounds/Chakras: "uh" / Throat Chakra

MEDITATION

The spear is an ancient symbol with powerful occult overtones. From the mighty spear of Athene, a symbol of her strength and protection, to the mystical spear of Longinus, the spear which pierced the side of the Christ, it has been a symbol of light, strength and power. Those of this name have come to realize that thoughts are things, and that we can project thoughts outward through the air to the target. Learn to control the thoughts and recognize that they are as important as our actions. Hating a person is just as detrimental as hitting a person. They both send blows to the other's energies. These individuals have a great capacity for thought projection, but it must be disciplined. Telepathy is but one way it will manifest. Lessons of power and its proper use will also be a part of these individuals' lives. They have come to manifest their own power so that they can be truly a spear and channel of light.

RONALD
(variations: Ron, Ronnie)

Meaning: "mighty power"
Suggested Affirmation: "I am Ronald. I am of mighty power!"
Primary Vowel/Element: O / Element of Water
Primary Sound/Chakra: "aw" / Solar Plexus Chakra
Other Vowels/Elements: A / Element of Ether
Other Sounds/Chakras: "uh" / Throat Chakra

MEDITATION

Those of this name could do no worse than to see the oceans of the world as their personal symbol or mandala. The great waters of the world are still powerful and mysterious. Their depths are unknown to a great extent, and yet they wield a power and life that is staggering. Lifeforms fill the oceans, foods that sustain humanity in plant and animal form. Most of the world is covered with water. Water is used to generate electricity, powering our cities and towns, and yet when uncontrolled, it can be destructive to life and to the Earth. To those of this name, there is a great store and depth of power and strength that never seems to be tapped. Caution must be exercised to not tap more than can be balanced and controlled. This innate power can be applied to any avenue or endeavor of life. There is nowhere where water does not exist in some form, even in the desert. These individuals can fit in anywhere to some degree and bring new refreshment and life to any area.

ROSE

(variations: Rosa, Rosalee, Rosamond, Roseanne,
Rosemarie, Rosemary, Rosette)

Meaning: "the rose; the giver of love"
Suggested Affirmation: "I am Rose. I am the giver of love!"
Primary Vowel/Element: O / Element of Water
Primary Sound/Chakra: "oh" / Spleen Chakra
Other Vowels/Elements: E / Element of Air
Other Sounds/Chakras: Silent

MEDITATION

Those of this name and its variations should meditate regularly upon the image of the rose, seeing themselves as roses coming into bloom. As each petal unfolds, so does the energies and abilities of the individual. This is a very powerful symbol. This and the lotus flower are very ancient symbols. The chakra is the spleen chakra, and when fully active, it opens one to communication with beings from other dimensions. The rose is a symbol that ties one to the angelic hierarchy, which works for humankind through other dimensions. Learning to breathe new life into emotional expressions will be the task of these individuals. Balancing the emotions for proper expression is not always easy. There can be a tendency to give too much. Remember that roses have thorns, and that those who do not treat the rose tenderly or gently deserve to be pricked by the thorn. Once pricked, they treat the rose differently thereafter. These individuals have a great capacity to love, but that love must also be extended to themselves. Love is the most dynamic healing force upon the Earth, and it is this that these individuals can manifest.

RUSSELL
(variation: Russ)

Meaning: "red-haired one; wise discretion"
Suggested Affirmation: "I am Russell. I am wise and discreet!"
Primary Vowel/Element: U / Element of Earth
Primary Sound/Chakra: "uh" / Throat Chakra
Other Vowels/Elements: E / Element of Air
Other Sounds/Chakras: "eh" / Throat Chakra

MEDITATION

Red, whenever associated with a person's name, usually reflects new energy, courage and strength. In the case of this name, it activates an energy in the individual's life so that new strength can be applied to all life circumstances, especially those which are the more practical. In other words, these individuals have a unique ability to take care of business. They are down to earth, and yet there is an inherent wisdom which lifts them above the average worker. Though their life task may appear to be mundane, there is an air of wisdom that surrounds them. They usually have a perspective that lifts them above the mundane. They have a unique ability that with time enables them to see things in more than just a superficial light. Knowledge and intelligence is important to them, although this side is often "silenced," and yet they must keep in mind that knowledge in and of itself is useless. It is only when knowledge is applied to normal living circumstances that it becomes true wisdom. And this is the natural ability of those with this name.

RUTH

Meaning: "compassionate and beautiful"
Suggested Affirmation: "I am Ruth. I am the compassionate
    and beautiful child of God!"
Primary Vowel/Element: U / Element of Earth
Primary Sound/Chakra: "oo" / Base Chakra
Other Vowels/Elements: ——
Other Sounds/Chakras: ——

MEDITATION

Those of this name have an earthy quality about them, and they
have a natural beauty and compassion that is grounded in the physical. Learning to keep their feet upon the ground is most important in
all endeavors. Many of these individuals have had trouble in past
lives in remaining grounded as they stretched themselves toward the
heavens, and thus this is their task. In Eastern philosophy it is said
that the way to heaven is through the feet. It is by utilizing the
energies of the Earth that we can propel ourselves to heaven. Thus
these individuals must understand that by fulfilling their daily
obligations and responsibilities with positive and creative zest, that
which is beyond the Earth opens to them. In this manner, then, not
only are the rewards of the Earth presented to the individual, but the
rewards of heaven as well. All energies of heaven flow within the
Earth, and thus those of this name must understand that it is important to tap the inner energies and manifest them in the outer world.
The intuition is very strong for those who wish to unfold it.

RYAN

Meaning: "little king; man of distinction"
Suggested Affirmation: "I am Ryan. I am a king of great
    distinction!"
Primary Vowel/Element: Y / Element of Fire
Primary Sound/Chakra: "eye" / Medulla Oblongata
Other Vowels/Elements: A / Element of Ether
Other Sounds/Chakras: "uh" / Throat Chakra

MEDITATION

Those of this name have come to take fully upon themselves the
mystical Quest for the Holy Grail. This is the quest for discovering
our true spiritual essence and how best to manifest it within this
lifetime. Anytime the Y is the predominant vowel, the chalice should
become a personal mandala. This is the cup of life from which we
must drink. Though initially its taste may be bitter, it fills and nour-
ishes the life essence of the individual with a honey—sweetened
energy that sustains one through all life circumstances. Kings have
great wealth, abundance and great responsibility. They must have a
great heart and be able to relate to everyone. They must not be locked
away within the castle but be out among the court's business. Those
of this name must remember that to them whom much is given, much
is expected. These individuals have the feminine energies of love and
intuition strong within them. They have the capacity to give new
birth and new life to those they touch. Just as a king passes favors, so
does the touch of those with this name.

SAMUEL
(variation: Sam)

Meaning: "his name is God; asked of God; integrity"
Suggested Affirmation: "I am Samuel. I am the integrity of
   God!"
Primary Vowel/Element: A / Element of Ether
Primary Sound/Chakra: "ah" / Throat Chakra
Other Vowels/Elements: U / Element of Earth
                     E / Element of Air
Other Sounds/Chakras: "oo" / Base Chakra
                     "eh" / Throat Chakra

MEDITATION

Those of this name have great responsibility. They have a name that activates much learning and application of learning within their lives. Clairaudience is often easily developed within them, but they must learn to discern what they are hearing. For these individuals, applying common sense to spiritual concepts is very important. It is equally important that they learn that the manifestation of the Creative Word of life revolves around integrity in life and with all individuals, and not upon self-sacrifice and martyrdom. Honesty is important, and these individuals must learn to be as honest with themselves as with others. They will have ample opportunity to demonstrate that integrity and truth do not hinder prosperity and fulfillment in any way.

SANDRA
(variation: Sandy)

Meaning: "helper; defender of others; compassion and humility"

Suggested Affirmation: "I am Sandra. I defend and strengthen others with compassion and humility."

Primary Vowel/Element: A / Element of Ether

Primary Sound/Chakra: "ah" / Throat Chakra

Other Vowels/Elements: A / Element of Ether

Other Sounds/Chakras: "uh" / Throat Chakra

MEDITATION

This is a name of great force in feminine expression. It takes the energies of the heart and gives them practical expression. It embodies the care of home and family, be it the biological family or the family of associates. There is a tremendous capacity in these individuals for healing and soothing others along many lines. In the case of those with this name, it becomes most evident when someone is being downtrodden. They are first to sense this and the first to offer compassion and assistance. They embody the principles of healing applied naturally. On some level they must come to realize that those whom they protect, they must also strengthen. There is a great sense of power awareness within these individuals, but they must learn humility with it. Strength in silence is a key trait with these individuals. They are the silent helpers and angels of the past. They often do not ask if help is needed, they simply respond because it is the right thing to do. Though quiet in their expressions, their energies ring out, having permanent effects in others' lives.

SARA
(variations: Sarah, Sharon)

Meaning: "princess; God's princess"
Suggested Affirmation: "I am Sara. I am God's princess!"
Primary Vowel/Element: A / Element of Ether
Primary Sound/Chakra: "ay" / Heart Chakra
Other Vowels/Elements: A / Element of Ether
Other Sounds/Chakras: "uh" / Throat Chakra

MEDITATION

Like the princesses of fairy tales, these individuals must come into their own. They may know that they shall inherit the kingdom, but it is necessary that they earn it through their endeavors as much as through their birthright. Most have the capacity for touching the hearts of others in very dynamic ways, but expressions of the heart must be true, or the innate power and strength becomes lost. These individuals must learn to step down from the throne to work with all others and yet keep in mind that the throne is theirs by right of inheritance. Princesses can grow to be queens of their own kingdoms if the training is right. Those of this name have come to undergo the necessary training and preparation that will make their time upon the throne beneficial to all concerned. Knowledge—both practical and mystical—is important. Just as the kings and queens of more ancient times were also priests and priestesses, so must the princesses be trained; then they may learn to rule and live in heaven and earth.

SCOTT

Meaning: "loyalty"
Suggested Affirmation: "I am Scott. I am loyal in all things!"
Primary Vowel/Element: O / Element of Water
Primary Sound/Chakra: "aw" / Solar Plexus Chakra
Other Vowels/Elements: ——
Other Sounds/Chakras: ——

MEDITATION

Those of this name have come to learn to control the emotions and balance their emotional ties to others by being loyal to their higher self. The solar plexus is a center that houses much of our emotions, both past and present. For many, our loyalties are determined by the emotional energy prevalent at the moment. Although that is a human trait, it is important to assert strength of will over impulses and to discern what is correct for the situation prior to attaching loyalties. Mind over the emotions is the key. For many, carrying the emotions in this way is like carrying a cross that can be quite heavy. For those of this name, the cross of emotions can be doubly difficult, as indicated by the cross of the double *T*'s in the name. Turning emotion into aspiration is the key. Creativity and empathy are strong in these individuals. There is always a tie between artistic energies and emotions. Working with the energies and beings of nature can assist those of this name, as they have a tie to the elemental kingdom of elves and fairies. As emotions are controlled, creative expression dominates dynamically.

SEAN
(variation: Shawn)

Meaning: "God's gracious gift"
Suggested Affirmation: "I am Sean. I am God's gracious gift!"
Primary Vowel/Element: A / Element of Ether
Primary Sound/Chakra: "aw" / Solar Plexus Chakra
Other Vowels/Elements: E / Element of Air
Other Sounds/Chakras: Silent

MEDITATION

Those of this name have come to link the mind and the emotions for balanced expression within their lives. The solar plexus is the seat of emotions and the silent *E* is the energy of the air, or mind. The heart bridges the two, and when the two are joined, new birth occurs. There must be a balancing of emotionalism with dogmatism. Overcoming self-doubts, possessiveness, fear and mistrust will be most important. Once accomplished, great compassion and healing can emanate from these individuals in whatever field of work or endeavor they are immersed. They have a strong idealism that is contagious to others, and prosperity comes through knowledge and art combined. Finding a way to synthesize the two will be the task of these individuals, but it will also bring the greatest rewards, physically and spiritually. They literally become a gift to those within their lives.

SHERI
(variations: Sherri, Sherry)

Meaning: "cherished womanly one"
Suggested Affirmation: "I am Sheri. I am the cherished child of God!"
Primary Vowel/Element: E / Element of Air
Primary Sound/Chakra: "ay" / Heart Chakra
Other Vowels/Elements: I / Element of Fire
Other Sounds/Chakras: "ee" / Brow and Crown Chakras

MEDITATION

Those of this name have an energy that can make them cherished by others. In order for this to occur, they must first come to cherish themselves. In order to cherish oneself, one must have the correct perspective. This is the influence of the brow and crown chakras. Fears, introversion, belittlement, martyrdom and envy must be overcome. The individual must come to understand that no one knows what's better for them than they themselves. They must also understand that we are never given a hope, wish or dream without being given opportunities to make them a reality, and the only thing that can shatter that possibility is compromise, settling for less. These individuals must recognize that within their hearts is all they need. As they recognize it within themselves, it manifests outside of them. This name gives great intuition, imagination and healing capabilities for those willing to unfold them.

SHIRLEY

Meaning: "from the bright meadow; the restful spirit"
Suggested Affirmation: "I am Shirley. I am from the bright meadow of God!"
Primary Vowel/Element: I / Element of Fire
Primary Sound/Chakra: "ih" / Throat Chakra
Other Vowels/Elements: E / Element of Air
                             Y / Element of Fire
Other Sounds/Chakras: "ee" / Brow and Crown Chakras
                             Silent

MEDITATION

Those of this name have a great capacity to influence the spiritual growth of others. A meadow is a place of rest. It is a place of color and energy, a place to build a new home, to establish home fires. Fire is the predominant element. Fire warms and soothes when kept alive within the home. It provides a security that allows others to grow out from it to establish their own fires. This is the passing of the Grail Cup of spirituality. The cup of life is passed on to others to drink from and discover upon their own. This is the significance of the *Y* at the end of the name. Silent and unspoken, it is an integral part of the life experience of these individuals, and it becomes an ethereal goal for others touched by those of this name. There is recognition that there is something special about these individuals—it is the influence of the spiritual being living through the fulfillment of responsibilities in the physical. It lays the foundation for the spiritual quests of others who are touched by those of this name. It awakens the intuition and creative and Christed imagination in those closest to them.

SONJA
(variations: Sonjia, Sonya)

Meaning: "woman of wisdom"
Suggested Affirmation: "I am Sonja. I am a woman of wisdom!"
Primary Vowel/Element: O / Element of Water
Primary Sound/Chakra: "aw" / Solar Plexus Chakra
Primary Vowels/Elements: A / Element of Ether
Other Sounds/Chakras: "uh" / Throat Chakra

MEDITATION

Those of this name have an energy that will enable them to express their energies and sensitivities in a practical manner. The sensitivity is strong within them. This is the influence of the water element. Water is a part of all life, and thus they can, if necessary, connect with all life to some degree. Learning to relate to all life and see others, once connected, through the heart is what must be developed. The heart accentuates and balances the energies of the solar plexus. It reveals what is hidden so that the individual can respond in the wisest manner. Learning to go within the temple of the heart to consider situations before being carried away by the emotions is part of discrimination. It is what leads to the manifestation of wisdom. This is what also leads to the transformation of the emotional psychic energies into true and wise spiritual expression. There is an innate wisdom about these individuals, reflected in how others often come to them for advice. This is healing, as all expressions of wisdom should be.

STACEY
(variation: Stacie)

Meaning: "resurrected; transformed heart"
Suggested Affirmation: "I am Stacey. I am the resurrected heart of life!"
Primary Vowel/Element: A / Element of Ether
Primary Sound/Chakra: "ay" / Heart Chakra
Other Vowels/Elements: E / Element of Air
                               Y / Element of Fire
Other Sounds/Chakras: "ee" / Brow and Crown Chakras
                               Silent

MEDITATION

Those of this name have an energy that will enable them to transform and re-express the energies of the heart. The heart chakra is the balancing center. If it is out of balance, the rest of our energy will be also. It holds most of the karma of the past, which we must someday cleanse ourselves of. It is the center through which we meet the Dwellers upon the Threshhold—those aspects of ourselves that we have painted over, glossed over, shoved to the back of the closet and pretended didn't exist in this life and past. Those of this name have come to deal with things from a new perspective, to open themselves more fully to the Quest for the Holy Grail (silent Y). Insecurity, self-doubts, fear, mistrust and the need for recognition must be overcome. As they are, these individuals will strongly manifest an idealism and a healing capability for themselves and others. It will open up intuition and vision of the path to come, instilling a new faith and inspiration in all life circumstances. They resurrect themselves on all levels.

STAN
(variation: Stanley)

Meaning: "one who lives at rocky meadow; sturdy in spirit"
Suggested Affirmation: "I am Stan. I am sturdy in spirit!"
Primary Vowel/Element: A / Element of Ether
Primary Sound/Chakra: "ah" / Throat Chakra
Other Vowels/Elements: ——
Other Sounds/Chakras: ——

MEDITATION

Those who have this name have an energy that will manifest opportunities to express the heart energies more strongly within their lives. This always involves tests of strength of will and individuality. These individuals have come to unfold their unique energies and to do so with control. This means they must often break bonds of security with others to find security in themselves. Learning not to allow others to dominate and control them and yet be flexible and open enough to listen and evaluate the opinions of others is part of their life lesson. These individuals usually learn to take full responsibility for their choices and decisions, whether they are good or bad. The heart is the balancing center of the body, and if this person's heart is in his or her activity, a sturdy foundation will be laid. Often these persons may seem like loners, but they have come to follow their own star and discover security within it. They will succeed, for they move forward always. They must remember that the past is past and yet keep in mind that it helped shape the present.

STEVE
(variation: Stephen, Stephanie, Steven)

Meaning: "one who is crowned"
Suggested Affirmation: "I am Steve. I am crowned with light!"
Primary Vowel/Element: E / Element of Air
Primary Sound/Chakra: "ee" / Brow and Crown Chakras
Other Vowels/Elements: E / Element of Air
Other Sounds/Chakras: Silent

MEDITATION
One who is crowned is someone who is a little special. Being crowned makes one stand out a little more than others, and these individuals often do. This, of course, makes them susceptible to attention that can be positive or negative. The chakras are the brow and crown chakras, which are the female and male centers, respectively. Whenever the male and female come together, there is the opportunity for new birth. When linked, these centers in the head create the "rainbow bridge"—a bridge of light—a crown. Thus the intuition and the imagination are strong within these individuals. There are strong male and female energies—sensitivity and assertion that must be balanced and employed according to the circumstances of the moment. These individuals have a great mental capacity, and no matter how mundane the task they are involved in, their minds are always whirling. They have great sensitivity, which must be protected at times (again the influence of the male and female), but it is both aspects that keep the "child" within alive and awakens that same child in others.

STUART
(variations: Stewart, Stu)

Meaning: "caretaker; the helpful spirit"

Suggested Affirmation: "I am Stuart. I am the helpful spirit of God!"

Primary Vowel/Element: U / Element of Earth

Primary Sound/Chakra: "oo" / Base Chakra

Other Vowels/Elements: A / Element of Ether

Other Sounds/Chakras: "uh" / Throat Chakra

MEDITATION

Those who take care of the Earth, tending to it and to what grows within it, must be knowledgeable about how to combine its various elements. This is the significance of the elements of earth and ether in this combination, side by side. The Earth needs air, water, etc. in order to make things grow. Too much of the others will destroy the life and prevent growth. Learning to combine all elements of life, learning to synthesize them, learning to see them as learning experiences for the soul, will provide the greatest growth for these individuals. It will enable them then to assist others in the tending of their earth (their lives) for greater fulfillment. These individuals can make excellent teachers if they synthesize their own life lessons first. When this is done, there is no one who can not learn from them. There is no one who will not be helped by them.

SUSAN
(variations: Sue, Suzi, Suzanne)

Meaning: "lily; full of grace"
Suggested Affirmation: "I am Susan. I am the lily of grace!"
Primary Vowel/Element: U / Element of Earth
Primary Sound/Chakra: "oo" / Base Chakra
Other Vowels/Elements: A / Element of Ether
Other Sounds/Chakras: "uh" / Throat Chakra

MEDITATION

Those of this name have a powerful personal symbol that should be used on a regular basis. The lily is a symbol of purity and is associated in occult Christianity with the Archangel Gabriel and the Christ energies activated within the heart of the Earth at the time of the Winter Solstice. The Winter Solstice was always a sacred festival. It was a time of the shortest amount of daylight upon the Earth, but a time when each day thereafter the Sun would shine brighter and longer. It is the time of the victory of the Sun over darkness, and it is this energy that those of this name have come to tie into and manifest within their own life circumstances. The predominant element is earth, and thus these individuals have come to bring new light, grace and purity into their little part of the Earth. The Earth is quiet, following its own cycle of growth and expression, and yet it manifests beauty in all seasons. This is the inherent energy and grace of those with this name. This is what they have the capability of achieving.

TAMARA
(variation: Tammy, Tami)

Meaning: "the twin; the seeker of truth"
Suggested Affirmation: "I am Tamara. I am the seeker of truth!"
Primary Vowel/Element: A / Element of Ether
Primary Sound/Chakra: "ah" / Throat Chakra
Other Vowels/Elements: A / Element of Ether
Other Sounds/Chakras: "uh" / Throat Chakra

MEDITATION

This name literally means "the twin," and thus it gives many clues as to the energies and lessons of those individuals who have it. In esotericism, the twin is the opposite that must be balanced—the male with the female, the electrical with the magnetic, the intuitive with the rational. Balance in all things is the key. The Hermetic principle of Polarity plays strongly in the life lessons of those with this name: "Everything is dual; everything has poles; everything has its pair of opposites; like and unlike are the same; opposites are identical in nature, but different in degree . . . " Hot and cold are but different degrees of the same thing—temperature. Nothing is truly opposite, and it is often the task of these individuals to balance and integrate opposing forces. They often then become the balance in others' lives. Truth is in everyone and in all situations. Everything has its grain of truth. As this is discovered by those of this name, great manifestations occur, for polarity operates most fully upon the astral plane. This plane opens all that we might call psychic gifts and the blessings of the angelic and archangelic hierarchy as well. Balance and integrate the energies of the heart, and new birth, new expression of truth will follow.

TANIA
(variations: Tonia, Tonya)

Meaning: "the fairy queen; noble in spirit"
Suggested Affirmation: "I am Tania. I am noble in spirit."
Primary Vowel/Element: A / Element of Ether
Primary Sound/Chakra: "aw" / Solar Plexus Chakra
Other Vowels/Elements: I / Element of Fire
                          A / Element of Ether
Other Sounds/Chakras: "ee" / Brow and Crown Chakras
                        "uh" / Throat Chakra

MEDITATION

Those of this name should spend as much time out around nature as possible. They have earned the right in the past to work with the elemental and fairy kingdoms of life, and have done so with great success. This must be earned again, but their name still resonates with these beings. There are tales of individuals being named by the fairies—blessed because of their strong spirit. Those that work with these beings of nature will increase their sensitivity—they will be able to "feel" their presence strongly (solar plexus), as those of the fairy kingdoms work with great feelings. As sensitivity grows, and as the individual establishes a sense of noble spirit in the way they live regardless of life circumstances, new sight and perceptions will also arise. For many this will be the inspiration for artistic endeavors and craftsmanship. For others it will manifest as a sensitivity toward all life upon the planet or within their realm.

TED
(variations: Teddi, Teddy, Theodora, Theodore)

Meaning: "gift of God"
Suggested Affirmation: "I am Ted. I am the gift of God!"
Primary Vowel/Element: E / Element of Air
Primary Sound/Chakra: "eh" / Throat Chakra
Other Vowels/Elements: ——
Other Sounds/Chakras: ——

MEDITATION

Those of this name have come literally to be a gift in the lives of others. The predominant vowel in this name or any of its variations are associated with chakra centers above the heart. These centers give strong perceptions, intuitions and imaginations. Those of the throat chakra involve the use of knowledge and the ability to manifest abundance in various forms, material or otherwise. This center, known as the cornucopia center, is the center where assertion of will is the key to manifestation. Clairaudience is also a strong potential, listening to that quiet inner voice, learning to wield the Creative Word of life. There will be lessons in developing proper strength of will in different areas of one's life. Those whose predominant vowel is the long *E* have a capability to envision much. Fear must be overcome by all and discipline developed for the higher understanding and intuition to fully manifest. Once accomplished, hidden abilities are realized and they become gifts in the lives of others.

TERRENCE
(variations: Terri, Terry)

Meaning: "smooth, polished one"
Suggested Affirmation: "I am Terrence. I am the polished gem of God!"
Primary Vowel/Element: E / Element of Air
Primary Sound/Chakra: "ay" / Heart Chakra
Other Vowels/Elements: E / Element of Air
Other Sounds/Chakras: "eh" / Throat Chakra

MEDITATION

Those of this name have a unique ability to relate to others. Like a rough stone in early life, life circumstances and situations serve to cut and polish that stone until it shines with a faceted brilliance. As these individuals get older they come more and more into their own. They have a capacity to read the hearts of others and respond accordingly. Regardless of life situations or environments, they have a charm that breathes new life into surroundings (element of air). They also have a capacity for learning and assimilating information, but only in regard to that which their hearts can be placed into. Dogmatism and dishonesty must be overcome—in themselves or in others. This implies overcoming personal insecurities and fears that can arise through comparisons and false pride. Once balanced, a healing and reverent compassion arises, instilling an idealism and an insight that grows with each day.

THERESA
(variations: Teresa, Terri)

Meaning: "the reaper; industrious one"
Suggested Affirmation: "I am Theresa. I reap the rewards of life!"
Primary Vowel/Element: E / Element of Air
Primary Sound/Chakra: "ee" / Brow and Crown Chakras
Other Vowels/Elements: E / Element of Air
                             A / Element of Ether
Other Sounds/Chakras: "uh" / Throat Chakra

MEDITATION
Those of this name have come to work with the law of cause and effect. This has been stated in a variety of ways in different societies and scriptures. In its simplest form: "what you sow, so shall you reap." Often these individuals seem to come in with a head start in some area of life, but this is because of previous sowing. What they have most come to learn and solidify in this incarnation is that their own industry is what will bring the rewards. For some this may be difficult, as they all have a visionary quality. They see very clearly what is capable of manifesting for them, but they often do not realize that physical effort and industry is what sets that vision into motion. Intuition and imagination are strong in these individuals, and if matched with equal industry, there is nothing that cannot be achieved by them. Not allowing fears of failure to interfere will keep their perspective clear and make their intuitive understandings and imaginings a realistic vision for the future.

THOMAS
(variations: Tom, Tommy)

Meaning: "the twin; the seeker of truth"
Suggested Affirmation: "I am Thomas. I am the seeker of truth!"
Primary Vowel/Element: O / Element of Water
Primary Sound/Chakra: "aw" / Solar Plexus Chakra
Other Vowels/Elements: A / Element of Ether
Other Sounds/Chakras: "uh" / Throat Chakra

MEDITATION
Those of this name have come to learn to balance the opposites that are within them. This links them to the Hermetic principle of polarity (see Tamara), but it also manifests lessons in balancing the emotions with the rational. There is a strong sensitivity in these individuals that can be overwhelming. The water element is strong within them, but it also ties them to others within their lives, enabling them to read others quite accurately. This is because all life is touched by water. Worry over what others think, overemotionalism and over-criticism will hinder the highest expressions of their energy. These are such things as enhanced communication ability, a sense of precision, creativity, expressiveness, and a strong sense of optimism. Clairsentience is strong within these individuals, and if they cannot see the actual auras of others, they can certainly feel them and read them accurately. Water is strong and yet adaptable. It can flow around or over objects, or if turbulent enough, it can wash them away. The energies and strengths of these individuals must be developed so that they can choose how their energy will manifest according to the situation.

TIMOTHY
(variations: Tim, Timmy, Timmi)

Meaning: "honoring God"
Suggested Affirmation: "I am Timothy. I am honoring God with my life!"
Primary Vowel/Element: I / Element of Fire
Primary Sound/Chakra: "ih" / Throat Chakra
Other Vowels/Elements: O / Element of Water
                       Y / No particular element in this case
Other Sounds/Chakras: "uh" / Throat Chakra
                      "ee" / Brow and Crown Chakras

MEDITATION

Those of this name or its variations have come to learn and live the process of spiritual alchemy. This does not occur in artificially contrived situations or through cloistered existences, but rather by living the normal day-to-day life circumstances. For these individuals the task is to learn to blend fire (*I*) and water (*O*) without extinguishing the flames. Together, if mixed properly, they generate steam, a great source of energy. The ancient alchemists mixed their elements in special containers. It is this container that is represented by the *Y*. The *Y* is the glyph of the Grail Cup, which holds the elixir of life where opposites are blended, creating new life. Those of this name or its variations have a capacity to stir new life fires and energies in others, but only so long as they keep their own strong and alive. Balancing their emotions and the high ideals will be the task. Dogmatism or overemotionalism will upset the chalice. If balanced, there will emerge sensitivity, creativity and great prosperity.

TODD

Meaning: "a fox; the wise one"
Suggested Affirmation: "I am Todd. I am the wise fox of life!"
Primary Vowel/Element: O / Element of Water
Primary Sound/Chakra: "aw" / Solar Plexus Chakra
Other Vowels/Elements: ⸺
Other Sounds/Chakras: ⸺

MEDITATION

Those of this name have come to unfold a strong sense of critical judgment. They have a strong sixth sense about most situations, but there is also a tendency to test it. Being overly critical or analytical may be a problem and must be balanced. At the same time they must keep in mind that there are circumstances where it does not matter what you choose or which way you go, but that you do choose. It is important to be active in the choice. Regardless of what direction they take, situations will unfold that can help them to grow and learn. One way may be easier than the next, but both will provide learning opportunities. Delaying decisions excessively simply to analyze them must be balanced against impulsiveness. When critical analysis and impulsiveness are balanced, there will emerge great confidence, self-awareness, intuition and expansion. These individuals should work with their dreams, for they will provide much insight into major decisions, etc. Spontaneity will be enhanced.

VALERIE

Meaning: "strong; of determination"

Suggested Affirmation: "I am Valerie. I am strong and determined!"

Primary Vowel/Element: A / Element of Ether

Primary Sound/Chakra: "aw" / Solar Plexus Chakra

Other Vowels/Elements: E / Element of Air
I / Element of Fire
E / Element of Air

Other Sounds/Chakras: "uh" / Throat Chakra
Silent
"ee" / Brow and Crown Chakras

MEDITATION

Lessons of strength and determination will predominate for those of this name. They must understand that they will not encounter anything that they cannot handle as long as they do not give up. Learning to stick to goals they have set for themselves is what will be most tested. At the same time there must be a flexibility to change if they find they are wrong, but such decisions should not be made quickly or without thinking. The elements are those associated with chakras above the heart, but the sound activation begins below the heart. This indicates that these individuals have come to learn to draw greater strength up from the depths for higher expression within their day-to-day lives. As this is developed, it will awaken great psychic sensitivity and intuition, and this can then build into an active clairvoyance. The key lies in controlling emotionalism and fears. It is then that initiative and hidden abilities emerge.

VICTORIA
(variations: Victor, Vickie, Vicki)

Meaning: "victory; conqueror; one who is victorious"
Suggested Affirmation: "I am Victoria. I am of victorious spirit!"
Primary Vowel/Element: I / Element of Fire
Primary Sound/Chakra: "ih" / Throat Chakra
Other Vowels/Elements: O / Water Element
                    I / Element of Fire
                    A / Element of Ether
Other Sounds/Chakras: "oh" / Spleen Chakra
                    "ee" / Brow and Crown Chakras
                    "uh" / Throat Chakra

MEDITATION

Those of this name have come to lay new foundations for victory of the spirit. There are four vowels within this name. Four in numerology is the number that signifies new foundations. For victory to occur, the passions and inner fires must be strong. The lower emotions must be brought into alignment with higher aspirations. This is the significance of the spleen chakra and the upper chakras. As they are balanced, the waters and fires combine, generating new steam and energy for greater strength. These individuals have a capacity for working and achieving from a variety of levels. They can employ emotional energy, either mental or spiritual, in order to achieve what is desired. This is the significance of the multiple elements within the name. Learning and discerning which to use and when and in what combination will be the greatest task. Once developed and focused in harmony, nothing can be withheld.

VIOLET

Meaning: "violet; humble"

Suggested Affirmation: "I am Violet. I am the humble wildflower of life!"

Primary Vowel/Element: I / Element of Fire

Primary Sound/Chakra: "eye" / Medulla Oblongata

Other Vowels/Elements: O / Element of Water

E / Element of Air

Other Sounds/Chakras: "uh" / Throat Chakra

"eh" / Throat Chakra

MEDITATION

Those of this name have come to unfold their abilities and
energies quietly and humbly. The violet is usually the first wildflower to
emerge in the spring. It does so quietly, oftentimes going unnoticed,
and yet it is the true herald of new energy about to manifest upon the
Earth. This is a flower sacred to the nature kingdom, particularly to
the fairies and elves. The violet was always a sacred flower to the
queen of fairies in ancient lore. That which was sacred to nature was
also blessed by nature. Living as nature does, molding one's behavior
after the wild violet, would be beneficial to those of this name. It
allows their energies to unfold in a manner that is protective and that
moves and flows with the universal rhythms of the Earth itself. The
violet is a gift of nature of great simplicity and beauty, and yet it holds
within it great power. No better symbol could be adopted by those of
this name.

VIRGINIA

Meaning: "maiden; the pure maiden"
Suggested Affirmation: "I am Virginia. I am the pure maiden of God!"
Primary Vowel/Element: I / Element of Fire
Primary Sound/Chakra: "ih" / Throat Chakra
Other Vowels/Elements: I / Element of Fire
                       A / Element of Ether
Other Sounds/Chakras: "ih" / Throat Chakra
                       "uh" / Throat Chakra

MEDITATION

Those of this name have come to unfold new fires of purity and service. This is not to imply that there has been no purity prior to this. Metaphysically, it is the purifying of emotions, of the astral body, that opens one to pure sight of the supersensible worlds. In esoteric Christianity, the Annunciation was a time of purification in which the feminine energies could be awakened and new birth occur. In Christian scripture this was the time in which it was announced to Mary that she would give birth. Meditation upon those scriptures will reveal much to those of this name, particularly that which has come to be known as the Magnificat (Luke 1:46). It was at this point, because of the purification, that sight of the angelic hierarchy occurred. Balancing and purifying the emotions is the task of those with this name. As this occurs, the influence of the angelic hierarchy within their lives will grow, blessing them and all they touch.

WALTER
(variations: Walt, Wally)

Meaning: "powerful warrior"
Suggested Affirmation: "I am Walter. I am the powerful warrior of God!"
Primary Vowel/Element: A / Element of Ether
Primary Sound/Chakra: "aw" / Solar Plexus Chakra
Other Vowels/Elements: E / Element of Air
Other Sounds/Chakras: "eh" / Throat Chakra

MEDITATION

Those of this name have come to embody the aspects of a true warrior. Being a warrior does not involve just physical strength; it involves so much more. It requires discipline, training, knowledge and finely honed skills. A warrior must be a tactician. It involves body, mind and spirit working in harmony. Those of this name have come to bring these three into harmony within their individual lives. There is inherent in these individuals great strength and power, especially when asserted through strength of will. It is this capacity that will be tested in the early years, so that harmony of body, mind and spirit can occur in some area of their life as they grow older. These individuals have the energies of the true spiritual warriors—an ability they can draw upon throughout their lives. In Persia, the third degree of initiation was known as the warrior. The warrior takes the occult teachings on life and presents them to the outer world, a world that may be more than a little antagonistic to something new. These are the revelators of spirit.

WANDA
(variation: Wendy)

Meaning: "wanderer; one who walks with God"
Suggested Affirmation: "I am Wanda. I walk with God!"
Primary Vowel/Element: A / Element of Ether
Primary Sound/Chakra: "aw" / Solar Plexus Chakra
Other Vowels/Elements: A / Element of Ether
Other Sounds/Chakras: "uh" / Throat Chakra

MEDITATION

Those with this name have come to walk with an inner peace. They often must discover that being alone and being lonely are two different things entirely. Inherent within these individuals is the ability to discern other life and other dimensions around them. This does not mean that they should preclude physical life, but as they recognize life operating around them at all times, they begin to unfold their energies and it draws those in the physical to them. Often these individuals follow the beat of a different drummer. There is that strong inner voice which they must come to recognize. These individuals have great sensitivity and often feel the full impact of whatever energy is around them. For this reason they must learn to balance themselves and control that "psychic" sensitivity. As they come to peace with themselves and their sensitivity, they then become catalysts for awakening that quiet sensitivity in others—teaching, nurturing and healing.

WILLIAM
(variations: Bill, Will, Willie, Willard, Wilma, Billy)

Meaning: "resolute, brave and protecting; secure spirit"
Suggested Affirmation: "I am William. I am the brave protector."
Primary Vowel/Element: I / Element of Fire
Primary Sound/Chakra: "ih" / Throat Chakra
Other Vowels/Elements: I / Element of Fire
                   A / Element of Ether
Other Sounds/Chakras: "ee" / Brow and Crown Chakras
                  "uh" / Throat Chakra

MEDITATION

Those of this name have come to learn to assert the fires of will for themselves and for others. Fire is the predominant element, but their fires must be contained and directed. Fire is both destructive and creative. It burns away the dross so that the gold can shine through. This gold must be protected, for it is the gold of the inner sun, the spark of the Divine. Strength of will will be a test for these individuals, be it in not allowing others to assert theirs and control them or in not allowing theirs to become a bullying and controlling force. Balance is the key. Doing what they know is right and sticking to it regardless of how others respond is often difficult, but it will unfold the greater potential within those of this name. This potential runs the gamut from higher intuition and inspiration to creative and artistic fires to psychic sensitivity and healing. These individuals must become sure in themselves, and then no matter what the field of endeavor, there will be success.

YVONNE

Meaning: "courageous heart and soul; the hero"
Suggested Affirmation: "I am Yvonne. I am of courageous heart and soul!"
Primary Vowel/Element: Y / Elements of Air and Fire
Primary Sound/Chakra: "ee" / Brow and Crown Chakras
Other Vowels/Elements: O / Element of Water
            E / Element of Air
Other Sounds/Chakras: "aw" / Solar Plexus Chakra
            Silent

MEDITATION

Any name whose predominant vowel is a Y have for themselves the personal symbol and mandala of the Holy Grail. The golden Chalice of Life and the quest for it involves the search for these individuals' true spiritual essence and how best to manifest it within their lifetimes. Those of this name are great healers. They have an empathic ability, and can see into the hearts, minds and souls of others with the proper training. Learning to assert their inner strength and courage, in spite of outside pressure, will unfold their potential. Often they must learn to follow their hearts, to recognize that we are never given a hope, wish or dream without also being given opportunities to make them a reality. The only thing that shatters that possibility is compromise, settling for less. It is the holding out for the ideal that demonstrates the true courage of the heart and manifests those dreams.

ZACHARY

Meaning: "Jehovah remembers"
Suggested Affirmation: "I am Zachary. I am remembered by God!"
Primary Vowel/Element: A / Element of Ether
Primary Sound/Chakra: "ah" / Throat Chakra
Other Vowels/Elements: A / Element of Ether
                          Y / Elements of Air and Fire
Other Sounds/Chakras: "uh" / Throat Chakra
                        "ee" / Brow and Crown Chakras

MEDITATION

Those of this name have great strength and power which must be controlled. Asserting one's strength of will over the situations and circumstances of life will be the task. Learning to exert that power and strength in a gentle manner is difficult, but it is this that brings the male and female energies together (*Y*). As the male and female forces are linked, new birth is manifested. When humanity is creative upon the earth plane, we are remembering our divine heritage. We demonstrate that the Divine remembers us as well by manifesting through that creativity. Those of this name are gifted with inner vision, but that inner vision must be brought out into the outer world or it is all for naught. These individuals are great at helping others succeed, and the arch of rainbows is a healing force for them. It will be important not to become introverted or reclusive, as the rainbow is for all people.

APPENDIX A

Index to Name Variations

This section applies to anyone who did not find his or her name in the Metaphysical Dictionary of Names. Many of the names listed here are simply variations of those that are listed in the Dictionary. Although the chakras may vary some, the meanings are essentially the same, and thus the affirmations and meditations will apply.

Next to each name variation is the name in the Dictionary that it is a variation of. If your name is not found in either the Dictionary of this work or within this index, consult your local library to discover your name's meaning. Then use the information from this book to unfold the sacred power within it!

Name Variation	Dictionary Name to Consult	Name Variation	Dictionary Name to Consult
Adeline	Adell	Alyssa	Alice
Adella	Adell	Ami	Amanda
Adellia	Adell	Amy	Amanda
Alec	Alexander	Andy	Andrew
Allan	Alan	Angel	Angela
Allen	Alan	Anita	Anne
Alexa	Alexander	Ann	Anne
Alexis	Alexander	Anna	Anne
Alicia	Alice	Annette	Anne
Allison	Alice	Arland	Arlene
Alyce	Alice	Audra	Audrey

Name Variation	Dictionary Name to Consult	Name Variation	Dictionary Name to Consult
Barb	Barbara	Chuck	Charles
Barbie	Barbara	Cindy	Cynthia
Bea	Beatrice	Claudia	Claude
Beata	Beatrice	Claudette	Claude
Ben	Benjamin	Claudine	Claude
Bernadette	Bernard	Cliff	Clifford
Bernice	Bernard	Constance	Connie
Bernie	Bernard		
Bert	Albert	Dan	Daniel
Bessie	Beth	Danielle	Daniel
Betsy	Beth	Danni	Daniel
Betty	Beth	Danny	Daniel
Bonita	Bonnie	Dario	Darren
Brad	Bradley	Darius	Darren
Bradford	Bradley	Darla	Darlene
Brandon	Brenda	Darryl	Darren
Brant	Brenda	Dave	David
Brendon	Brenda	Davey	David
Brent	Brenda	Deb	Deborah
Bryan	Brian	Debbie	Deborah
		Debra	Deborah
Candace	Candice	Dennis	Denise
Candi	Candice	Derryl	Darren
Candy	Candice	Diane	Diana
Cara	Kara	Dianne	Diana
Caroline	Carol	Don	Donald
Carolyn	Carol	Dora	Dorothy, Ted
Carrie	Carol, Carla	Doris	Dorothy
Cathi	Catherine	Doug	Douglas
Cathy	Catherine		
Charlene	Charles	Ed	Edward
Charlie	Charles	Eddie	Edward
Charlotte	Charles	Edgar	Edward
Cheri	Cheryl	Edith	Edward
Cherise	Cheryl	Edmund	Edward
Chris	Christine	Edna	Edward
Chrissie	Christine	Edwin	Edward
Christopher	Christine	Eleanor	Eileen

Name Variation	Dictionary Name to Consult	Name Variation	Dictionary Name to Consult
Elinore	Eileen	Howie	Howard
Ella	Ellen		
Em	Emily	Jack	Jacob
Ema	Emily	Jackie	Jacob
Emil	Emily	Jacqueline	Jacob
Emma	Emily	James	Jacob
Ericka	Eric	Jamie	Jacob
Eva	Evelyn	Jan	Janet
Evan	Evelyn	Jane	Janet
Eve	Evelyn	Janell	Janet
		Janice	Janet
Fay	Faith	Jean	Janet
Flo	Florence	Jeanette	Janet
Flora	Florence	Jeff	Jeffrey
Fran	Frances	Jenny	Jennifer
Francis	Frances	Jerold	Jeremy
Frank	Frances	Jerome	Jeremy
Frederick	Frederic	Jerry	Jerome
Fred	Frederic	Jesse	Jessica
		Jessie	Jessica
Gabe	Gabriel	Joan	Janet
Gayle	Gail	Joanna	Janet
Geneva	Gene	Joanne	Janet
Georgia	George	Jodie	Jodi
Geraldine	Gerald	Jody	Jodi
Gerard	Gerald	Joe	Joseph
Gertrude	Gerald	Joey	Joseph
Glenda	Glen	Johan	John
Glenn	Glen	Jon	John
Glenna	Glen	Jonathon	John
Greg	Gregory	Jonetta	John
		Josephine	Joseph
Harlan	Harold	Josh	Joshua
Harley	Harold	Joyce	Joy
Harriet	Harold	Joylynn	Joy
Harry	Harold	Juanita	John
Hank	Henry	Judi	Judith
Henrietta	Henry	Judy	Judith

Name Variation	Dictionary Name to Consult	Name Variation	Dictionary Name to Consult
Julian	Julia	Lori	Laura
Julianne	Julia	Lorna	Laura
Julie	Julia	Louis	Lois
Juliet	Julia	Louise	Lois
Julius	Julia	Luci	Luke
		Lucille	Luke
Karen	Kara	Lucy	Luke
Kari	Kara	Lynda	Linda
Karin	Kara	Lynette	Linda
Kathi	Catherine	Lynn	Linda
Kathleen	Catherine		
Kathryn	Catherine	Marc	Mark
Kathy	Catherine	Marcia	Mark
Katie	Catherine	Margie	Margaret
Kay	Catherine	Marguerite	Margaret
Kelly	Kelley	Maria	Mary
Ken	Kenneth	Marian	Mary
Kimball	Kim	Marie	Mary
Kimberly	Kim	Marietta	Mary
Kris	Christine	Marilyn	Mary
Krissie	Christine	Marlene	Mary
Kristi	Christine	Marsha	Mark
Kristin	Christine	Matt	Matthew
Kristine	Christine	Michaelina	Michael
Kristy	Christine	Michelle	Michael
		Mike	Michael
Larry	Laura	Miriam	Mary
Laurel	Laura		
Lauretta	Laura	Nan	Nancy
Laurie	Laura	Natalie	Nathan
Lawrence	Laura	Nate	Nathan
Leon	Leo	Nathaniel	Nathan
Leona	Leo	Neil	Neal
Leonard	Leo	Nelson	Neal
Leslie	Lesley	Nick	Nicholas
Lin	Linda	Nicole	Nicholas
Lora	Laura	Norm	Norma
Loren	Laura	Norman	Norma

Name Variation	Dictionary Name to Consult	Name Variation	Dictionary Name to Consult
Olive	Olivia	Sarah	Sara
Oliver	Olivia	Sharon	Sara
		Shawn	Sean
Pam	Pamela	Sherri	Sheri
Patricia	Pat	Sherry	Sheri
Patrick	Pat	Sheryl	Sheri, Cheryl
Paula	Paul	Sonjia	Sonja
Pauline	Paul	Sonya	Sonja
Peg	Margaret	Stacie	Stacey
Peggy	Margaret	Stanley	Stan
Pete	Peter	Stephanie	Steve
Phil	Phillip	Stephen	Steve
Philip	Phillip	Steven	Steve
Phillis	Phyllis	Stewart	Stuart
		Stu	Stuart
Rachael	Rachel	Sue	Susan
Ray	Raymond	Suzanne	Susan
Rebekah	Rebecca	Suzi	Susan
Ronda	Rhonda		
Rich	Richard	Tami	Tamara
Rick	Richard	Tammy	Tamara
Ricky	Richard	Teddi	Ted
Roberta	Robert	Teddy	Ted
Robin	Robert	Teresa	Theresa
Robyn	Robert	Terri (masc.)	Terrence
Ron	Ronald	Terri (fem.)	Theresa
Ronnie	Ronald	Terry	Terrence
Rosa	Rose	Theodora	Ted
Rosalee	Rose	Theodore	Ted
Rosamond	Rose	Tim	Timothy
Roseanne	Rose and Anne	Timmi	Timothy
Rosemarie	Rose and Mary	Timmy	Timothy
Rosemary	Rose and Mary	Tom	Thomas
Rosette	Rose	Tommy	Thomas
Russ	Russell	Tonia	Tania
		Tonya	Tania
Sam	Samuel		
Sandy	Sandra		

Name Variation	Dictionary Name to Consult
Vicki	Victoria
Vickie	Victoria
Victor	Victoria
Wally	Walter
Walt	Walter
Wendy	Wanda
Will	William
Willard	William
Willie	William
Wilma	William

APPENDIX B

Phonetic Guide to
Pronunciation of the Vowels

A

    [e] bait, fade

    [æ] bat, fat

*   [ə] about

    [ɔ] autumn, law

E

    [i] bead, feet

    [ɛ] bed, bet

    [ə] camel

I

    [I] bid, fit

    [ai] bide, buy

    [ə] robin

O

    [o] boat, note

    [ɔ] cot, autumn

    [a] fodder

    [au] loud, cow

    [ə] carrot

U

    [u] boot, food

    [ʌ] but, bud

    [U] book, foot

    [ə] circus

---

* The schwa sound is a common component of all the vowels (tuba, camel, robin, carrot, circus). Its sound is similar to the sound of the OM or HUM, which is often given as the source of all sounds within the Universe.

phthongs

[ai] bide
[ɔi] boy
[ei] bay
[æ:] fairy
[au] loud
[Iu] few
[ou] blow

Diphthongs have at their core a very sonorous effect. They are two vowels in one syllable. One of the two will always have greater sonority. One vowel is always subordinate to the next, although some can take on a gliding sound. Assimilation often occurs. This is the tendency of one vowel sound to become similar to those next to them. Variations in these sounds are due to the mechanics of their vocalization and production.

APPENDIX C

The Chakra System

Mediating the energies of one's subtle bodies (subtle energy fields) and linking them to the physical body are energy distribution centers called *chakras*. This is a Sanskrit term meaning "wheels," which reflects the manner in which they circulate energy into, out of and around the body. They are linked to the physical body primarily through the endocrine and skeletal systems, and although they are not part of one's physical being, there is an intimate connection with it (see Figure 1).

There are actually hundreds of energy distribution centers (often known as acupuncture and acupressure points) connected to the physical body, but there are seven primary ones. Their location varies, depending on whether one is oriented to Eastern philosophy or Western esotericism. In either case, these are points near the body where there is a greater amount of electromagnetic energy (which now can be measured by modern science). Any discrepancies in their actual location exist only because people from different areas of the world utilize their energies differently.

The chakras are linked to the neurological ganglion along the spine and to the endocrine glands. They extend both in front of and behind the body. These vortices of biochemical and electromagnetic energy rotate in a clockwise manner, circulating and distributing the life force throughout the body for physical, emotional, mental or spiritual purposes.

By learning which functions each chakra governs within us, we can maintain balance and health. They can then be activated for purposes beyond the physical—for unfolding our highest potential.

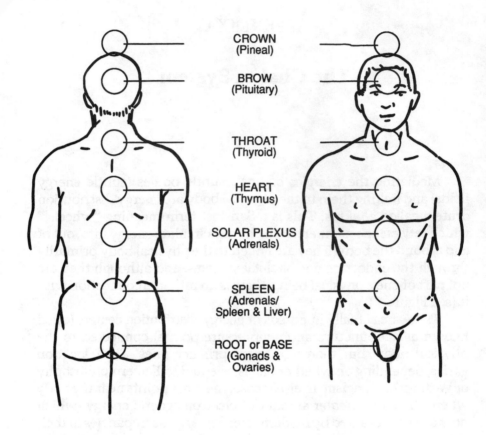

CROWN
(Pineal)

BROW
(Pituitary)

THROAT
(Thyroid)

HEART
(Thymus)

SOLAR PLEXUS
(Adrenals)

SPLEEN
(Adrenals/
Spleen & Liver)

ROOT or BASE
(Gonads &
Ovaries)

Figure 1. The Chakra System

BIBLIOGRAPHY

Ames, Winthrop. *What Shall We Name the Baby?* New York: Workman Publishing, 1941.

Anderson, Christopher P. *The Name Game.* New York: Simon and Schuster, 1977.

Bardon, Franz. *The Key to the True Quabbalah.* Germany: Dieter Ruggeberg, 1986.

Baskin, Wade. *The Sorcerer's Handbook.* Secaucus, NJ: Citadel Press, 1974.

Bischoff, Erich. *The Kabbala.* York Beach, ME: Samuel Weiser, Inc., 1985.

Browder, Sue. *New Age Baby Name Book.* New York: Workman Publishing, 1974.

Busse, Thomas V. *The Professor's Book of First Names.* Elkins Park, PA: Green Ball Press, 1984.

Cottle, Basil. *Names.* London: Thames and Hudson, 1983.

Crandall, Joanne. *Self-Transformation Through Music.* Wheaton, IL: Theosophical Publishing, 1986.

da Silva, Andrew J. *Do From the Octave of Man Number Four.* New York: Borderline Press, 1985.

Dunkling, Leslie Alan. *First Names First.* New York: Universe Books, 1977.
———. *Our Secret Names.* Englewood Cliffs, NJ: Prentice-Hall, Inc. 1981.

Godwin, Joscelyn. *Harmonies of Heaven and Earth.* Rochester, Utah: Inner Tract, International, 1987.

Gray, William. *Concepts of Qabalah.* York Beach, ME: Samuel Weiser, Inc., 1984.

Kalisch, Isidor. *Sephir Yezerah,* New York: L. H. Frank and Co., 1987.

Katsh, Shelley and Merle-Fishman, Carole. *The Music Within You.* New York: Simon and Schuster, Inc., 1985.

Khan, Hazrat Inayat. *The Mysticism of Sound.* Geneva: International Headquarters of the Sufi Movement, 1979.

Langacker, Ronald. *Language and Its Structure.* New York: Harcourt, Brace and World, Inc. 1968.

Palmquist, Al and Harzell, John and Francis, Linda. *What's in a Name?* Minneapolis: Ark Products, 1976.

Robertson, Stuart. *The Development of Modern English.* Englewood Cliffs, NJ: Prentice-Hall, Inc., 1954.

Schneider, William Alan and Gray, Aline R. *Handbook for Numerologists.* Indiana: Schneider Corp., 1980.

Sepharial. *The Kabala of Numbers.* North Hollywood, CA: Newcastle Publishing, 1974.

Smith, Elsdon C. *American Surnames.* Baltimore: Genealogical Publishing Co., 1986.

Tracy, Martita. *Stellar Numerology.* California: Health Research.

Waite, A. E. *The Holy Kabbalah.* Secaucus, NJ: Citadel Press.

Wells, Evelyn. *What to Name the Baby.* New York: Doubleday and Company, Inc., 1946.

STAY IN TOUCH

On the following pages you will find listed, with their current prices, some of the books and tapes now available on related subjects. Your book dealer stocks most of these, and will stock new titles in the Llewellyn series as they become available. We urge your patronage.

However, to obtain our full catalog, to keep informed of new titles as they are released and to benefit from informative articles and helpful news, you are invited to write for our bi-monthly news magazine/catalog. A sample copy is free, and it will continue coming to you at no cost as long as you are an active mail customer. Or you may keep it coming for a full year with a donation of just $2.00 in U.S.A. ($7.00 for Canada & Mexico, $20.00 overseas, first class mail). Many bookstores also have *The Llewellyn New Times* available to their customers. Ask for it.

Stay in touch! In *The Llewellyn New Times'* pages you will find news and reviews of new books, tapes and services, announcements of meetings and seminars, articles helpful to our readers, news of authors, advertising of products and services, special money-making opportunities, and much more.

The Llewellyn New Times
P.O. Box 64383-Dept. 012, St. Paul, MN 55164-0383, U.S.A.

•   •   •

TO ORDER BOOKS AND TAPES

If your book dealer does not have the books and tapes described on the following pages readily available, you may order them direct from the publisher by sending full price in U.S. funds, plus $2.00 for postage and handling for orders of $10 and under. Orders over $10 will require $3.50 postage and handling. There are no postage and handling charges for orders over $100. UPS Delivery: We ship UPS whenever possible. Delivery guaranteed. Provide your street address as UPS does not deliver to P.O. Boxes. UPS to Canada requires a $50 minimum order. Allow 4-6 weeks for delivery. Orders outside the U.S.A and Canada: Airmail—add $5 per book; add $3 for each non-book item (tapes, etc.); add $1 per item for surface mail.

FOR GROUP STUDY AND PURCHASE

Because there is a great deal of interest in group discussion and study of the subject matter of this book, we feel that we should encourage the adoption and use of this particular book by such groups by offering a special "quantity" price to group leaders or "agents."

Our Special Quantity Price for a minimum order of five copies of *The Sacred Power in Your Name* is $38.85 cash-with-order. This price includes postage and handling within the United States. Minnesota residents must add 6% sales tax. For additional quantities, please order in multiples of five. For Canadian and foreign orders, add postage and handling charges as above. Credit card (VISA, Master Card, American Express) orders are accepted. Charge card orders only may be phoned free ($15.00 minimum order) within the U.S.A. or Canada by dialing 1-800-THE MOON. Customer service calls dial 1-612-291-1970. Mail Orders to:

LLEWELLYN PUBLICATIONS
P.O. Box 64383-Dept. 012 / St. Paul, MN 55164-0383, U.S.A.

SIMPLIFIED MAGIC
by Ted Andrews

In every person, the qualities essential for accelerating his or her growth and spiritual evolution are innate, but even those who recognize such potentials need an effective means of releasing them. The ancient and mystical Qabala is that means.

A person does not need to become a dedicated Qabalist in order to acquire benefits from the Qabala. *Simplified Magic* offers a simple understanding of what the Qabala is and how it operates. It provides practical methods and techniques so that the energies and forces within the system and within ourselves can be experienced in a manner that enhances growth and releases our greater potential. *A reader knowing absolutely nothing about the Qabala could apply the methods in this book with noticeable success!*

The Qabala is more than just some theory for ceremonial magicians. It is a system for personal attainment and magic that anyone can learn and put to use in his or her life. The secret is that the main glyph of the Qabala, the Tree of Life, is *within* you. The Tree of Life is a map to the levels of consciousness, power and magic that are within. By learning the Qabala you will be able to tap into these levels and bring peace, healing, power, love, light and magic into your life.

0-87542-015-X, 210 pgs., illus., softcover $3.95

GODWIN'S CABALISTIC ENCYCLOPEDIA
by David Godwin

This is the most complete correlation of Hebrew and English ideas ever offered. It is a dictionary of Cabalism arranged, with definitions, alphabetically, alphabetically in Hebrew, and numerically. With this book the practicing Cabalist or student no longer needs access to a large number of books on mysticism, magic and the occult in order to trace down the basic meanings, Hebrew spellings, and enumerations of the hundreds of terms, words, and names that are included in this book.

This book includes: all of the two-letter root words found in Biblical Hebrew, the many names of God, the Planets, the Astrological Signs, Numerous Angels, the Shem Hamphorash, the Spirits of the Goetia, the Correspondences of the 32 Paths, a comparison of the Tarot and the Cabala, a guide to Hebrew Pronunciation, and a complete edition of Aleister Crowley's valuable book *Sepher Sephiroth*.

Here is a book that is a must for the shelf of all Magicians, Cabalists, Astrologers, Tarot students, Thelemites, and those with any interest at all in the spiritual aspects of our universe.

0-87542-292-6, 500 pgs., 6 × 9, softcover $15.00

IMAGICK: THE MAGICK OF IMAGES, PATHS & DANCE
by Ted Andrews

The Qabala is rich in spiritual, mystical and magickal symbols. These symbols are like physical tools, and when you learn to use them correctly, you can construct a bridge to reach the energy of other planes. The secret lies in merging the outer world with inner energies, creating a flow that augments and enhances all aspects of life.

Imagick explains effective techniques of bridging the outer and inner worlds through visualization, gesture, and dance. It is a synthesis of yoga, sacred dance and Qabalistic magick that can enhance creativity, personal power, and mental and physical fitness.

This is one of the most personal magickal books ever published, one that goes far beyond the "canned" advice other books on Pathworking give you. You will learn how the energies reflected in such things as color vibration, names, letters, tarot associations and astrological relationships radiate from the "temple" of each sephiroth.

0-87542-016-8, 6 x 9, 312 pgs., illus. $12.95